Creativity and Writing

What is the role of creativity in the teaching of writing?

> The authors are very close to the needs and aspirations of teachers, so that the tone of this book is accessible as well as stimulating. It will make an important, well-timed contribution to language and literacy in education.
>
> Eve Bearne, University of Cambridge

This accessible yet authoritative book affirms the vital role of creativity in writing and considers and encourages flexible, innovative practice in the teaching of writing. Importantly, the book reflects upon teachers' imaginative and artistic involvement in the writing process as role models, collaborators, artists and writers themselves.

Arguing that children's creative use of language is key to the development of their language and literacy skills, this book focuses on the compositional process and children's own ideas. The authors examine the many voices that influence the inner and outer voice of the child, through reading, investigating, imagining, talking and taking part in a range of engaging and inspiring learning experiences.

Illustrated throughout with many examples of children's writing and drawing, and with suggestions for the classroom, this book is for any teacher wanting to deepen their understanding of theory and practice in the teaching of writing.

Teresa Grainger, **Kathy Goouch** and **Andrew Lambirth** all work at Canterbury Christ Church University College, UK.

Creativity and Writing

Developing voice and verve in the classroom

Teresa Grainger,
Kathy Goouch and
Andrew Lambirth

 Routledge
Taylor & Francis Group

LONDON AND NEW YORK

First published 2005
by Routledge
2 Park Square, Milton Park, Abingdon, Oxon, OX14 4RN

Simultaneously published in the USA and Canada
by Routledge
270 Madison Ave, New York NY 10016

Routledge is an imprint of the Taylor & Francis Group

Transferred to Digital Printing 2010

Typeset in Palatino by
HWA Text and Data Management Ltd, Tunbridge Wells

British Library Cataloguing in Publication Data
A catalogue record for this book is available from the British Library

Library of Congress Cataloging in Publication Data
A catalog record for this book has been requested

ISBN 0–415–32885–3 (pbk)
ISBN 0–415–32884–5 (hbk)

Publisher's Note
The publisher has gone to great lengths to ensure the quality of this reprint
but points out that some imperfections in the original may be apparent.

Contents

Foreword

A delicate tension

If you were asked to name the teacher who inspired you most when you were at school, who would it be? Would it be the one who told you about cycling round 1930s Europe and witnessing the growth of fascism? The one whose hands and gestures fascinated you? The one who excelled at a sport you enjoyed? The one who made you feel that you mattered? The one who 'did all the voices' when reading aloud to the class? And when you try to analyse why these teachers are memorable, what can be distilled as the essence of inspiration? It's tricky. It could be the stories they told, the spells of enchantment they wove, the inner energy of conviction. It might be that they fed the imagination or offered the sense that you could do what they did. It's probably all of these. But I suspect there's something more – something about trust and about respect. In telling stories about their own lives, exposing their efforts to the gaze of their pupils, being patient beyond the bounds of expectation, they were honouring their classes with trust, sketching out landscapes of possibility and offering a structure for potential futures. Such tributes from adults to children stay in the memory.

I wonder if the teachers whose work is described in this book have given any thought to the seeds of memory they have sown, the future possibilities they have offered? It's intriguing to speculate that at some time in the future, someone will reminisce about an experience from the We're Writers project, remembering a personal moment of realisation. Stories such as those deserve to be told. Harold Rosen points out that:

> There is a huge reservoir of innovatory teaching experience which is never drawn on because it is never translated into stories.
>
> (Rosen, 1988a: 172)

Creativity and Writing does, in fact, tell the story of such teaching experience. Rosen continues to flesh out just what 'innovatory' might mean and provides detail which is spelt out in this book. The important point is not so much about stories, but about the 'delicate tension between reproduction and invention' (p. 171) which is the mark both of creative teaching and creativity in writing. In bringing together these two elements: *reproduction* which suggests something emerging from existing material and *invention* which indicates adding something new, Rosen highlights the balance which is explored in *Creativity and Writing*. However, he also points out that 'teaching and learning never change without a special kind of imaginative act' (p. 172). The project outlined in this book gave the opportunity for the teachers involved to engage in that special kind of action. Behind action, however, there is thought. *Creativity and Writing* offers a window into that thinking.

One of the great strengths of this book is that it brings together action and reflection, practice and theory, heart and mind, children and teachers. It offers an integrated view, supported by impressive and wide-ranging scholarship, of the dynamic relationship between teaching and learning. Whilst teaching will, it is hoped, result in learning, the learning itself then prompts further teaching. And, of course, this is not just a matter of first the one and then the other; teaching and learning exist in harmonic counter-point, mingling with each other in duet then separating to solo, reverting to duet again and again. And like any satisfying music, teaching and learning combine technique and performance, appealing both to emotion and thoughtful imagination. In this brief foreword I want to concentrate on that combination which results in professional creativity.

Trust and possibility

The dualities of teaching and learning depend on a delicate balance if they are to be productive, but the tensions inherent in everyday teaching experience may not always be healthy or creative. The OfSTED report on creativity in teaching *Expecting the Unexpected*, identifies some of these 'barriers to creativity' (OfSTED, 2003: 18). There are those which are related to the teacher's own sense of security, for example, 'not recognising the "creative moment"' or 'not letting go' (p. 18) but other constraints are more structural in terms of school or curriculum organisation. Most notable, and unsurprising, is the imperative on teachers to reconcile:

> the demands of high test and examination results or the demands of public accountability for improving performance ... with a creativity agenda.
>
> (OfSTED, 2003: 19)

Certainly, it is not an easy balance and requires much trust on the part of teachers as they engage in creative teaching – trust in their pupils and trust in themselves. Much of the language of creativity implies trust, suggesting expansiveness and readiness to open oneself out to experience, for example, Craft's 'possibility thinking' (Craft, 2000: 1) and Robinson's views of being 'innovative and flexible' (Robinson, 2001: 1). What conditions might promote that kind of trustful and risky teaching? With the demands and sometimes unproductive judgements of current educational practice, teachers may be inclined to close up like sea anemones when they feel threatened. Trust, then, goes beyond the classroom walls to the public environment in which teachers are working.

To trust means being able to feel some security, yet it is clear that innovation thrives best in an atmosphere of risk and insecurity. There seems a paradox here. One of the underlying themes of this book is about the professional value of ambiguity and uncertainty. Whenever teachers embark on a curriculum development project like We're Writers there is an inevitable sense of insecurity and sometimes an urge to hang on to established 'certainties'. Some of these might be worth hanging on to, but the trick is in recognising what is worth keeping and what can be cast aside. The whimsical – and certainly inventive – artist and architect Antonio Gaudi recommends a return to 'early solutions' when making such decisions about innovative practice:

> Originality consists of return to the origin. Thus originality means returning, through one's resources, to the simplicity of the early solutions.
>
> (van Hensbergen, 2001: 54)

As advice towards creativity, this is intriguing. Just what might 'returning to the origin' mean? And what are 'the early solutions'? The key, it seems to me, lies in the central placing of the phrase 'through one's own resources'. Stripping away preconceptions and the accretions of unexamined habits can help in identifying just what matters, what is at the centre of beliefs about teaching, what has to go, what is worth keeping and how that core of personal resources can be energised.

These resources will not be the same for everyone. As Ken Robinson points out, 'we all have creative abilities and we use them differently' (Robinson, 2001: 12). This is equally true of learners at whatever age – the teachers who put themselves in the position of learners in their own classrooms alongside their pupils. This diversity is also found in the 'many different areas of a person's experience and intelligence' (Robinson, 2001: 12) and helps illuminate the sometimes difficult concept of 'risk-taking'. One of the problems associated with encouraging creative approaches to teaching can be the potential for misunderstanding 'risk'. It would be easy to assume that risky teaching depends on 'performance' or some element of the slippery term 'charisma'. But there are many teachers whose strengths are reflective and 'low key' or those who do not easily expose their feelings and ideas to others. What does 'risk-taking' mean for them? This book carefully and perceptively describes how all teachers can push at the boundaries of practice by realising – making real and coming to understand – their own varied strengths and resources. The dual meaning of 'realisation' which involves both action and understanding is very like Bruner's two landscapes: of action and consciousness (Bruner, 1986: 14). These are essentially interwoven in making sense of experience, offering worlds made possible by knowing and feeling.

Structures for potential

There can sometimes be resistance to talk of developing creativity and writing because of the association with the (probably mythical) flavour of permissiveness of the 'let it all hang out' creative writing movement of the 1960s. Current views of creativity, however, turn their back on *laissez faire* notions, offering a sturdy and robust vision of harnessing, not just releasing energies (Robinson, 2001). Another shift from earlier perceptions sees these energies not as springing solely from individual qualities but as part of the collaborative generation of ideas:

> Creativity is not purely an individual performance. It arises out of our interactions with ideas and achievements of other people. It is a cultural process. Creativity prospers best under particular conditions, especially where there is a flow of ideas between people who have different sorts of expertise. It requires an atmosphere where risk-taking and experimentation are encouraged rather than stifled … Creativity flourishes where there is a systemic strategy to promote it.
>
> (Robinson, 2001: 12)

Significantly, Robinson emphasises the need for structures to support creative endeavour. However, the notion of structures can suggest the possibility of confining ideas, highlighting another apparent paradox in creativity education. How can there be a free flow of ideas within systems? Bourdieu tackled this opposition as he outlined his theory of social practices as 'regulated improvisations' (Bourdieu, 1977: 78). Just as play depends on 'rules' in order to liberate inventiveness, creative improvisation obeys certain kinds of regularities in making sense of experience. Such practical theory offers a sound basis for professional development.

The view of creativity as a cultural process emphasises the importance of whole-school commitment in establishing the 'particular conditions' to foster innovative teaching approaches. I'd like to push the notion of culture and community further, however, to suggest an even more pressing imperative for initiatives like the We're Writers research and development project. Just as creativity is differently nuanced for different individuals, the creative arts as a whole act as a focus for celebrating diversity as well as commonality. In a speech given in March 2002 entitled *Beyond Boundaries*, Peter Hewitt, the Chief Executive of the Arts Council, argued for the value of art in society in a turbulent world:

> Art helps us to understand what we have in common and where we differ, what we like and what offends us, what excites us and what leaves us cold. We come together around art without having to agree about it. Art helps to populate and energise an open public space for reflection, expression, empathy, dissent and disagreement.
>
> (Hewitt, 2002: 2)

Art and creativity are powerful. This book, with its emphasis on the significance of creative teaching for both teachers and children, recognises the value of an open public space where the energies and potentials of all the learners involved can be explored and expressed.

I haven't said much about the children involved in this work, partly because their voices in the pages which follow speak clearly, poignantly, thoughtfully and vigorously for themselves. However, it's worth considering how they found their voices. Their teachers planned for them, worked sensitively and reactively during sessions, offered them a classroom space which promoted risk but provided structured support. They listened to them, prompted them further, led them up to and beyond boundaries. The teachers themselves took some chances, not always knowing where the work might lead. Throughout the work they returned to writing in its many forms – as generating ideas, reflecting on them and communicating them to others. And it paid off. I'd like to return to that list and ask how many of those experiences the teachers themselves had during their work on this action research project. It is my sense that the authors of *Creativity and Writing* offered the teachers just the same professional challenges, structures and opportunities for imaginative flight as the children experienced. They planned, listened, prompted, stepped into the unknown with them.

There's much in this book about ambiguity and 'not knowing'. There's also a lot of strong language like *passion, power, potential* and *principles*. And this is perhaps the final 'delicate balance'. Whilst it is essential to know with passion just what principles drive our professional actions – the inner conviction born of reflection and experience – it is equally important at other times *not* to know exactly what the outcomes might be. Writing can be like that. Sometimes it is important be sure of just what the written outcome will be; at other times it is absolutely crucial not to know and to allow writing and thought to work together creatively. So it is with teaching, as this book so thoughtfully explains. And it matters. The children whose work rings out of the pages of *Creativity and Writing* are the future.

They deserve to know that some kinds of certainties are not creative and to have the inspiration and example of their teachers to give them the courage to trust themselves.

Eve Bearne
University of Cambridge

Acknowledgements

We would like to thank all the children and teachers who have contributed their time, talent, energy and enthusiasm to working with us, both those in the We're Writers Research and Development Project and our Advanced Certificate and Masters' colleagues over the years. We are particularly grateful to the children for their engaging writing, inspired and supported by the creative teachers who have allowed us into their classrooms, shared their children's ideas with us and influenced our thinking. We also want to acknowledge the influence of our external examiners on the Masters' programme: Margaret Meek, Barry Steirer, Eve Bearne and Judith Graham, who have guided and shaped our work. We sincerely hope that the voices of the children who have taught us, with their words and wisdom, and the colleagues who have collaborated with us, sing out from these pages, without them this book could not have been written.

The We're Writers Research and Development project involved the following schools: St James C.E.J., St James C.E.I., St Matthew's C.E.P., Bishops Down Primary, Claremont Primary, St Mark's C.E.P. and St Luke's C.E.I.

Introduction
Looking back to travel forward

Children's voices ring and resonate in playgrounds and classrooms, in their homes and communities. Their conversations, quick-fire repartee, chants, jokes and even whispers reflect their energy and vitality, their strongly held views and concerns, their unusual ideas and intriguing insights. In their writing too, we sometimes feel their voices vibrate off the page with conviction, with surety and an engagement born of passion. Such writing is likely to have benefited from full involvement in imaginative contexts, from extended contemplation upon experience, from oral as well as written drafting. In their writing they demonstrate their knowledge about language as they seek to engage and interest others. For many young writers, and certainly for most professional authors, the compositional process encompasses significant gestation time, an extensive rehearsal period. This may involve observation and the gathering of ideas through participation and position taking, reading and reflection and the process of writing and redrafting. If children's writing is to demonstrate their creativity, individuality, voice and verve, then the seeds of their stories and other forms of writing need constant nurturing and support as well as time to evolve and reverberate.

In this book we argue that to help children find their voices, a better balance between knowledge about language and creative language use must be sought in the primary years. Teaching writing is a complex process and ideas can emerge from imaginative activity and the desire to communicate as well as from leaning on examples. Shape too can come from engaging with experience as well as from convenient blueprints. Much will depend on whether we are seeking to produce 'battery hens or free range chickens' (Abbot, 2001). Developing children's knowledge and skills also enhances their ability to write creatively, but balanced provision is the key and many teachers are rightly concerned about 'the apparently imbalanced emphasis on literacy skills at the seeming expense of purposes and creativity' (Dadds, 1999: 16).

As a society, we rightly value both the first order skills of composition, and the second order skills of transcription, including grammatical conventions. However, we have generally taught the second strand, the transcription skills and conventions, more fully and explicitly than the other.

(Frater, 2004: 81)

We too perceive an over-emphasis on the technicalities of writing, as one teacher colleague in our research expressed it, *I feel as if I've been teaching the full stop for too long*. So our book seeks to profile the significance of children's creative engagement in the compositional component of writing and also examines teachers' imaginative involvement in the writing process as role models, collaborators, artists and writers themselves.

The seeds of our argument were sown many years ago when we worked with teacher colleagues reflecting upon their creative practice in literacy learning. Their pleasure in engaging personally and imaginatively in their own learning was so marked that the transfer of principles to the classroom context was made with relative ease. At the close of the various courses, the teachers had shifted so much professional ground that many of them signed up for a Masters degree in their desire to understand this transformation and to explore the connections between practice and theory more fully. Such creatively fulfilling journeys were somewhat sidetracked however in the late 1990s by the increased pressure of assessment and the heavily monitored requirements laid out in the National Literacy Strategy (NLS) *Framework for Teaching* (DfEE, 1998). At this time our professional development work became oriented towards supporting teachers in flexibly interpreting and developing the NLS, but the professionals we worked with seemed reticent to grasp the challenge, they were concerned to 'get it right', and felt both pressured to conform and driven by tests and targets. As the millennium approached, we were invited to work with a consortia of primary schools, positioned in this accountability culture, whose head teachers expressed the view that their children's writing was *competent yet uninspired*, and who were concerned about the increasingly negative attitudes towards writing expressed by their young learners. As one teacher noted at the time, *The children are simply playing the game called writing – like us I suppose – and the energy has gone out of their writing*.

The two-year research and development project 'We're Writers' was consequently established (2001–3) to examine both teachers' and children's perceptions about writing and current practice and to ascertain some of the critical influences upon this. We also sought to explore how the children's written voices might be enhanced by empowering teachers to use and develop their own and their children's creative potential. Whilst the book draws upon more than the We're Writers research project, most of the children's work used to illuminate our argument is drawn from this work, so a brief outline of it is offered to contextualise this text.

We're Writers: a research and development project

The educational and political context in which this project was undertaken, was, as already noted, unusually full of tension, pressure and contradiction, which probably reflected the status quo in other parts of the country, as well as in this part of southern England. The NLS had been in operation for two years, and the tunnel vision experienced elsewhere was in evidence here also. The project was undertaken in three phases.

Stage One – the initial phase involved an audit to capture the current context in terms of attitudes and perceived practice: teachers questionnaires (n: 65), children's writing surveys (n: 390), samples of children's writing and teachers' commentaries (n: 130) and factual information about the schools.

Stage Two – the development phase involved the formation of a Project Focus Group (PFG); two teachers from each school worked as action researchers case studying three children in their classrooms. The PFG explored their understanding of creativity in writing, developed their own creativity personally and professionally, and worked on various school-selected foci such as drama and writing or storytelling and story writing. The teachers kept professional logs, were regularly interviewed, and retained evidence of the case-study children's writing and their reflective commentaries upon it. Towards the end of the project, writing workshops for the PFG were also established and the group began to write alongside their children. The overall consortia focus moved from increasing autonomy and dialogue in writing in Year 1, to a focus in Year 2 on integrated units of work which encompassed more open-ended and creative practice within an extended process of composition. Consortia development days, staff meetings, interviews with the case-study children and meetings with head teachers were also held and a parent/governor leaflet was produced by the PFG to explain the innovative development work being undertaken by the schools.

Stage Three – the evaluation phase involved collecting similar data to that gathered in Stage One, and in addition, PFG members and their case-study children were interviewed. A final celebration conference was held by the consortia, which was run by the PFG members and other school staff who organised workshops and shared their practice and insights, demonstrating the children's not inconsiderable achievements. Video and audio recordings captured the children's voices in action and evidence of their written voice and verve was shared. A consortia anthology entitled *We're All Writers* was also published.

The research was a time of genuine enquiry as we sought to develop ways of reflecting upon creative engagement in writing, and considered creativity in writing, by both the children and their teachers. Frameworks for observation and commentaries on creativity in writing were developed and refined, as together we listened to the children and helped them shape a sense of themselves as writers with something to say and a voice to convey it. As researchers and university tutors we also needed to tune into the teachers' voices and understand their vehemently expressed sense of professional compromise and challenge.

Professional autonomy in teaching writing

The powerful influence of high-stakes assessment, detailed literacy curricula and the marked reduction in teacher professionalism in the UK which characterised the beginning of the twenty-first century, has undoubtedly influenced the teaching of children's writing (Packwood and Messenheimer, 2003).Perhaps the most significant marker has been the increasing tendency for teachers to request permission to be autonomous as teachers of literacy; such has been the influence of accountability and prescription in this domain. The initial audit in the We're Writers project revealed that the teachers, concerned to cover the NLS requirements and to prepare their children for the official assessment tests, were tentative and lacked confidence as teachers of writing. They frequently asked *are we allowed?* and sought permission to employ their professional knowledge, experience and understanding. Around the same time, it was also argued that the professional self-confidence of teachers had been drained and their love of language and literature suppressed by the prescriptive culture, the degree of surveillance and the control exerted by the externally evaluated system (Frater, 2000; Anderson *et al.*, 2000). This may have prompted the profession to stay within the safe boundaries of the known and officially supported pedagogical practices of the day and is likely to have reduced the use of creative and innovative teaching approaches. During this period, the teaching of writing arguably became more standardised, homogenised even, as test criteria were specified more closely and the writing curriculum became entwined with detailed objectives and particular pedagogic practices. Teachers in England, through extensive training and support, undoubtedly developed their knowledge of form and function, grammatical features and linguistic terminology and many adopted different classroom practices and raised the standards of writing, as measured by the national tests. The ongoing evaluations of the NLS by the Ontario Institute for Studies in Education (Earl *et al.*, 2000, 2001) also indicate that there is much to celebrate. However, many of the significant challenges that existed in 2000 still remain and must be confronted if we are to take practice forward from the current apparently safe, but somewhat formulaic status quo. It is to these challenges which we now turn.

The influence of assessment and reification of knowledge

When comprehensive curricula for literacy and the presence of prescribed objectives for the teaching of writing at text, sentence and word level combine, then the coverage of such objectives can come to dominate teachers' concerns. This is particularly likely in an accountability culture, with closely monitored and inspected teaching and the requirement to provide detailed plans and reach set targets. The teachers surveyed and interviewed in the We're Writers project, perceived that the coverage of curriculum content and the explicit teaching of knowledge about written language had become reified in a system which regularly checked and assessed such knowledge. They felt pressured to concentrate on the writing objectives at the expense of exploring the process by which children become writers. The first samples of writing, collected back in Spring 2001, revealed some interesting data in this regard. All the teachers collected the most creative work of two randomly selected children in their class at the end of a half term and added their own contextual notes. The analysis showed that these pieces of writing had arisen from writing practice activities, practice in response to a skill, or a recently introduced genre or practice for assessment purposes. Guidance, when given prior to this writing, focused on the key technical features of the particular genre, although frequently no support at all was given. Follow-up discussions suggested that these 'one time only' writing opportunities (Smith, 1982), were likely to be assessment preparation exercises or short-story writing practice for children to demonstrate their knowledge of a genre. These teachers, in manner similar to those observed by Frater (2000), seemed preoccupied with the prescribed content and appeared to perceive the NLS framework as a plan itself; they certainly followed it carefully and consciously. Frater found that those schools where such a literal interpretation of the NLS prevailed were those in which the children made least progress in writing. The We're Writers teachers appeared to believe that they should deliver the writing curriculum and teach in accordance with what was to be assessed, they did not feel their role involved developing the curriculum in interaction with their learners and creating autonomous young writers.

As Packwood and Messenheimer acknowledge 'teachers expectations of children as writers are increasingly framed by educational knowledge determined by external agencies' (Packwood and Messenheimer, 2003: 144) and it seemed that in this consortia of seven schools, high-stakes assessment coupled with prescription and accountability had influenced both their expectations and their practice, fostering a rather surface approach to teaching writing. This profiled forms and features of texts at the expense of meaning and message, so from the children's perspectives, naming and knowing appeared to be given precedence over understanding and applying language in meaningful contexts. As the teachers sought to enrich their children's knowledge about language, the analysis of language as an abstract object had, they realised, come to dominate the agenda. Yet research evidence has shown that effective teachers of literacy place a high value on composition and prioritise text level work, embedding their teaching of linguistic features in whole-text activities which are meaningful and clearly explained to the learner (Medwell *et al.*, 1998). The teachers in the We're Writers project acknowledged that they were somewhat dependent upon publishers' materials and decontextualised text extracts, which they used to illuminate points of grammar or language knowledge, yet recognised that such a 'sound bite' approach to teaching literature denies fiction and poetry the opportunity to inspire, engage and challenge young writers (Messenheimer and Packwood, 2002). However, these professionals lacked both the confidence and permission to inhabit other creative spaces to develop their pupils' written competence, voice and verve in writing. Evidence from national evaluations of the NLS also indicates that teachers may have become more competent in teaching sentence and word level work, but still find supporting children's compositional development more challenging (Earl *et al.*, 2003).

Misunderstanding the nature and purpose of writing

The public disclosure of test results, as already noted, inevitably leads to teachers teaching to the tests and taking from the test criteria what they need to ensure success for their children (Madaus, 1994; Dann, 2001; Messenheimer and Packwood, 2002). Classroom practice thus becomes shaped by assessment criteria which may lead to an instrumental approach to teaching writing and a focus on 'construction and correctedness' which, D'Arcy (1999) argues, the national tests profile at the expense of content and conviction. One of the consequences of this situation is that the perceived nature and purpose of writing can become skewed. For example, a nine-year-old in the We're Writers project, in response to a test question, *Why did the author use the phrase 'frozen with fear?'*, wrote *Because he wanted to get a level 4*. This sobering response serves to remind us that children construct their understandings from the opportunities, experiences and priorities created in their schools. Such a zeitgeist should warn us all.

The pre-eminence of test criteria also appeared to influence the teachers' understandings of the nature of writing. Initially, the teachers in the consortia described quality writing merely in terms of the national test criteria with which they were evidently very well acquainted (Grainger *et al.*, 2002). No mention was made of the engagement of the reader, the content or meaning of their writing, the writer's style, their ability to take risks, their authorial voice or commitment to the writing. Writing seemed to have been redefined for these teachers and merely encompassed easily observable and testable features such as: a clear structure, a range of adverbs and adjectives, good punctuation, dialogue, a range of connectives and the use of complex sentences. These experienced professionals were working towards prescribed levels and perceived that in the teaching of writing they tended to foreground the demonstration and practice of text, sentence and word level features of different genres, in line with what they believed was required of them. Through discussion, they acknowledged that audience and purpose were largely ignored. As Bearne (2002) has observed, the profiling of textual elements and the absence of ideational and interpersonal elements of writing in the NLS framework, has shaped not only perceptions of writing but practice also. Using Halliday's (1978) functional model of language, Bearne shows how the NLS short-changes the ideational element, the significant role of the writer's ideas and intentions and ignores the interpersonal component, the sense of audience/reader (Bearne, 2002: 13). Yet these elements play a significant role in the process of finding a voice and becoming a writer.

The model of writing reflected in the practice of these hardworking professionals was one of a toolkit, suggesting that once the children had a command of a range of specific tools, then their competence as a writer was assured. Through observation in project classrooms, it became clear that some of the teaching of writing at this time was atomistic and disembodied, as writing objectives were focused upon in a discrete and rather detached manner and then practised repeatedly. The consequences of this practice were evident in the children's views recorded in the surveys and follow-up interviews. They put their voices on the line and expressed their perspectives with a marked degree of coherence and real strength of feeling. In essence, the younger learners, aged 5–7 years, were more enthusiastic about writing than the older pupils and had more positive views of themselves as writers. The children aged 7–9 years expressed predominantly negative attitudes to writing, typically describing it as boring, whilst a small, but worrying proportion of those aged 9–11 reflected an indifferent, somewhat detached disposition. *More writing? Who cares? What difference does it make what I think? We have to do it – it's part of school.* Had they become schooled writers, products of the conventional game called writing played out in school? The teachers were concerned to realise that these pupils seemed to see themselves as passive recipients, disengaged from the process of becoming writers and with little sense of their own agency or empowerment. They perceived that the contrasting attitudes and less positive self-perceptions expressed by the 7–9-year-olds may have been linked to the fact that in the NLS (DfEE, 1998a) there are 43 more objectives listed for 7–8-year-olds than for 6–7-year-olds. Since 89 per cent of these transitional increases relate to word and sentence level objectives, it is possible that teaching in these years may become disproportionately focused on transcription skills and short-change the importance of meaningful composition.

Research into the influence of literature on the writing of 7–11-year-olds has focused on the development of an ear for written language and on the role of quality literature in the interaction between reading and writing (Barrs and Cork, 2001). In the We're Writers project, we planned to build on this work and focus on the creative engagement of the children and the role of talk in the extended process of composition. Children write more powerfully when they are fully involved in the compositional experience and are not outside the frame, handling the tools of written communication in a distant or apparently academic manner. There is a pressing need to attend to children's ideas, their generation, incubation and contemplation, since without these they have nothing to say, even if they do have appropriate linguistic knowledge and editorial skills. Without the desire to use this knowledge and communicate with others for their own purposes: to persuade, cajole, tempt, castigate, inform, annoy, amuse or whatever, they may merely be playing the game called writing.

Writing involves us in communicating, conveying meaning to ourselves and others and the act of writing itself can help us refine our thinking and reshape our views, since it allows us to hold our ideas in our hands and consider them as they unfold. Just as a woodcarver discovers their subject in the wood, in its knots, lines, shades and patina, so too writers begin to discover what they want to say through an extended process of composition which is just as central to the final writing as knowledge of the conventions and structures of the form. Writers shape and rehearse their texts through reading, investigating, talking and taking part and through playing with possible tunes, themes and issues. As this process unfolds their confidence grows and their capacity to sharpen their communication increases. The tenor and tune of this book has also emerged through an extensive rehearsal process which has challenged us to stand in the footsteps of the teachers in the project and see the world through their eyes. We were privileged to work with them as they travelled and reflected on the process of teaching writing, as they overcame some of the barriers to their own creative engagement and as they took risks, gradually exerting the right to choose their own pedagogies and teach writing creatively according to their own beliefs and principles.

Emerging voices

This book focuses on the development of voice and verve in children's writing and considers the contribution that flexible, playful, dialogic and imaginative practices can make to children's creative capacity, linguistic potential and growth as writers. We hope it will enable both teachers and children to harness the power of creativity and become rejuvenated in the process. As they explore form and freedom, structure and innovation in teaching and learning about writing, we trust they will exercise their own voices and discuss the implications and ideas with others. Initially we introduce some of the theoretical background with regard to creativity, talk and writing and explore contemporary understandings of creativity, its role in writing and the interdependence of the language modes. We go on to examine the myriad of voices which influence the inner and outer voice of the child and the cultural practices of today's young writers, and consider the role of talk in the social process of writing as a tool for generating ideas, for rehearsing the tunes created and for reflecting upon and evaluating their written texts. We then move on to consider literacy practices which imaginatively develop voice and verve in the writing classroom. The need for genuine autonomy is initially profiled through a discussion of the relationship between choice and voice and the importance of open-ended practices, such as writing journals. We also show how children can extend their voices, both spoken and written, through full social and emotional engagement in a range of playful and investigative responses to text activities, such as discussion, drama, storytelling and poetic performance. A range of engaged artistic children's voices are included and the multimodal nature and social context of their writing is described to illuminate its development. Much of the children's writing collected in the We're Writers project was fictional but where possible non-fiction pieces have also been included.

Our text then turns to reflect upon the role of teachers as fellow artists, personally and professionally involved as role models, engaged collaborators and genuine writers in the classroom. We consider the importance of teachers' emotional and artistic engagement in the extended process of composition and examine the implications for classroom practice, arguing that teachers can extend their own and the children's creative potential by making more extensive use of the language arts. In our last chapter we seek to highlight the principles and practice of creative teachers of writing and suggest that if we want creativity, voice, verve and passion on the page then we must model such writing from inside texts, and voice our collective view that such writing takes time to develop and is supported by imaginatively involving contexts and powerfully engaging texts, explored in an environment of possibility, creativity and challenge.

Chapter 1

The potential of creativity

Teaching is an art form, an imaginatively engaging and creative endeavour, which relies upon the creative capacity, autonomy and intuitive knowledge base of the profession. Yet in recent years pressure on the curriculum has arguably resulted in a narrowing of learning experiences, so that emotional engagement, full participation, experiential and inquiry based learning, as well as spontaneity and creativity have been pushed to the margins of learning (Sedgwick, 2001; Craft, 2000; Puttnam, 1998) As the Design Council (1999: 83) state, 'the more prescriptive the curriculum, the greater the need to be explicit about creativity and not leave it to chance'. If teachers are to find innovative ways forward in teaching writing, they need to recognise that the currently directive discourse and imposed assessment structure demands an imaginative and enterprising response. Teachers need to be encouraged to take part in professional dialogue, to seize opportunities to assert their knowledge and understanding and to develop new insights in order to plan more holistically and creatively. Professional aspirations to increase creativity and raise test results are not irreconcilable, but we need to be convinced of this in order to find effective and inspiring ways forward.

To increase their flexibility, teachers need more than knowledge of curriculum requirements; they need pedagogical knowledge and subject knowledge, encompassing an understanding of both principles and concepts in teaching English. More significantly perhaps, they need to recognise the potential of creativity and be able to develop it in young learners, as OfSTED observe in *Expecting the Unexpected*, a recent report on creativity in schools.

> Teachers who inspire creativity have a clear understanding of what it means to be creative ... even though they are not always able to put this into words.
>
> (OfSTED, 2003: 8)

Greater creative assurance will place teachers in a stronger position to offer scaffolds and spaces for growth in writing. In this chapter we focus on the nature of creativity and its importance in developing young writers, especially their ability to write with voice and verve. In arguing for a better balance between developing children's knowledge about written language and their creative language use, we highlight the importance of the imaginative involvement and motivation of young writers. We explore the creative act of writing, and the importance of purpose, relevance, control and innovation, and outline creative and playful approaches, arguing for recognition of the extended process of composition. These issues are all developed further in later chapters, as is the emergence of voice through children's cognitive and affective involvement in artistic learning encounters.

Redressing an imbalance in the teaching of writing

In recent years the dual pressures of prescription and accountability have tended to lead teachers towards a more standardised approach to teaching writing, at least in England, where the main pedagogies of shared, guided and independent writing have become institutionalised in the context of the literacy hour. The NLS Framework (DfEE, 1998a) has profiled the teaching of different genres of writing, both fiction and non-fiction and introduced the profession to writing frames developed from the work of Wray and Lewis (1997). The features of each genre have been explicated in publishers' materials, assessed in national tests and assiduously taught to young writers, creating a somewhat formulaic approach to teaching writing (Frater, 2000), since 'under the guise of developing writer's linguistic awareness', as Myhill (2001: 19) observes, 'it is all too easy to reduce writing to a set of formulae taught through a series of exercises'. A better balance needs to be struck between teaching the important skills of form, grammar and spelling for example, and providing opportunities for children to undertake purposeful writing which satisfies their need to communicate and harnesses their individuality and creativity. As Boden has argued, knowledge is a necessary precondition for creativity, but, she warns, it can be taught in such a way that it ends up 'killing the creativity' (Boden, 2001: 102). Helping children find a voice involves supporting them in developing their ideas, opinions and possibilities and being concerned with what they are saying, not merely with how they are communicating. As the original National Curriculum for England and Wales, back in 1989, stated:

> The best writing is vigorous, committed, honest and interesting. We have not included these qualities in our statements of attainment because they cannot be mapped onto levels. Even so all good classroom practice will be geared to encouraging and fostering these vital qualities.
>
> (DES, 1989: 17.31)

There are at least three paradigms of teaching writing which are evident to differing degrees in current practice, including the genre paradigm, the skills paradigm and the process writing paradigm, developed by Britton *et al.* (1975) and Graves (1983). The first sees literacy as social practice and highlights the importance of teaching certain forms as a way of empowering children, the second focuses on a range of discrete language skills which populist perspectives view as common sense, and the third 'positions the writer as an individual author and theorises writing as a recursive, cognitive process' (Robinson and Ellis, 2000: 73). The genre movement and the skills based approach are clearly enshrined in the NLS, but, as Robinson and Ellis observe, the process writing approach is short-changed and an emphasis on form and feature dominates. We believe that teachers need to work towards a more appropriate balance between teaching knowledge about the linguistic features of different forms and exploring and supporting the content and meaning of children's writing. It is more than possible to teach such knowledge in a manner that encourages flexibility, judgement and imagination and simultaneously fosters the development of voice and verve, since it is not only what we teach that counts, but how we teach it that shapes the abilities and attitudes of our young learners. In adopting a socio-cultural perspective, we focus on context and text and highlight meaningful communication, thus linking writing closely with speech, with reading and practical open-ended activities of all kinds. There is no formula for developing voice in writing, but when we exploit the potential of creativity and enhance children's knowledge about language in engaging collaborative contexts, providing opportunities for them to communicate purposefully about topics that have salience for them, their voices emerge with an energy, vitality and authenticity which reflect their creative engagement. As creative professionals we too are part of this inspiring and involving journey.

Creativity

The place and purpose of creativity in the broader curriculum needs to be understood against the background of competing conceptions of schooling and literacy. Bell (2001) describes functional literacy as the mastering of basic skills and contrasts this with cultural or critical literacy. He suggests this goes beyond the basic competences and includes visual, aural and tactile skills which 'liberate and enable individuals to transform their modes of thinking, acting and expressing themselves in ways that would otherwise be impoverished and limit their lives' (Bell, 2001: 87). Others have also argued that there is more to intelligence than academic ability and suggest that in order to develop lifelong learners, who can cope with the uncertainty and speed of technological and economic change, we need to turn our attention to the potential of creativity (Robinson, 2001; Gardener, 1999).

Yet there is a danger, as OfSTED (2003) acknowledge, that the development of creativity is not seen as an essential element in education, but is viewed merely as a modish concept or yet another thing to add to schools' lists of priorities.

The concept of creativity is widely recognised as challenging and complex and is a term so variously employed that it is often used and abused by the media, politicians and policy makers (Prentice, 2000). As the government's committee on creative and cultural education made clear, misconceptions about creativity abound; these include: the misguided perception that creativity is the province of the few, the view that it is associated with particular people, and the perception that it is synonymous with the arts (NACCCE, 1999). In addition, a further misunderstanding aligns creativity with childlike play that is intuitive and undisciplined, a quality of childhood that must not be intruded upon. Yet research evidence suggests that creativity is possible 'whenever human intelligence is engaged' (Robinson, 2001: 7) and that it is a human capacity which can be both developed and enriched in each individual. Furthermore, creative play is unusually serious, thoughtful and demanding, arising out of our interactions with others, with ideas and with experience. Bronowski (1978) sees the creative mind as one which looks for unexpected likenesses and connections between disparate domains and highlights creativity as a way of thinking. If children erroneously perceive writing as the domain of a lucky few, a gift possessed by others, and experience real difficulty or failure, they are likely to be less confident which will influence their attitude to writing. This was the case in the We're Writers' project, in which many of the KS2 children perceived themselves to be weak writers and some of them showed the early stages of a potentially long-term negative disposition towards writing (Grainger et al., 2003).

Developing creativity in writing is not a fanciful extra in learning to write, but is central to children's growth as writers and to their self-esteem. To develop their creativity in and through writing, children need skills and knowledge of the form they wish to compose in, a growing assurance of themselves as writers, and the space and opportunity to develop their voices with support and encouragement. Craft (2000) posits the process of 'possibility thinking' at the core of creativity and highlights the role of problem finding and problem solving as well as having novel and valuable ideas. Certainly composition involves a willingness to take risks, to try alternatives and impose some form of order on our thoughts, as well as accepting a degree of uncertainty as our words and meanings emerge. It involves the process of raising questions about our intended meaning, about the audience, form and purpose of our writing as well as the production of possible ways to respond. The creative process of writing involves us in making choices about our stance, content, structure and language, and creating combinations and connections between ideas and images.

Creativity as a social and cultural process also involves the production of outcomes. In seeking to find a balance between the process and the product and between the individual and the wider value system, the authors of *All Our Futures* adopted a definition of creativity as 'imaginative activity fashioned so as to produce outcomes that are both original and of value' (NACCCE, 1999: 29). We have chosen this definition to lean upon in examining creativity in writing as it suggests creativity is a multifaceted capacity of human intelligence, which is relevant to everyone and encompasses both individual and collaborative activities. It highlights five key concepts which we need to understand: using imagination, the creative process, originality, the pursuit of purpose and judging value.

Using imagination in the creative process of writing

Imaginative activity takes many forms, drawing on a more varied range of human functioning than linear, logical and rational patterns of behaviour (Claxton, 1997). It is essentially generative and may include physical, musical, aural or visual thinking, involving children in activities which produce new and unusual connections between ideas, domains, processes and materials. Physical engagement and learning through our minds and bodies, eyes and ears provides a balance to the sedentary and often abstract nature of much modern education and enables children and their teachers to step outside predictably bound and previously rehearsed supports for writing. In less conventional contexts, new insights and connections can be generated, perhaps through analogy and metaphor, and alternative understandings and positions adopted which feed into writing. Children also need help to understand the nature of communication conventions so that they can deliberately play with these and produce novel and original outcomes in their own terms.

There is a close relationship between imaginative activity and a playful attitude of mind; conjuring up possibilities and selecting from amongst these is a theme running through the book. Playful approaches support active and experiential learning and build upon children's curious and exploratory nature. Yet play is not necessarily creative. The kinds of play relevant to literacy are those concerned with the imagination, play with language, and sounds, multimodal explorations, visual and bodily play: the development of creativity in handling words, ideas and feelings. Play constitutes a significant part of the compositional process. In the transition from playful improvisation to composition children begin to play with ideas, structures, patterns and combinations of words and sounds. In examining the serious play of writing, Gurevitch (2000) distinguishes between disciplinary seriousness, taking on the responsibilities of an adult expert, and poetic seriousness, revealed from the point of view of the child whose play has been exposed. He describes writing as originating from moments of broken play and following Derrida (1991), argues that 'poetry (vs. science) is not only emotion and selfhood; it is ritual, magic, voice, dance, tongue, the rhythm of heartbeat' (Gurevitch, 2000: 6). Poetic speech, he suggests, is neither talk – ethnography, narrative, theory – nor dance – magic, trance, play – but is between them. In his terms both talk and dance combine to help writers find their voices as they engage imaginatively in the serious play of writing. This creative process involves the writer in seeking solutions or a different perspective and involves them in actively fashioning, shaping, moulding and refining the ideas generated.

Purpose, outcomes, originality and value in writing

Creative activity is goal oriented and the creative act of writing self-evidently involves making; making connections, making meaning, composing and communicating. The outcomes produced may fall anywhere on the 'private–public' spectrum (Craft, 2000) and may be expressed internally, verbally within the peer group or publicly in written form. A child who has developed an idea or insight about a character in drama, but has not yet shared this with others, will have produced an outcome on the private end of the spectrum. At the other end of the spectrum, the public end, the same child may have had an original poem published in the school anthology. Creativity usually encompasses some kind of 'performance' which demonstrates the degree of understanding and mastery achieved through the creative process (Perkins, 1998) and writing is no different in this regard. The nature of the final piece will not, however, always be known at the outset, and the mental and practical activities through which the writing evolves need to remain open to the unexpected and be perceived as part of the creative process. Writing is shaped through the generative and reflective processes of production, as writers create and critique their compositions, both consciously and unconsciously, as they write. This involves the two modes of creative thinking: the 'imaginative-generative' mode which produces outcomes and the 'critical-evaluative' mode which involves consideration of originality and value (NACCCE, 1999: 30). These operate in close interrelationship and need to be consciously developed to ensure children can both generate and evaluate their writing. This ability to give and receive criticism is an essential part of creativity in writing and needs careful modelling and nurturing in the classroom; it is explored further in Chapter 3 on the role of talk in writing.

Whilst writing relies upon the ideas, language and literary styles of others, to be creative it must also be original for the individual, in the context of the peer group or within its particular field. Young writers can strike up new and unexpected connections and images, which sing off the page with authenticity and originality, and although as Craft (2000) acknowledges, the spectrum of originality is vast, children should be encouraged to improve on their own previous work and come up with new and original ideas, moving beyond their existing understanding or use of language. The aesthetic dimension of value forms a criterion for evaluating the quality of writing and demands the fluent use of a critical language to reflect upon it. It also requires confidence and the persistence to see a piece through to completion, and a sense of fair mindedness and a respect for others' opinions, views and ideas (Nichersen, 1999). In relation to writing at the poetic end of the continuum (Britton, 1993), this issue of value was viewed as challenging by the teachers in the We're Writers project, since it involved their subjective responses and drew upon their aesthetic sensibilities. In contrast, they reflected more confidence with the labelled features of writing examined in the national tests in England, but such assessment tests do not encompass the criterion of originality or even attend seriously to the issue of imaginative content. However, as teachers we must reward experimentation, allow failure, and be prepared to be involved and surprised as we work creatively with young authors.

Teachers' own creativity

Since creativity is not an event, but a process, it follows that teachers can adopt a creative disposition and choose a creative path in any given situation, since it is less a matter of their ability to do so and 'more a mind set or attitude', as Craft calls 'little c creativity' (Craft, 2000: 9). Teachers, in working to foster children's creativity in writing will want to build creative teaching contexts, use imaginative approaches, expand their children's knowledge about language and celebrate their creative development. As the government's strategy for primary schools, *Excellence and Enjoyment* (DfES, 2003) acknowledges, making learning vivid and real and developing understanding through enquiry and creativity are critical principles of learning and teaching. Such learning can enhance literacy skills and improve self-esteem, motivation and achievement (DfEE/QCA, 2003), although arguably this is only possible if teachers themselves are creatively engaged. As teachers our own creativity is central to the enterprise of developing voice and verve.

> Young people's creative abilities are most likely to be developed in an atmosphere in which the teacher's creative abilities are properly engaged.
>
> (NACCCE, 1999: 90)

Our ability to interest and inspire young writers deserves attention and development. Our playfulness, openness and innovative bias also need to be nurtured and enriched if we are to contribute imaginatively to the construction of creative, competent and curious learners. As artists in our classrooms, telling tales or writing alongside the children, we are freed from the traditional patterns of classroom interaction and are more personally and affectively involved, using our knowledge and skills, as well as our intuitive insights based upon experience (Grainger, 2002). In this way we can shift from being 'presenters of content to becoming leaders of an exploration' (Black *et al.*, 2002: 7) and are more open to children's creative use of language, noticing the poetic in children's speech and providing plenty of playful opportunities for discussion, drama, storytelling and other explorations in order to ensure deep learning in and through writing. We will also be teaching about forms, functions and features of writing, but within a motivating and empowering context which demonstrates the potential of creativity and profiles meaning. Teachers' involvement as language artists and the characteristics of creative teachers of writing are explored more fully in Chapters 9 and 10.

Developing autonomy, relevance and control in writing

Relevance, ownership and control of learning, as well as innovation, have all been identified as key issues in creative learning in children (Woods and Jeffrey, 1996; Jeffrey and Woods, 2003).

So in order to foster creativity in writing we need to encourage self-directed learning and the agency of the individual. Children must be given opportunities to draw from their linguistic resources and experience, to grasp and shape the purpose of the writing activity and become involved in their writing and in sharing it with others. If, however, the classroom is predominantly teacher controlled, then as Dyson (2000) observes, the learners will develop little sense of what they are doing or why. In contrast, more imaginative approaches involve individuals and groups in initiating questions and lines of enquiry so that they are more in charge of their writing; such collaboration and interaction helps to develop a greater sense of autonomy in the literacy events which unfold. The development of ownership, responsibility and relevance in writing can also be realised through the creation of an open environment in which the learners can seize the initiative. It is further enhanced through genuine choice, since this 'transforms writing from an assigned task into a personal project' (Calkins, 1986). Such autonomy is in evidence in classrooms where young children independently produce their own magazines, comics or newspapers for example, perhaps turning to the school for support with copying or advertising, but creating their own team of editors and writers and enjoying the independence of such self-initiated projects. Figures 1.1 and 1.2 show the front covers of two issues of *Bonkerz*, published every six weeks or so over a period of 18 months by a team of initially 9–10-year-old

Figure 1.1 Front cover of *Bonkerz*

boys. The seven young men wrote their material in the computer suite at lunchtimes and at home and sold their popular magazine with all profits going to FROGS, Friends of Gambian Schools. Another context in which young learners have the opportunity to choose their form, audience and purpose in writing is in the role play area; this can increase the children's sense of volition and create a more inclusive and enabling agenda. Vygotsky (1978), in describing the potential of imaginative play, reminds us that desire

Figure 1.2 Front cover of *Bonkerz*

and self-discipline play an important part in this activity. Autonomy also needs to be implemented through thoughtful teachers' intervention: through respecting children's interests and selections, providing opportunities for experimentation, and letting the learners decide how to take their writing forward and when their work is complete. Increasing independence and self-direction foster both fluency and ownership in writing and enrich the learner's sense of their own voice.

In the context of teaching for creativity, teachers need to encourage innovative contributions and pass control back to the learners. For example, in an improvised drama session, the teacher is likely to follow the children's interests and needs, enabling them to take a full part in the learning encounter and experience increased agency. In this 'no penalty zone' (Heathcote, 1980) learners think laterally and write in different roles and with different viewpoints as part of their world making play. The imaginative freedom of such playful contexts, in which genuine choice exists, appears to prompt unexpected ideas in writing. As Craft and Jeffrey (2003) show, in flexible situations, in writing journals for example, when high value is placed on the children's ownership and control, innovation and enterprise are likely to follow. It is in such open-ended scenarios, in discussions, unstructured investigations and in exploratory encounters with literature for example, that children stretch their voices and engage with enthusiasm, fluency and flair.

> Reading the word is not preceded merely by reading the world, but by a certain form of writing it or rewriting it, that is transforming it by means of practical work. For me, this dynamic process is central to the literacy process.
>
> (Freire, 1972: 35)

Through engaging in creative and practical activities and considerable conversation, children transform their understanding of texts and develop their imaginations; this encourages them to deliberately structure 'the web of meaning' for themselves (Vygotsky, 1978). However, writing that is imposed upon children in a mechanistic way and tested formally against set criteria may have the reverse affect and prompt them to focus on passing the tests and pleasing their teacher. In order to enhance creativity in writing, teachers need to include children's own ways of coming to know the world representationally, for example through language play, drawing and storytelling, whilst also giving some consideration to unofficial and unexpected agendas, such as their pleasure in revisiting others' tunes and voices, their enthusiasm for the world of popular culture and their ease in designing mutimodal texts. In the act of composing, young children negotiate the multiple textual and social worlds they inhabit and make their writing have relevance and resonance for them (Dyson, 2000). When they discover literacy's relevance to their current interactions with friends and family, and perceive its value in reflecting on experience, they learn that reading and writing can be used as tools to make sense of the world and to express meaning. Relevance, Jeffrey and Woods (1997) suggest can be achieved in four key ways: responding to children's emotions; engaging in their interests and having 'fun'; giving ideas and stimulating their imaginations; and by maintaining their individuality and encouraging their criticality.

Children's natural disposition to learn about what they are interested in deserves to be capitalised upon in the teaching of writing; this ensures literacy is powerfully learnt and language is explored as salient, meaningful and engaging. The influence of popular culture on children's interests is well documented and we are now beginning to understand the role of the media and popular cultural texts in children's writing (Marsh and Millard, 2000). Creative and imaginative approaches to literacy learning have the potential to link the literacies of everyday life with the world of schooled literacy. Children have a vast reserve of visual experiences which shape and influence their interpretation and production of texts and if a broader conception of literacy is adopted, this wealth of multimodal forms can be embraced and the texts and literacy practices which they engage in at home can be explored in school. As teachers we need to work hard to connect the literacies of home and school, offering rich textual encounters that bridge the gap between the children's own 'cultural capital' (Bourdieu, 1977) and the culture of school, as these affectively involve all our learners. The issues of relevance, autonomy and interest are explored in more depth in the following two chapters and run throughout the book.

Affective engagement, participation and motivation

In response to the apparent emphasis on measurable performance and the marked reduction in the artistic and affective side of teaching and learning (Ball, 1998), many schools have worked hard to recapture some of the elements of a more child-centred philosophy and have retained a role for creativity, participation and motivation (OfSTED, 2002). Their work acknowledges that learning involves engaging students emotionally, physically and aesthetically as well as cognitively. The work of Craft (1997) and Fryer (1996) also indicates that the most creative professionals place the people in the learning process above the curriculum, and in fostering creativity in writing, 'it is clear teachers need to be geared towards individuals, their passions, capabilities and personalities' (Barnes, 2001: 27). Children deserve to be invited into the learning experience as individuals, to become fully involved in their learning so that they can exercise their imaginations and stretch their intellectual and affective muscles in creative contexts. Teachers know that children's emotional engagement makes a difference to their propensity for learning and their openness to new insights and we believe this must be explicitly tapped in the context of developing young writers. Creative endeavour exploits and enhances the energy of both children and teachers and ensures high levels of involvement, a key indicator of quality in learning. It encompasses full pupil participation and promotes a more interactive discourse in which there is a tendency to look at things from different angles and express alternative and original perspectives which contribute to the development of voice.

Acknowledging the affective dimension in writing is important, since children's attitudes to writing influence their ability to take risks and persevere. Some of the KS2 children involved in the We're Writers project, initially felt detached from the process of writing, influenced perhaps by their teachers' lack of ownership of prevailing orthodoxies. Later, however, when their teachers developed more creative approaches to the teaching of writing and contextualised the teaching of skills in emotive and engaging contexts, the same learners became more positive about writing and their competence as writers grew. Personal choice writing was also profiled to foster the connections between identity and self-expression and the learners began to want to write, to desire to communicate, knowing they had something to say and readers who were interested in their ideas, their concerns, their raps, their stories and their lives. Through creative endeavour and full participation, we believe writers can be brought to the brink of writing, with a need to write, a sense of what they want to convey and an awareness of both their purpose and perspective. The animation in their faces and the speed at which they write in such situations indicates that at these moments there is no holding them back, they are perhaps continuing to experience the 'state of flow' that develops through creative play (Cziksentmihalyi, 2002). In this state, characterised by concentration and motivation, 'the meanings of words and ideas are felt more strongly and deeply' and their voices ring with conviction and their individuality (Laevers, 2000: 24). In addition, their involvement in imaginative and open-ended contexts and their reflection upon experience supports the development of their ideational fluency and helps them make unusual associations and connections as they compose.

Expanding the concept of composition

Historically, the idea that children could write something of their own was not apparently considered or valued in the nineteenth century, and as Hannon (2000: 19) notes, writing was conceived as writing from dictation. It was many years before 'composition itself was considered appropriate in the elementary school curriculum, and then at first only for the older pupils'. Many generations later, perceptions have changed, but nonetheless children are held back in their growth as writers where narrow interpretations of the writing curriculum persist and a focus on testable skills prevails.

> Children need more time to think about the processes involved in finding ideas, composing and expressing meaning, rather than being hustled from one skills based task to another.
>
> (Marsh and Millard, 2000: 61)

Time is a critical issue in relation to creativity in writing since meaningful composition needs careful nurturing, support and development. This inevitably lengthens the process of composition, and involves the children in more extended writing journeys, in which they can take risks and take their time, letting ideas emerge, live, be rejected or selected as they travel. Such time offers them the chance to generate and evaluate their developing stance and meaning and prioritise the content of their writing. Whilst it seems innocuous to suggest that serious writing – composition – requires a respectful amount of time, time to talk, to read, to play, to imagine and inhabit, to dream, ponder and share ideas, as well as to draft and reconstruct, this is not always easy to achieve, as the following vignette from the classroom indicates. In a class of five- and six-year-olds, after an involving beginning to a lesson, the children went to their tables to compose their poetry. Henry was confused about where he should sit; he was unsure if he was a 'tiger' or in the red group. An assertive girl pulled him toward her table and informed him sternly *you're a tiger now and in red for maths!* Henry wrote the date and started to think again about his poem. He had written one line by the time the teacher started to reassemble the class for a plenary. Henry complied; shuffled his pencils and book into the middle of the table, and was observed grumbling aloud *I never have time to finish me bits!* If writing is rushed, it can become superficial and unsatisfying. We need to offer an extended process of composition; time to journey towards writing. This provides children with the chance to play with ideas and possibilities through oral drafting and enables them to investigate ways to communicate and shape their writing through conversation and discussion. The critical role of talk in developing children's voices in writing should not be underestimated; it plays an important part in an expanded concept of composition. The argument for an expanded process for teaching writing is made by Bearne (2003), who recognises the importance of the early stages in the writing journey, and the time needed for familiarisation and capturing ideas for writing. We have added keywords to her model to highlight the complexity of travelling between reading and writing (Figure 1.3).

Current advice on writing (DfEE, 1998, 1999) does not, we believe, give sufficient weight to the initial stages of writing which focus on the genera-tion of ideas and involve children in a range of creative contexts in order to generate thinking and capture ideas. Influenced by the assessment system in England, planning for writing may have become dominated by written tasks, such as spider diagrams or lists with key words pertinent to the genre. Planning should also include oral, kinaesthetic and visual activities of various kinds which may be combined with written ones in imaginative and creative contexts. A creative context implies an environ-ment of possibility which offers choice and encourages children to experiment with ideas, take intellectual risks and find innovative ways forward in speech and writing. Such an environment is both supportive

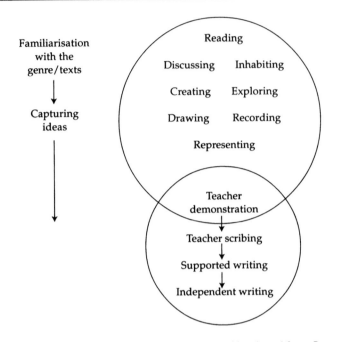

Familiarisation
with the
genre/texts

↓

Capturing
ideas

Reading

Discussing   Inhabiting

Creating   Exploring

Drawing   Recording

Representing

Teacher
demonstration

↓

Teacher scribing

↓

Supported writing

↓

Independent writing

Figure 1.3 An expanded process of composition (developed from Bearne, 2003: 32)

and challenging although is not without frames of reference. Creative teachers of writing do not ignore form and function, rules or conventions of language but seek to help children explore these in meaningful and engaging contexts. Open-ended approaches, involving all the learners in a stimulating process of exploration and experimentation, can be planned and developed from set learning objectives and can embed learning about conventions and codes within them. Language arts activities in particular, enable both children and their teachers to inhabit creative contexts, generating alternatives and selecting from among those alternatives. The tools of the hand and body, as Vygotsky (1978) asserts, can become the tools of the mind, and what is first done in physically engaging, active and interactive ways can become the source, frame and substance of writing. The later stages in the extended process of composition also involve a considerable amount of talk and inner speech as young writers re-read their own work and reflect critically with others on their written drafts. This reviewing process, when changes are made as a consequence of this evaluative thrust, makes a significant contribution to the final piece and continues to involve readers in responding to their own voices. Again this is an issue developed further in later chapters.

Literature discussions, oral storytelling, both personal and traditional, poetry performances and improvisational drama all provide potent contexts for learning about language, learning through language and developing creativity in writing. Such writing will not however be confined to writing in the poetic or expressive mode, since it is more than possible to speak with voice and verve in the context of a letter to a friend or to make one's voice heard in a letter of complaint written in the transactional mode (Britton, 1993). In addition, a range of other practices, such as writing journals, explorations and connections to the world of film, television and the internet, as well as making full use of school trips and collaborative ventures of various kinds can help create the conditions for the development of voice and verve. In this book we have chosen to focus on those contexts developed more extensively by the teachers in the We're Writers project, namely explorations through the use of writing journals, literature, drama, storytelling and poetry. We are conscious however that creativity in writing is not exclusively developed through these particular environments of possibility and expectation. Film making, multimedia authoring and non-fiction investigations offer children opportunities for developing creativity in written communication, but in drawing on our research it must be acknowledged they are not well represented here.

Echoing voices

Our written voices are intimately linked to the oral voices of others since, as Bakhtin suggests, most written genres have been framed and shaped by absorbing and digesting simpler, usually oral genres (Bakhtin, 1986: 62). A veritable 'sea of voices' therefore consciously and unconsciously supports young writers as they become apprenticed to the craft and read, hear, watch and imagine, also receiving responsive help from adults and each other (Dyson, 2000). Powerful voices from the world of literature and the rhythmic voices of poets, storytellers and singers, as well as individuals from film and TV, combine with the more personal and intimate voices of family and friends to fill the ears of young people. Their own oral voices also contribute to the oceans of talk which surround them and through which they travel as readers, writers, speakers and listeners. Thus meaning makers lean on both oral and written voices and assimilate and transform the tenor and tunes of their texts. The many voices which we glimpse in children's texts are examined more fully in the following chapter, but an example may help to show how the extended process of composition contributes to the development of voice and verve, although each piece of writing will experience a different trajectory. In a class of 8- and 9-year-olds, the teacher had been reading and exploring a number of Alan Ahlberg books with the class. This significant children's author has written extensively and his picture books as well as more recent novels were read, shared, discussed and enjoyed. Role play and other drama conventions were employed to investigate various characters and plots and prompted by

The Jolly Postman, *Peepo* and some of his other rhyming texts, the class had generated lists of playground songs and rhymes. These rhythms were revisited with pleasure and many found their way into the children's writing journals and were beautifully decorated. The teacher established that the children could use their writing journals to follow up any aspects of this three-week unit of work that they chose, and also worked with them to create their own monsters, resonant of Ahlberg's creatures in *The Dark and Stormy Night* which was the class reader at the time. Shannon became interested in the weird creatures described in the book and she shared the pictures in her mind's eye with others, generating these initial ideas and images and later choosing to draw two monster pictures. The class later created some of their monsters in group freeze frames and were invited to describe their creature's appearance, supported by teacher modelling. On another day in small groups, the children began to invent stories about their creatures and moved around in a storybuzz retelling their tales and listening to others. Whiteboards were used to capture opening sentences and the following day the children returned to this work and began to record initial plans. Whether this was for themselves or for their teacher is perhaps debatable, Shannon however, returned to her visuals, adding details and poring over her drawings in a determined manner. In the playground at break time she was observed playing 'monster games', probably triggered by her drawings, no doubt this imaginative and collaborative play also fuelled her eventual written composition. Her work and this brief description of the extended context through which it emerged, shows the diverse activities she engaged in. Over time, these helped her develop, refine and evaluate ideas for her delightful story, The Mischievous Moat Monster King!

The Mischievous Moat Monster King!

Long ago before any maps had been drawn and any lands had been named, there lived a king who had the most beautiful wife and a handsome young son. He was very proud of them both, but he was most proud of his precious crown which had opals, lapis lazuli, diamonds and pearls surrounding the white tiger skin base. His favourite part of the crown however was the rich red satin which was draped in the middle of it, it kept his head warm and made him feel important.

One day the handsome young prince, who liked to play with all the creatures in his father's castle, found a rather fat newt in a muddy puddle and fed it on blood red wine from the cellar. Unfortunately, when he was up at the topmost turret naming his newly found newt, he dropped it down down down into the moat! After a few months the newt grew into a monstrous creature, but it never forgot the taste of the red wine and was always attracted to anything red.

The monstrous newt had eyes as black as midnight, skin as slimy as a slug's trail, and big dinosaur nails on its small claws. It lived in the deepest murkiest part of the moat and acted like a fearsome tiger hunting for its prey. It drew near to anything which was the colour of blood. This ghastly creature ate whatever it could lay its claws on, but was particularly fond of human flesh. Sadly, it caused the death of a foolish guard who poked it with a stick. Often this flesh eating mogglemump was to be seen sharpening its vicious claws, they were like razors able to slice through the toughest iron. The moat monster was feared by all the members of the castle apart from one, that of course was the handsome prince who had created this terrible tortuous thing.

One day after the prince's 21st birthday, the foolish heir poured a bottle of the best red wine into the moat. This was when disaster struck! The mutant newt leapt from its lair and seized the king as he passed by. It had spied the rich red satin of his crown and snatched its prize off the monarch. Triumphantly, it placed the precious crown upon its own warty head, which was as bumpy and green as a tired old avocado. Everyone fled from the castle and the victorious monster was left to reign over the beautiful castle and the horrible moat. The mischievous moat monster king lived there forever with his prize possession, the crown of all crowns.

The pleasure in reading Shannon's tale lies in her ability to entertain, to draw her readers in and share a good yarn, building as it does on her experience of hearing stories and retelling them. She transformed her previous visual, oral and imaginary experiences in the extended process of composition, and employs similes as modelled by her teacher, using tunes from the world of folk tales, such as 'the crown of all crowns' and her opening sentence 'long ago before any maps had been drawn and any lands named, there lived a king'. It is clear she is also drawing on her reading, and is beginning to unconsciously imitate phrases she has read or heard, the 'flesh eating mogglemump' is reminiscent of the Roald Dahl's descriptions of the giants in *The BFG* and Mugglewump, the monkey from *The Twits*, both of which she had read and enjoyed. Her drawings also influenced her composition; the casually drawn crown became a central motif or object in the tale. The story is well structured and paced and was redrafted through working with a response partner, who helped her mostly with editorial decisions. Her voice and verve are evident as she spins her tale, a tale born of an extended process of composition through which she developed her growing expertise and assurance in narrative writing.

Shannon's 'Mischievous Moat Monster' also demonstrates verve, in that it reflects the energy, commitment and flair of this young writer and indicates a clear sense of her involvement in writing. Such energy is most likely to be evoked by creative texts and contexts which, as we have argued, foster relevance, autonomy and affective engagement and encourage children to use their imaginations. When we recognise verve in children's writing and in their attitude to writing, we are often able to hear their smile in their voices or feel their anger and empathise with their stance. We are also able to observe their involvement in the extended process of composition and appreciate their persistence and desire to communicate. At the start of the We're Writers project very few children, particularly in the later primary years, expressed or demonstrated either voice or verve in their written work. Their writing, as described by their teachers was lacklustre, competent perhaps, but dull and uninspiring and their attitude to writing was of considerable concern. Many found writing boring and others felt constrained by the clear boundaries and prescribed expectations that their teachers felt obliged to impose upon them. When their views were known and their most creative pieces of writing were analysed, it became evident that conversations and innovations in the teaching of writing were needed. The teachers in the project focus group, working as action researchers, experimented with alternative practices, such as writing journals and using drama to prompt and empower writing, and closely observed their case-study children, analysing their writing on the way. We found no easy solution for enabling children to write with voice and verve, but working collaboratively we all developed new insights, knowledge and understanding about creativity and writing which are shared in this book. Echoes of all our colleagues' voices are, we hope, present in the final text, alongside their children's energetic and inspiring writing.

Conclusion

When learners are engaged in mindful, negotiated, interactive and creative literacy practices which encompass writing, their oral and written voices reflect their affective and authentic involvement. Participation in such practices can extend children's communicative competence, their understanding, their self-esteem and sense of agency in writing and enable them to adopt a more creative stance towards writing. Teachers too, if artistically involved, can plan more extended writing journeys and adopt a more creative state of mind. 'Promoting creativity is a powerful way of engaging pupils with their learning' (DfES, 2003: 34) and can make a marked difference to children's commitment to and interest in writing, as well as influence their ability to write with voice and verve, with authenticity and vigour. There is no formula for voice, but the potential of creative

approaches which enable us to see the world differently and make connections must be recognised and developed in our classrooms. In the next
chapter we examine the many voices which children assimilate in their
writing and the complex process of finding their own.

Chapter 2

The 'voice-strewn landscape'

Children engage with many texts to help them understand the world and are assisted in this task by a wealth of different voices that are part of the busy forum that is culture (Bruner, 1986). If culture is seen as a forum of voices negotiating, renegotiating and agreeing meanings and 'realities', then these voices are the starting point for children's own written contributions to the forum. What children want to talk and write about is influenced by the texts that they have heard, seen, read, watched and played with: the books, stories, rhymes, songs, television, film, dramas, video games and artefacts that make up their dialogue with their culture. Children appropriate voices from these various texts in their writing, transforming and re-shaping their own voices in the process. If, when they compose, they lean on the 'voice-strewn landscape' (Bakhtin, 1986) for their own purposes and creatively employ the processes of transformation or transduction (Kress, 2003) then their voices are flexed and exercised.

Bakhtin (1981: 293) argues that 'the word in language is half someone else's' and in this chapter we explore others' words and voices which children creatively assimilate and rework in their writing, and examine the changing nature of this landscape of literacy highlighting the influence of popular consumer texts on children's compositions. We begin our discussion, which is extended throughout the book, of other voices found in written fiction, oral stories, poetry and drama and reflect upon the fact that children are part of a cultural forum far larger than present-day curricula suggest. We propose both a widening of literacy horizons and an increased awareness of the need to develop authenticity, conviction and individuality: voice in writing.

The changing landscape of voices

Outside school, children are exposed to an ever-increasing forum of voices. As technology develops, the landscape of communication expands and children experience others' voices through communication in web chat rooms, blogging, email and texting (Snyder, 2003). In this new world, driven by social and economic change, forms of meaning-making and communication are rapidly increasing and much more extensive use is made of the image, not only on the computer, but also in newspapers, advertisements, pamphlets and printed information texts and narratives of various kinds. In such texts, the image no longer just illustrates the written word or repeats what the written text has conveyed (Barthes, 1967), but plays a more central and complex role (Kress, 1997). The 'voice' of the image and its affordance is different to that of the written word, for each mode of representation has its own affordance (Kress and Van Leeuwen, 1997). These changes have reconfigured the nature of reading and text production, and mean that the children we work with think and work differently from us as adults (Bearne, 2003a).

> Children live in a highly complex visual world and are bombarded with visual stimuli more intensely than most preceding generations. Yet few teachers spend time helping children sort out, recognise and understand the many forms of visual information they encounter, certainly not in the same way teachers deal with print literacy.
>
> (Kiefer, 1995: 10)

The diversity of multimodal texts extends well beyond illustrated books and includes for example: newspapers and advertisements, computer games and graphics, films and television in all their genres, magazines and comics, pop videos and song lyrics as well as environmental print. The range can sometimes overwhelm and challenge teachers who are likely to have experienced a smaller range of textual forms as young readers and writers. In addition, the often negative connotation applied to popular cultural and consumer texts can influence their use in school. This was evident in the early stages of the We're Writers project, in which we found some teachers who were alienated by the unknown world of multimedia and multimodal texts and inclined to make unquestioned assumptions about them (Lambirth, 2003). Some of the difficulties children experience in expressing themselves using the conventions of the written word may derive from their considerably greater experience and interaction with other modes. When invited to write, today's children may find it difficult to translate their aural words and their images held in the mind's eye into written words. They may be moving between rapid film or comic-strip images and the written word and 'deserve to be given the key to translating their inner text making into coherent communications' (Bearne, 2003a: 99), which may be achieved through discussion of both written and multimodal texts and their different but complementary communicative potential.

Children's writing often reflects their experience of multimodal communication and they move apparently seamlessly from mode to mode as they seek to make meaning, using image for representing spatial arrangements and speech-like writing for representing temporal arrangements (Bearne and Kress, 2001). Image, speech, and writing as a mixed mode are in part speech-like and in part image-like, and offer different logics for reading and for representing. Young people's competence in borrowing, adopting and adapting different modes for their own purposes is considerable, yet whilst they are becoming increasingly multi-modally literate, many of their teachers remain relatively print bound (Millard, 2003). Public domains of communication do, however, utilise a more multimodal approach to text, with a particular emphasis upon the image, so as teachers we need to challenge conventional conceptions of literacy based primarily on the written word and expand the literacy curriculum in school to reflect these changes (Marsh and Millard, 2000; Millard, 2003; Kress, 1997). Children have much to say and deserve a chair in the forum for their often multidimensional and multimodal literacy practices. The inclusion of non-print literacy in schools can complement work around written texts and reveal more numerous voices reflecting and validating children's diverse literacy experiences. As forms and modes of communication continue to change and are transformed through use, new intonation patterns, different volumes and voice flavours will emerge in the 'voice-strewn landscape', these deserve to be respected, recognised and built upon in the context of schooling.

Acknowledging diverse voices in school

It is widely accepted that models of literacy evolve and exist within power structures and reflect the interests of different power groups, but if literacy is understood as a social practice 'defined by the social and communicative practices which individuals engage in the various domains of their life world' (Barton and Hamilton, 1998: 9), then a wider range of practices and voices need to be acknowledged in school. Literacy is not a unitary, neutral entity, but a rich and varied activity, driven by the context within which it occurs and shaped by the purposes for which it is used, so curricula based on research into actual literacy practices are needed (Street, 1997). In exploring some of the literacy practices in their research sample, Barton and Hamilton (1998) show how the human factor and voice ring through and reveal various individuals' 'ruling passions' as they make sense of their lives and participate socially. Yet such vernacular literacies often have very little formal status and are frequently undervalued in schools (Luke and Carrington, 2002).

Current literacy curricula in English primary schools (DfEE, 1998b, 1999) fail to reflect the growing number and diversity of voices that children engage with outside school, and as a result there are a number of vacant chairs in the forum of school. Advice advocates the inclusion of a particular set of written text types and medium-term planning is often sculpted around these. Teachers are expected to undertake units of work and immerse children in certain text types leading them towards an imitative recreation of the chosen form (DfEE, 1999). According to this pedagogical approach to writing, based on genre theory, knowledge about form and feature enables children to express themselves appropriately. However, this model is at present biased towards printed genres and does not encompass all the multimodal forms of communication available (Millard, 2003; Bearne, 2003a). In addition this paradigm tends to view genres as fixed, when in reality they are often blurred and the form must be made their own. Children who engage with and learn about the conventions of 'unofficial texts' at home may become alienated from school literacy practices if these remain narrow or static. Yet children continue to be schooled in a relevant but somewhat detached and limited set of disciplines that may be perceived by them as simply the 'stuff' of tests and exams. Their conceptualisations of literacy open and close possible avenues of communication, and in order to develop their voice and verve in writing we must seek to recognise the diverse landscape of literacies that currently exist and encourage them to draw on these.

In the We're Writers schools, many teachers, in response to the children's requests for increased autonomy and choice in writing, established writing journals. These are examined in more detail in Chapter 4, but it is worth noting that in this, their own work, the children made full use of their knowledge and experience of multimodal texts and frequently drew on popular cultural and consumer texts in their writing. Nathan's hilarious cartoon of Hairy Potty and the Justice of Captain Underpants, Figure 2.1, highlights this practice and the children's ability to draw on diverse and contemporary voices and visuals. This 10-year-old took particular delight and some considerable time to complete his ingenious work of art, in it he demonstrates his own 'cultural capital' (Bourdieu, 1986). Composed at the time that the second Harry Potter movie, based on J.K. Rowling's book *Harry Potter and the Chamber of Secrets* hit the cinema, his cartoon's title amusingly combines Harry Potter and the phrase 'hairy botty' which had street cred in the school at the time. It also involves the popular character Captain Underpants, from Dav Pilkey's books. These were admired by the boys in his class and were passed around his peer group through 'the underground network' in the classroom. Nathan had just finished reading *Captain Underpants and the Wrath of the Wicked Wedgie Woman* and was keen to start another. His cartoon is an original idea, well executed, reflecting his knowledge and enthusiasm for the world of cartoons, for he was an avid Beano reader, a silver Beano club member in fact. His enthusiasm for Pilkey's zany books is also reflected in this work. The storyline documents a young man who flushes his hair cream down the toilet, the toilet grows hairier and hairier and bigger and bigger, until Hairy Potty bursts out into the world and runs around causing mischief. Finally Captain Underpants

Figure 2.1a Hairy Potty and the Justice of Captain Underpants

outwits him, using an electric cable to put the beast to rest! For Nathan, this work represented a real step forward. He had initiated it, clearly enjoyed working through it, and demonstrated considerable persistence which is a key feature of creativity. He makes unexpected connections between unrelated pieces of knowledge and his work creates an 'effective surprise', which Bruner (1962: 18) sees as the 'hallmark of creative enterprise'. The fact that his teacher and, probably more importantly, his peers took pleasure and delight in reading it, also helped Nathan. He began to experience a sense of himself as an author, an entertainer in this context

Figure 2.1b *Hairy Potty and the Justice of Captain Underpants*, continued

and he responded enthusiastically to the request for further narratives about his hairy toilet monster. His own unique voice in this work and the diverse and multimodal voices of all children deserve to be heard in school and in addition, as Bearne (2003c) argues, mixed modes of communication should be incorporated into assessment arrangements, so children's competences and skills are not short changed. Contemporary discussions of the 'reader in the writer' must also take into account such alternative modes of representation and communication.

The myriad of others' voices

In school, children's voices, like Nathan's, echo the voices of others, gleaned from their active engagement with particular people and texts that have helped shape their identities. Their written and oral voices are peppered with others' words and voices. Bakhtin (1986) points out that 'chuzhaia rech' – quoted speech – permeates all our language activities in both practical and artistic communication, and through an examination of Rabelais' use of the language of the marketplace and Parisian street cries, he shows that we are more often dealing with someone else's language than with our own.

> Our speech is filled with others' words, varying degrees or otherness or varying degrees of our-own-otherness, varying degrees of awareness and detachment. These words of others carry with them their own expression, their own evaluative tone, which we assimilate, rework and accentuate.
>
> (Bakhtin, 1986: 89)

Other people's speech makes it possible, Bakhtin argues, for us to generate our own and thus it becomes an indispensable factor in the creative power of language. Classrooms have a rich diversity of socio-cultural differences based on the languages spoken, the cultural styles of communication and familial and gender differences. This diversity of experience provides the classroom with different perspectives, different voices and a plethora of possibilities. As Dyson observes, however, these differences are seldom viewed as resources and are 'primarily viewed as "problems" that more affluent (and homogeneous) schools do not have' (Dyson, 1997: 168). Socio-cultural differences need to be recognised and transformative and transductive possibilities seized (Kress, 2003), if we are to build on children's early oral and aural experiences and encourage them to draw from the 'voice-strewn landscape' in the context of their writing.

In the We're Writers project we asked the children in the initial survey where they felt their ideas for story writing came from. Their responses were predictably varied, over half perceived that ideas just arrived, dawned upon them or popped up in their minds. The reminder mentioned the influence of television and film, their teacher and books in that order. Several stated that they invented their own ideas and in the follow-up interviews many of the young people voiced the view that to borrow ideas from other writers, from TV or life was to cheat, to steal and was neither original nor acceptable. Some theorists have argued that the world of ideas seems to recycle itself and is unable to avoid the continuous use of the same bank of ideas, with constant retelling and self-referencing (Kearney, 1994). But intertextuality can engender originality, when the connections stem from the being of the creator. Creativity does call upon socially established forms but 'it incorporates the original when the private imagination generates alternatives and extensions' (Cremin, 1998: 11). Such alternatives and extensions will be influenced by the myriad of voices with which the children are acquainted. Mostly unconsciously they will appropriate these, exploring them and trying them on for size, before transforming them as they shape and tune their own voices, both oral and written.

Various authors and educational researchers have commented on the concept of voice and we have examined their thinking and listened to them in order to develop our own understanding. Graves (1983) for example, suggests voice is the imprint of ourselves in writing and Bearne too, highlights voice as a quality which is individual and convinced, one that reflects 'the ring of conviction of a writer' (Bearne, 2002: 10). The connection to the oral voice of the writer is clear in Olson's (1997) work also; he suggests that the written text preserves not the word, but the voice itself. In Native American cultures and elsewhere, each stone, tree and element is attributed its own voice, and so perhaps it is with writers who successfully convey that sense of individuality and uniqueness in their writing, marking their work out as different, as their own. Part of learning to read and write involves us in learning to hear the tunes in texts (Barrs, 2000) and learning to use the available resources to find the tunes and rhythms in our own voices. Reading aloud for example, can help children hear the author's voice, and if this voice is brought to life through a teacher's performative reading, it can make a marked contribution to the quality of children's writing (Barrs and Cork, 2001). These researchers suggest that the development of an ear for language is one of a reader's and a writer's most valuable attributes, and show that the development of this 'inner ear' for language is enhanced by extensive aural experience of language. It is also likely to be extended through children experiencing language themselves, through personally reading literature aloud, through poetry performances and through engagement in drama and oral storytelling. Full engagement in these and other creative language practices motivates learners and encourages playful experimentation and innovation as well as increased agency and control. As teachers we need to help children hear, notice and experience language emotionally, aesthetically and artistically, so that their voices ring with authenticity and individuality and carry a sense of this full participation and experiential engagement. As children compose and communicate, they reshape the dimensions and tunes of texts they know and with support will find their own voices in this process. As Britton has observed, 'trying other people's voices may be a natural and necessary part of the process of finding one's own' (Britton, 1970: 57). It is to examples of these different voices which we now turn.

Literary voices and the voices of storytellers

Children imitate, emulate and appropriate different voices through their engagement in the world of fiction and through their experience of oral stories, anecdotes, reminiscences, gossip and traditional folklore of many kinds. As they become well acquainted with literary rhythms and patterns, they play with these forms and begin to innovate and borrow ideas, images, structures and tunes to enrich their own writing. This process is examined in more detail in Chapters 5 and 7, on written literature and oral stories respectively, but it is worth noting here that the influence of reading on writing is well documented, and authors are widely recognised as mentors to young writers (e.g. Harwayne, 1992; Fox, 1993; Mallet, 1997). Recent work shows convincingly how children draw on literature with which they have imaginatively engaged, and how the literary texts they have been exposed to 'encourage them to write differently, moving out of what might be termed their "home style" into new areas of language' (Barrs and Cork, 2001: 210). Experience of many authors' voices and thoughtful teaching which highlighted particular literary voices helped the 9–11-year-olds in this research to write with voice and verve; they took on the language of the text and echoed the author's style. As Jill Paton Walsh (1996) observes, a 'narrative voice might mean the strategy deliberately adopted by the writer, fully self-aware, for telling a story, and it might mean that indefinable quality which makes it possible to recognise small fragments of a writer's work, which distinguishes it, even in dialogue, from the works of other writers'. Our sense of voice in writing relates to the latter of these possibilities, and involves, we perceive, a real sense of individuality reflecting their creative engagement and fully adopted stance. Becoming aware of their own and others' voices, intonation patterns and impact can enrich children's creativity in writing. This is assisted through 'public reading', which Alberto Manguel (quoted in Barrs and Cork, 2001) suggests is an important form of publishing as it offers the writer the chance to bring the writing to life and 'give the text a tone'. As children read their own work aloud to interested others, they hear their own voices and may begin to evaluate their writing, appreciating moments in the text when their voice is clear or confused.

In describing the diversity of social speech types used by novelists in their writing, Bakhtin notes that authors orchestrate a vast array of 'social voices and a wide variety of their links and interrelationships' (Bakhtin, 1981: 144). Novelists use these, he suggests, for their own artistic purposes as they are not constrained by any particular form of language use. He champions the freeing of consciousness through language and foregrounds the author's relative freedom to select from the 'voice-strewn landscape', believing that aesthetic intentions are compromised by having to sculpt a piece of writing in the image of a particular form, although he does accept that breaking frames depends on the existence of them. A pedagogy that severely restricts a writer's freedom, however, and insists upon a specific use of language, runs the risk of cleansing the author's voice from their own work. Children, like adult novelists, can make language work for them and develop their individual voices by drawing on their knowledge and galvanising diverse voices for their own intentions. Through listening to the music of oral stories and through telling and writing tales of their own lives as well as folk tales, children may find their voices as they share their individual frames of reference and experience with others. In particular, stories which celebrate and recognise the cultural histories and voices of all ethnic groups are important as they make learning socially, emotionally and culturally relevant. Through such oral storytelling, children learn to hear the rhythms and cadence of different tales and make links between their spoken language and the texts they write, often creating close personal connections with the plights of particular characters (Fox, 1993). As children participate in and explore the tradition of oral story-telling, through play, through retelling and through re-enactment, they appropriate the materials and the modes of telling, and inhabit the voices of the tellers in the social process of production. This demonstrates their agency and volition in the extended process of composition and enables them to exercise and develop their authorial voices.

Voices from the world of popular culture

The world of popular culture includes some of the most urgent and compelling voices for children: television programmes, music, advertising, comics, magazines, film, merchandise from films, foods, drinks, clothes and sports. Although many of the texts and practices in this world are transitory in nature (Bernstein, 1996), children take considerable pleasure in them and are adept at manipulating them for their own devices. Yet adult understanding of popular culture is elementary in comparison to the 'real-time' knowledge possessed by the young, and teachers need to be aware that children may not wish to discuss openly 'that which they hold sacred and important in their world outside the classroom' (Alvermann et al., 1999: 22). Popular culture is sometimes used as a means into the traditional literacy curriculum as it captures the interests of the children and can enable teachers to introduce aspects of the English curriculum that may initially appear unpalatable to children, particularly those whose home literacy practices are not reflected in the normal diet of school life. Marsh and Millard (2000) reflect on the benefits of tuning into the voices inherent in popular cultural texts and of recontextualising these into officially recognised generic forms. Bromley (2002) gives an example of this kind of practice using the popular cartoon show 'The Simpsons'. Utilising the website, she offers children brief biographical information about each character and suggests that they discuss these and use their own knowledge of a chosen Simpsons character to create an autobiographical account. This transformative activity draws on children's existing knowledge from the show, motivates them by linking to the worlds of TV and comics and explicitly connects the work to teaching about the genre of diary writing. But is the use of popular culture in this particular instance no more than a bait to lure children into traditional forms of literacy (Lambirth, 2003)? The rich semiotic of popular cultural texts can do more than motivate learners, who have the potential to work transductively across many modes and make their own animated cartoons or who can script and produce their own Simpsons movies for example. As teachers we must ensure new-technology mediated practices in classrooms engage with and explore new ways of working. As Lankshear and Knobel (2003: 29) acknowledge, 'school routines are highly regular forms of practice that are intimately linked to what we call the "deep grammars" of schooling, as well as to aspects of policy development and imposition'. They believe that classrooms are unlikely sites for 'new literacies', but teachers can encourage children to flexibly mix semiotic modes and make full use of transductive opportunities which have the potential to feed and fuel their writing. In doing so, children may reconceptualise communication for the adults around them as they move between modes, exploiting image, sound and movement and creatively using language in the process. This issue of how children lean on the voices of popular cultural texts is examined more fully in Chapter 4 with particular reference to writing journals and autonomy in writing.

Poetic and musical voices

Children's early induction into their culture is often packed with speech events; their conversations and banter are full of word play, jokes and nicknames, anecdotes and idioms, rhymes and riddles. These verbal art forms are potentially fluid and fed by the media as well as the oral tradition and children's own modifications are often playful, transformative and transductive as they draw on music, song and dance to spin new songs and rhymes into existence. Such performance poetry creates meaning through a combination of rhythm, intonation, gesture, music and song and depends on the interaction between text, audience and performer for its efficacy (Hoyles and Hoyles, 2003). As performance poet Linton Kwesi Johnson (1975: 12) remarks, 'my poems may look sort of flat on the page. Well, that is because they're actually oral poems, as such. They were definitely written to be read aloud, in the community'.

The oral tradition ensures children hear a diverse range of poetic voices through conversation and word play in the home (Grainger and Goouch, 1999), in the playground (Grugeon, 1999) and in the community. These voices are often vital and energetic and are frequently experimented with and manipulated, borrowed and subverted for their own purposes and for the sheer pleasure of playing with sounds and savours, words and tunes. In analysing the oceans of everyday talk in the CANCODE Corpus, Carter (2004) shows that language play is a creative social practice which pervades many aspects of everyday life. Meek too, demonstrates that as children learn to handle the language of the taken-for-granted in their culture, they 'experiment with parody and impropriety, guile and authority baiting' (Meek, 1985: 47) and become wordsmiths, whose voices creatively undermine or challenge existing forms and function almost as an element of the carnivalesque (Bakhtin, 1986). The world of popular music also offers rich rhythms and powerful voices which children unconsciously learn to recite, sing and subvert in the company of others. Yet in the context of school, poetry may be divorced from music and song, physicality and performance, obliging children to separate their experience of the vital voice of poetry from the earnest study and production of this literary form. Chapter 8 explores possible ways to retain the potent voice of language play and poetry in the writing classroom and examples elsewhere show how catchphrases, songs and chants that express the children's inner voices are recorded by them to retain, to revisit and to share.

Imagined and inhabited voices

Imaginative play, whether in the context of the playground, the role play area or in improvisational classroom drama, involves making and shaping new worlds, investigating issues within them and returning to the real world with more understanding and insight. It also offers a rich context for creating and hearing others' voices and perspectives and, as in ordinary, creative conversation, children 'move between voices as the context changes, developing in the process a kind of multi-voicing' (Carter, 2004: 68). The complex web of different sign systems which drama employs, including facial expression, body language, words and their intonation, gesture, mime and movement and space, combine to communicate in sound, image and movement. As an intertextual art form, drama encompasses these many 'dramatic literacies' (Nicholson, 2000) and provides a clearer than usual sense of perspective and voice and an opportunity for authentically engaging in writing, reading, speaking and listening. In role, the voices of the characters and their inner and outer lives are explored, which can help give shape, content and an emotive stance to any writing and a clearer sense of voice to the writer. In role play in the playground, in classrooms and in home contexts, children re-enact and rehearse familiar scenes, and invent imaginary others based on media texts or known narratives, exploring the voices of different characters in each setting. As they play they often narrate the events, experience a sense of authorship and employ a narrator's voice in the process (Grugeon and Harding, 2004).

The plurality of such voices from a wide range of texts, be they fictional, poetic, popular or imagined are assimilated, appropriated and reshaped in both speech and writing, and they contribute considerably to the development of children's own voices.

Developing our own voices

Semiotically, continuity exists between reading and writing, for writing, like reading, is the production of new signs from existing and available resources. Readers internally produce such signs, whereas writers externally produce them, often for a multiple readership (Kress, 1995). When writers weave in their own experience of materials read and absorbed, they transform the writing and make new resources out of already existing ones, drawing on their own identity, personality and subjectivity in the process. Such transformation, Kress (2003) suggests, occurs within each mode of communication and makes links between categories, but operates in only one mode at a time. Transduction, on the other hand, is the process of possible shifts across different modes and involves something that has been configured or shaped in one or more modes, being reconfigured and reshaped according to the affordances of a different mode. Kress's (2003) theory of transformation and transduction shows how writers are able to stamp their own mark on their meaning making and create a clearer culturally and socially individual voice.

> Voice is the imprint of ourselves on the writing. It is the part of the self that pushes the writing ahead, the dynamo in the process.
>
> (Graves, 1983: 227)

If the author's voice is to ring with conviction and meaning, then the writer's own individual imprint needs to surface in the writing. But written conventions tend to standardise language and as we move from speech to writing we lose the immediacy and interpersonal contact with our audience, and run the risk of losing our individuality and personal voice. At school, children are currently assessed on their ability to standardise their writing to different degrees, yet successful writers appear to speak through the conventions that their mode of representation dictates and still retain their individuality and uniqueness. Skilful writers may expose the roots of their writing – themselves as individuals, speakers and listeners – and instil this energy into their written words. Heaney seemed to perceive this and argued accordingly.

There is a connection between the core of the poet's speaking voice and the core of his poetic voice, between his original accent and his discovered style. I think that the discovery of a way of writing that is natural and adequate to your sensibility depends on the recovery of your own unique voice ... that is the absolute register to which your proper music has to be tuned.

(Heaney, 1980: 72)

In the past, writing that came close to speech was often hounded out of public domains of communication, which demonstrates the power and influence of formal writing, writing marked by power difference. However, the social relations of writing appear to be changing for, as Kress (2003) argues, academic writing and professional writing of various kinds, including official writing, were once all demarcated by strict observance of this power differential. Now this is beginning to disappear, albeit at different paces in different domains, which may help to develop the inhabited voice of young writers. Some purposes and forms may, however, reduce the writer's voice. Factual writing of textbooks for example, tends to increase the distance between the author and the reader (Buckingham and Scanlon, 2003), since this kind of writing can 'separate speech from speaker, and that separation in itself may make the words impersonal, objective, and above criticism' (Olson, 1980: 192). A personal voice, on the other hand, increases the solidarity between readers and writers and may make connections between them (Van de Kopple and Crismore, 1990). When children realise their inner worlds can be successfully converted into writing, through the practice of using writing journals for example, and that their work can be shared, recognised and celebrated by their friends, then 'the true power and joy of writing is experienced' (Johnson, 2003: 7). If the old Arabic proverb that says 'Man is hidden behind his tongue' bears any truth, then teachers need to find the people behind the words and help their young learners carefully convey their individuality and uniqueness, their sense of self in writing.

Whether the roots of writing are in speech (Graves, 1983; Rosen, 1989), is an issue we examine further in the next chapter on talk and writing. Writing does use some of the same materials: words, order and organisation, but there are clear differences between them due to the functional load of each medium. In conversation, we present ourselves in multimodal ways: our clothes, accent, dialect, gestures and facial expressions all speak volumes, and we interact with our audience to create shared meanings. But when we communicate through writing, we are faced with trying to share much of this layered knowledge through the logic of the written word to an unknown audience. Rosen (1989) argues that children are introduced to the conventions and logic of the written mode too soon and proposes that their entry into writing should be linked explicitly to the spoken word.

> Children need to discover that 'exactly what they say' can be represented on the page right from the start. They need to carry on doing that among the other kinds of writing they learn as they get older. In this way children will have a foundation of literacy based on the competence they already possess: their oral language.
>
> (Rosen, 1989: 34)

The relations between written and spoken genres deserve further examination, but as teachers we must guard against writing practices which cause 'genre theory to descend like a suffocating blanket on the ways we approach stories and poems with young primary children' (Martin, 2003: 17). From a genre perspective, as noted earlier, writers apparently find their voices through the systematically practising of different text types. 'Just as the voice of a trumpet rings out clearer and stronger for being forced through a narrow tube' (de Montaigne, trans. Screech, 1987), so the voice of the writer purportedly develops through widening children's knowledge about and adherence to the disciplines of different genres. But such an approach, if adopted too literally, carries the danger of authorial cleansing – the removal of the individual's voice, and if our aim is 'not to impart knowledge about language but to develop every child's individual writing voice' (Hilton, 2001: 9), then we need to offer freedom alongside form and support for playful innovation as well as imitation.

> For children, as for adults, freedom is a verb, a becoming; it is experienced as an expanded sense of agency, of possibility for choice and action.
>
> (Dyson, 1997: 166)

Such freedom, however, does not involve providing children with pen, paper, keyboard or a screen and leaving them to their own devices. It needs to help children sense a whole realm of possibilities beyond their current borders and must provide support for their endeavours. Knowledge about language in this context is essential, but purpose and audience determine the choice of textual features and children deserve to experience to communicate the desire in imaginatively engaging and creative contexts. Motivated, they are free to play with ideas, images and issues and inhabit and transform their own and others' voices in the process.

Conclusion

Many voices reverberate across the changing landscape of literacy, yet only certain voices are heard and valued in school. Children engage in a dialogue with a wide range of communicative modes and their compositional competence needs to be celebrated and developed so they can draw more fully on the 'voice-strewn landscape'. The inclusion of multiple modes of communication in the classroom validates children's implicit knowledge and experience and enables them to assimilate and build upon the voices of others to explore their ideas and connect their inner and outer worlds. Children absorb and develop others' voices and add to their creative potential for composition in sometimes unrecognised ways. Through the processes of transformation and transduction, children can find their personal writing voice and express something of themselves in their writing. Their own voices resound clearly when the journey between speech and writing has been an engaging, creative and reflective one, undertaken through the extended process of composition. It is to the issue of the role of talk in writing that we now turn.

Chapter 3

Talking and writing

Oracy is a crucial foundation for the development of literacy. From their earliest encounters, young children learn to engage in joint constructions, learn to negotiate meaning and actively seek to solve problems. In the process they make full use of oral competencies which are the basis of literate behaviour (Geekie, 2003). As they develop their oral voices, they prepare the ground for their later entry into written language, although as Vygotsky asserts:

> unlike the teaching of spoken language into which children grow of their own accord, the teaching of written language is based on artificial training (which) relegates living written language to the background.
> (Vygotsky, 1978: 105)

If we wish to develop children's voice and verve in writing, this living language deserves our serious attention, for as we have argued already, it is possible to teach knowledge about writing in ways that foster flexibility and increase children's agency. But such teaching depends in large part on the oral culture of the classroom, as well as on the teacher's subject knowledge, pedagogical understanding and awareness of the need for creativity in teaching writing. In this chapter, we explore the early development of children's voices, their playful interactions and purposeful behaviour which set the stage for later development, both oral and written. We highlight the importance of oral stories, play and drawing as early symbolising activities and examine the significance of intentionality and autonomy. The constraints and challenges of developing integrated literacy practice, with a high profile for talk in school are examined and teachers' perspectives are shared. Generative talk which can nurture children's voices, increase their involvement and help them shape ideas and play with possibilities is considered and the importance of scaffolding children's understanding is explored. We also argue that children need to develop a reflective metalanguage to talk about writing and themselves as writers, so they can voice their views and respond reciprocally to one other. In addition, the practice of writing collaboratively with others is examined as a valuable example of the significance of talk in developing writing.

The early development of voice

Soon after birth, infants develop a voice, their individual voice, in the company of others and facilitated by more experienced family and community members. Although this may initially be used for functional purposes, the voice of the child is soon employed to express emotion, to make choices, to manipulate others and situations and to express a sense of their growing identity. It has been shown that during the last months in the uterus, the foetus develops a growing sensitivity to the unique qualities of its mother's voice and the rhythms of her native language, as if the foetus is busy 'eavesdropping on its mother's conversations' (Karmiloff and Karmiloff-Smith, 2001). This early introduction to the nature of the primary carer's voice carries with it messages of enculturation as, after birth, the baby will consolidate and extend this learning through experience (Greenfield, 2000). Babies arrive primed for attachment and interaction, and their primary carers, predominantly their mothers, are able to tune into conversations with them. These often wordless conversations, which include 'cooing' and 'motherese' operate as if mother and child are taking part in an intimate dance (Gopnik *et al.*, 1999). Such protoconversations in the first year of life show that infants are able to take turns, predict and infer from the sounds and patterns of language that they hear (Trevarthen and Aitken, 2001). Through jointly employing sounds, gestures and facial expressions, infants and their carers develop relationships, reciprocity and intersubjectivity (Murray and Trevarthen, 1985).

A developmental pathway may be drawn from crying to babbling to the development of voice, with babies operating as prime movers able to exert considerable influence over their lives. They realise early on that what they *say*, that is the noises they make, and what they *do*, can change the behaviour of others and affect the context and the environment in which they are living. The range of sounds, patterns, tunes, language and scenarios of families feed the naturally curious nature of babies and their knowledge of language and literacy grows in such safe and familiar cultural contexts as they take up a role within the drama of family life (Bruner, 1986; Gopnik *et al.*, 1999). Alongside this development, babies are also learning to reach and later point, creating communicative gestures. Vygotsky suggests that 'the gesture is the initial visual sign that contains the child's future writing as an acorn contains a future oak' (Vygotsky, 1978: 107) and highlights the role of interaction and physical engagement. Children's early language and literacy learning is bound by the models and practices they encounter, which enable them construct meaning from experience, make inferences and shape their intentions. Such opportunities shape their oral and written voices and it is to these which we now turn.

Play, drawing and story making

As children grow and learn, with approval to sustain them, they begin to use concrete experience and a developing knowledge of the world in their play. The transformative act of reconstructing the narratives of their lives into symbolic acts in play, happens in a variety of imaginative ways, as children work with one or more of the 'hundred languages of children', for example, dancing, singing, storying, patterning, model making, mark making or talking (David *et al.*, 2003). Through play, they negotiate meaning and learn to symbolise by making one thing stand for another, for example, a scarf may become a table cloth, a Lego brick may become a cake and a pair of cupped hands may stand for an imaginary, yet steaming cup of tea. Such symbolism in play is the origin of composition and is often accompanied by 'story muttering' when children are playing alone. This may include commentary and dialogue or more developed oral storying in the company of others. Such talk is often almost inaudible when children play alone, but in some of the deep play of childhood, in the 'third space' as Winnicott (1974) describes it, their play may involve others and their language may be heard. Young children energetically and enthusiastically exploit the potential of narrative and use it to construe their world (Moffett, 1970; Egan, 2003), and fortunately for many of them, their explorations are modelled, mediated and scaffolded by parents, carers and siblings who offer them verbal and non-verbal support. Even without such support, young children's imaginations are strong and committed when they are engaged in serious play, as they conjure up possibilities, manipulate objects and tell stories to themselves or others. The role of metaphor is central to children's imaginative development and is used with ease and understanding within their oral cultural life, in narrative play, in word play and when they subvert language patterns and forms. Their 'delight in utterance' (Oakeshott, 1959) and playful engagement with the lore and language of the culture is well known (Grugeon, 1988) and provides much pleasure and satisfaction to the young who make seamless links between different modes of communication and invent and create their own meanings within family groups or other contexts. As Carter's analysis of everyday adult speech reveals, 'creative language is not a capacity of special people but a special capacity of all people. It shows speakers as language makers not simply language users' (Carter, 2004: 215). This creative capacity begins in the early years as children symbolically play with ideas, feelings and meanings.

Children's symbolic play can be understood, Vygostsky (1978) suggests, as a complex system of 'speech' through gestures that communicate; he argues that representation in play is essentially a particular form of speech which leads directly to written language and he discusses how gesture, drawing and play are closely linked. Vygotsky proposes that as children become symbolists, the marks they make become 'mnemotechnic symbols' or 'gestural depictions', so their early mark making and drawing can be seen as indicatory gestures as they attempt to fix their play in time and space and represent what they know. The importance of such early 'written' pieces, whether they are represented as marks, drawings, symbols, alphabetic print or as maps of play (Barrs, 1988), is in the chosen form and the process undertaken to construct the narrative. Attempting to understand and interpret children's marks and drawings requires some understanding of their community and culture, as Barrs' (1988) account of 5-year-old Ben's maps of play indicate.

> The roots of writing lie in the other forms of symbolising (drawing, modelling, play, drama) that children engage in before they come to the abstract symbolic system of writing.
>
> (Barrs, 1988: 114)

Play, drawing, exploration, talk and interaction form the basis of culturally bound communicative acts and as Malaguzzi claims, children constantly construct and reinvent their own ideas, for they are 'apt to explore, make discoveries, change their points of view and fall in love with forms and meanings that transform themselves' (Malaguzzi, 1998: 75). Through such explorations, different shapes and forms of expression emerge and become part of children's repertoires of stories. Early drawing and play prepare children for the development of written language, and later their knowledge continues to be actively constructed through interaction with others, giving rise to the intra-personal development of the individual.

Intentionality and autonomy

A crucial issue in children's early oral encounters with text is that of their autonomy and intentionality. When given space, time and appropriate resources, children attend voraciously to what interests them and naturally and purposefully engage in literacy practices, involving both oral and written events. Three-year-old Billy, for example, came into the nursery yard nearly every morning with a gang of girls running after him wanting to play kiss-chase. On one occasion, he ran inside to the writing corner, made some marks on a page, folded this up and placed it in an envelope. He then gave it to his teacher saying *Can you give it to them, it says they can kiss me later.* Billy was already discovering the symbolic power that writing can provide! In recording his 3-year-old granddaughter's literacy practices,

Campbell (1999) too found that these were almost exclusively initiated and managed by her. By availing themselves of the 'cultural litter' of their homes (Pahl, 2001) and other familiar sites, children learn to work within the social frame that has been constructed for them, and are often observed seizing the initiative in these contexts and using language and literacy for their own purposes. In supportive situations, even very young children take risks and push boundaries as they explore the potential for power and influence that oracy and literacy can provide.

At home and in nurseries, children engage in 'free flow play' (Bruce, 1987; Bruce and Meggitt, 2002) and are seen to 'externalise' their thoughts, voicing ideas that have occurred to them and developing concepts. In such self-directed play, children construct and manipulate situations incorporating a range of communicative acts, cultural rituals and texts, and 'engage in semiotic worlds in which texts in different modes are conceptually linked' (Marsh, 2003: 43). Their early literacy practices are seamlessly woven together with actions, dramas and reconstructions, with talk, visual creations and printed versions and their experience of selecting particular representations or modes in their playful activities are a strong foundation for expressing themselves in our changing world. Although, initially, as Kress (2000) observes, children plausibly relate voice with image, in alphabetic cultures such as ours, they are required to crack new codes relating sound with image (the image of a letter), which may be less plausible to them. The way in which this understanding is mediated socially will determine children's levels of affective engagement and their ability to make sense and meaning as they are introduced to writing.

What young children choose to represent, as well as the form they choose to communicate in, will be influenced by the resources they encounter as well as the social interactions in which they engage. For example, the maps that children draw in the Reggio Emilia settings in Italy are almost exclusively constructed in the shape of a square, 'piazza' style, influenced by their experience of visiting city squares, of seeing such representations and talking about them. Children's representations depend on the 'cultural tool kit' available to them and the level of approval, support and space provided by significant adults (Bruner, 1986). There are interesting connections here between the early development of semiotic systems in young children and Mercer's (2000) close examination of adults at work, whom he observes use language, gesture and drawing tools for making meaning, as they connect the symbolic world with the concrete. The opportunity for such an interconnection of expressive modes may help fluent journeys to be made between early literacy events and later writing events in official school contexts. However, much will depend upon the practice, policy and understanding of the teachers in school.

Talking and writing in school

When children enter school their early interactive and vocal encounters with texts and contexts need to be sustained in order to enhance their development as language users. Knowledge from the world of neuroscience suggests that 'as far as the brain is concerned, stimulation is provided by conversations, experiences and encounters' (Greenfield, 2000: 63), and as teachers we need to provide a wide range of these throughout the compositional process, since each text they commit to paper or screen floats, as Britton described over thirty years ago, on a 'sea of talk'.

> All that the children write, your response (as educator) to what they write, their response to each other, all of this takes place afloat upon a sea of talk. Talk is what provides the links between you and them and what they write, between what they have written and each other.
>
> (Britton, 1970: 29)

Conversations about writing, whether to generate ideas or to reflect upon them, give children access to others' experience and through this interactive discourse they learn from the comments and understandings of more experienced others (Vygotsky, 1978). In this social constructionist model, responsibility for learning about writing and through writing is shared, despite some degree of asymmetry in the roles and responsibilities of those involved. Such an interactive pedagogy is dependent on the children's active involvement and sees learning as a transformation of participation (Rogoff, 1990). Playful and creative writing activities such as the exploration and presentation of poetry as adverts, or the re-creation of non-fiction facts in TV documentaries can prompt quality interaction and pupil participation, both of which are widely recognised as central elements in learning (Cambourne, 1995; Geekie et al., 1999; Mercer, 2000). For learning about written language involves far more than learning a new code for representing meaning, it involves entering new and social dialogues with oneself and others.

In view of the wealth of research relating to the social construction of knowledge, it is surprising that the 67 objectives for speaking, listening and learning in England (DfEE/QCA, 2003) were not published until the NLS had been in place for half a decade. For the teachers on the We're Writers research project, the lack of official support for oracy had, they perceived, led them to profile reading and writing objectives and reduce the time spent on interaction, creative exploration and discussion. Far from being integrated, their planned units of work tended to focus on tightly defined models of reading and writing which short-changed the role of talk in learning. Perhaps, like the teachers observed by English et al., they also regarded teaching for understanding as 'an optional extra, permissible once the objectives had been met' (English *et al.*, 2002: 25). Both studies show that these primary professionals felt compromised and believed that they needed to give precedence to curriculum coverage and test preparation. Partly as a consequence of such pressures, practice in the UK and elsewhere frequently centres on individual performance, personal achievements and individual skill based targets take priority. Yet teachers intuitively know that learning is often a mutual accomplishment and that collaboration is a critical way to build intellectual insight and understanding.

In attempting to ensure progression and raise standards in England, shared and guided writing have been identified as the preferred writing pedagogies, with an emphasis on whole-class interactive teaching and guided group work undertaken with the support and intervention of the teacher. In practice, however, the understanding of such pedagogical principles has been limited (Fisher, 2001) and evidence suggests that the discourse of the literacy hour in relation to the whole-class teaching remains squarely in the teacher-led recitation format of question, response, feedback (Mroz *et al.*, 2000; Hardman *et al.*, 2001). Recent research into guided work also indicates that the teacher leads from the front, does most of the talking and controls both the agenda and the turn taking (Skidmore *et al.*, 2003). Such transmissive practice reduces the chance for all children to participate interactively in shared and guided contexts and in relation to composing, such teacher-controlled practice offers limited opportunities for children to generate ideas; to draw from their own experience; to adopt the roles of actor, tale teller, reader, writer or critic or even to understand the purpose of writing (Dyson, 2000). Yet pleasurable interactions and close collaboration over writing can help involve and motivate children, enabling them to focus on the content, the process, the audience and the purpose of their writing. If we want children to engage cognitively, emotionally and aesthetically as writers and we want children 'to talk to learn – as well as learn to talk, then what they say actually matters more than what teachers say' (Alexander, 2000: 33). As the Essex Writing Project found, talking about writing, before, during and after writing is not only essential, it also raises standards (Bearne, 2002; Essex County Council, 2003). This issue was raised at the close of the first year of the We're Writers research by teachers in the project focus group, who perceived that their learners were both more motivated and more involved in their writing, and that this was due in no small part to the considerable increase in interaction, small-group discussion and playful engagement with texts in their classrooms.

Generating writing: talking together

In this book we emphasise the importance of finding a voice through creative engagement and considered reflection; we believe talking towards writing in playful and generative contexts is crucial, as is time to reflect upon ideas and options. In such contexts, children are able to share ideas, understand others' perspectives, amend and develop their opinions and try out new possibilities as part of the extended process of composition. Stepping in and out of texts to play with ideas, to understand characters, to create connections, to map emotions, or imaginatively extend their understanding of a glossary for example, involves the serious play of creativity, and spoken dialogue has a central role in this endeavour. A conversational context supports children creative development and their understanding of particular stories, poetry or non-fiction and generates possibilities for written responses. In one class of 5–6-year-olds, following a focus on sharing personal stories, the children were given the chance to select a member of their family or a friend and were invited to draw them. They took their pictures to a friend in the class storybuzz and talked about their chosen person. As Figure 3.1 shows, Graham, aged 6, chose not to draw his nan, but drew himself instead. His tears and sense of loss are evident in this picture poem which he executed with considerable care.

Through his drawing, almost more than his words, Graham reinforces the sense of separation and loss that he feels; his nan had moved from a nearby flat to another part of the town with her new husband, and had left her grandson feeling bereft and alone. Writing as spectator of his own experience, Graham uses the poetic mode to convey his feelings through both words and pictures. The empty bird cage and single chair, the discordant directions of the animals in the wall display and the dramatic tears on his face convey his raw emotional state as he looks at the picture of nan and him once so close together and now so far apart. His complex multimodal text is layered with meaning and reminds us that twenty-first-century learners like Graham draw on a wide range of textual forms. The emotional engagement engendered by talking about his nan to friends undoubtedly supported Graham in articulating his voice, his position and his concern. Whilst the rest of the class wrote descriptive words around their pictures or retold anecdotes, he chose poetry to powerfully convey his sense of loss and separation. His feelings for his nan and the opportunity to reflect upon them through talking around their photographs, appears to have released his creative energy and demonstrates the affective as the dynamic force or thrust of this text. The consequences of this work triggered another stage in Graham's relationship with his nan, since after his mum read it at parents' evening, his nan was prompted to renew contact with him and invited him to visit. For Graham, the conversations that surrounded this text and its consequences arguably helped him interpret his life; he was certainly proud of his work which was published in a class anthology.

Open-ended oral activities can encourage creativity, for inherent in being creative is the absence of a precise goal, although the problem-solving

Figure 3.1 Happy times

nature of generative activities, experienced in storytelling or drama for example, do involve certain constraints and rules. In such contexts, children may use exploratory talk as they discuss ways of sharing the chosen tale or prepare to sculpt a freeze frame depicting the themes of the text. They will be generating ideas and options and engaging critically, but constructively, with each others' thoughts. Some suggestions may be challenged and alternatives may be voiced with reasons offered since, in open-ended contexts, agreement will need to be sought as a basis for moving forward. This process of selection and refinement of ideas and meanings prepares children for writing and must be recognised as a critical part of the compositional process. As Bearne observes, 'the outer experience of discussion, justification, role play and drama feed into the inner voices of a critically reflective writer' (Bearne, 2002: 25).

When children reflect laterally and envisage other possibilities they are involved imaginatively, using 'little c creativity' (Craft, 2001) both orally and in writing, as they take risks with ideas, words and images. Creative approaches motivate children and help learners realise the potential of multimodal play which engages and invigorates, enriching the journey towards writing. Playfulness, knowledge and judgement are all necessary elements of writing and are woven through the process in spoken threads. Children need sustained time within the extended process of composition to use talk to play their way forward, to experiment and reflect in order to develop ideas and select from among them. Through this process, thoughts and feelings, attitudes and information will be shared and the substantive content for the written communication may be generated, as encourage-ment and critique are offered by both peers and adults alike. This conver-sational journey is explored in relation to literature, drama, storytelling and poetry in Chapters 5 to 8. However, the bridge between oral interaction and the written script should not cease as literal writing materials appear, for much critical conversation will also take place during this later part of the compositional process.

Responding to writing: talking together

Young children often talk as they commit to paper; such self-regulatory behaviour can help them plan and evaluate their efforts. It also frequently involves others, reflecting the responsive interchanges experienced with adults. In conversations about writing, adults can 'lead by following' (Wood, 1988) which involves very careful observation, listening and working with the child's intentions in order to help them develop their ideas in a purposeful manner. Such contingent instruction should assist the gradual transfer of responsibility for managing the writing to the child and in such interactions, like the infant caregiver years before, the adults or other experts 'loan' children their consciousness about literacy and language use, and help scaffold their understanding as they select and reflect upon their choices (Bruner, 1986).

> Just as young children test their hypothesis about spoken language through the feedback they receive during conversations with interested and competent adults, so must novice writers have opportunities to test their hypothesis about written language by writing and receiving feedback as they write.
>
> (Geekie, 2003: 162)

When we are engaged in communication we need a response or some form of feedback, whether from our own inner voices or from another human being to reassure us that we are having some impact on the world. Children too need opportunities to talk over their writing during the process, perhaps with talk partners, adults or children. In the We're Writers research, the children perceived that their teachers talked to them most *after* their writing was completed, in order to mark or grade it, and requested more time to discuss their writing as they shaped their ideas and not necessarily with an adult. If, as teachers, we seek to work towards mediation, reflection and response through a range of opportunities and 'teach the writers, not the writing' (Calkins, 1986), then we must be sure to encourage and support children working together as readers of each others' writing and as response partners. When children engage together in dialogues focused on their evolving writing, the nature of this conversation will be substantially different from a teacher–child dyadic discussion. Together, two peers can more informally explore ways of using language to clarify each others' ideas and can also support one another secretarially. If strong relationships of trust and respect are created in the classroom, then young writers can learn to respond to one another's work with interest and insight, responding to the human who wrote it as well as developing their critical awareness of its features, function and purpose. In discussing their writing, children need the chance to talk about what they were trying to achieve and the strategies they employed to keep the reader interested; this can help them develop a clearer sense of audience and tone. Through considering problems, toying with alternatives, drawing on their knowledge and previous experience and their involvement in creative encounters, children learn what it is like to be an author; part of this will involve them in responding to others' critical comments.

Through examining their own writing in an evaluative and reflective manner, teachers can model and frame the thinking that will ultimately be needed to help children make judgements about their own work. In verbalising our thoughts as we write in front of the class, we need to focus on the core message or meaning, the construction and the language as well as at other times on planning, drafting, editing and proofreading.

Working with response partners, children can learn to celebrate their success, reinforce what they have learnt and identify areas for development or aspects which may need attention. Such conversations need a supportive frame and benefit from the use of prompt sheets to encourage active reflection; Sharples (1999) describes this reflection as the key to breaking through the 'what next?' stage. This focus on the evolving text, its emerging meaning and on the reader's needs and responses is very important, as is a growing awareness of writing conventions and the writer's craft; such reflection enables children to recognise what they or others have achieved. Even more significantly, however, children need to appreciate that what it means to be a writer is very different from learning to write, and they must be helped to develop a positive sense of self-esteem. As social beings, young writers carry a sense of themselves as writers which will markedly affect their views of their writing. Whether this reflects disaffection and disinterest or pleasure and delight can make all the difference to their growth as writers, as we show in the next chapter. Their thoughts and feelings about writing are important and offer significant insights to which teachers must respond.

> The interpersonal then, comes before and goes beyond 'communi-
> cation' … it operates as part of the sense of what it is to be a writer, not
> just part of the process of actually putting a text together.
>
> (Bearne, 2002: 16)

Children bring their own unique experiences to writing and must be allowed to build on these social, cultural and linguistic differences in the context of the classroom, so they can develop their own voice, that sense of the self in their writing. As they develop as writers, they are able to engage in a discourse of their own learning, and can be helped to use an appropriate metalanguage when discussing their written texts. However, they also need to reflect on the process of writing and on being a writer. Such engagement encourages deep, rather than surface learning, and is crucial if children are to become creative writers who exert their autonomy and use their voices for their own personal and epistemic purposes (Packwood and Messenheimer, 2003). Through quality discussions with teachers and peers, children can learn to describe their learning reflectively and develop a metalanguage to talk about writing. As 9-year-old Lauren noted in conversation with her teacher, *I think I have got better in my writing because I can describe how an author manages to make me feel now. And then I can do this in my own writing. I didn't really see this until I wrote that one about the girl who ran away. It makes my writing much more interesting – at least I think it does.* Through talking about her writing, Lauren has begun to make her thinking more visible and shape her understanding. Corden's research (2000, 2003), suggests that with careful teaching, children can comment upon the compositional features of literary and non-literary texts and can then integrate these and other metalinguistic insights into their personal repertoires and use them successfully in their own writing. If children articulate a sense of themselves as growing writers and make their knowledge about writing more explicit, they will be more able to take risks as writers, and will be better placed to play with forms, features and styles; this will also put them in a stronger position to evaluate their work. As Boden argues 'the better the person's grasp of the conceptual space concerned, the more likely that they will be able to judge the worth or worthlessness of new ideas' (2001: 98). Through focusing on the meanings that children express, and discussing their texts, especially at the draft stage, Barrs and Cork (2001) found that writing can be improved, particularly if the teacher reads the work aloud, giving it life and breath and helping the children hear the tunes and patterns they have created. Other work also shows that teacher intervention and peer discussions during drafting can facilitate reflective activity and enrich the quality of writing (Wells *et al.*, 1990; Corden, 2000).

Writing conferences represent a rich opportunity to discuss writing and set targets for improvement; these can be undertaken individually, in pairs or groups. Shared and guided writing sessions can also be used as a forum for demonstration, discussion and feedback. Such spaces help children articulate their awareness of the process and the craft of writing and foster a more evaluative and self-critical stance in safe and supported contexts. Children's perceptions of their development as writers are influenced by their teachers' comments so our initial response will often need to be as readers, engaging aesthetically with the text's meaning, and then considering the writer's achievements which enabled our engagement (D'Arcy, 1999). As many research projects and surveys have shown, the most effective teachers of literacy profile the meanings that texts seek to convey (Medwell *et al.*, 1998; Frater, 2000), and whilst linguistic analysis has a place, meaning needs to be foregrounded in responsive comments to the writer. Some of the teachers in the We're Writers project tracked their comments on children's writing, whilst others analysed the targets they had set individual writers. Many found that their targets focused on word, sentence and text level features of writing at the relative expense of the meaning or the impact on the reader. The teachers felt they needed to remind themselves that successful writing, in whatever form, conveys meaning which holds the reader's interest and attention, and worked to avoid a 'features first' attitude to writing, promulgated in response to accountability and skills-oriented objectives. It appeared that their understanding of 'good writing' had become somewhat divorced from the meaning, purpose and audience of the children's writing.

Writing is not good or bad *per se*: it is effective or ineffective, elegant or inelegant, powerful or puny in relation to its purpose and audience. To be literate is to be able to identify one's purpose, to recognise predominant social conventions and expectations and to use language in order to achieve a desired outcome; whether this is to inform, direct, persuade, entertain, shock, challenge conventions or overturn the status quo.

(Corden, 2000: 150)

Collaborative writing

Whilst the act of literally writing may be quiet and individual at times, effective writing classrooms include a strong element of response and collaboration, increasing children's security and reflexivity in the community of writers (Barrs, 2000). Collaboration over writing can also take the form of composing together, dancing a rap into existence, for example, or working in small groups to write a pamphlet or a news broadsheet. Such texts may speak with many voices, those of the composers, the illustrator, the designers and the editor, for example. Genuinely collaborative work can be enhanced by the opportunity to be both author and audience. As the children read and hear their work they take part as engaged participants, sharing the tenor and tune of their choices, and as spectators, critically evaluating their work. Writing with a partner involves children in composing processes that make more explicit the social nature of writing, for in working reciprocally children take part in a dialogue mirroring the internal dialogue writers have with themselves. In joint activities in the 'intermental development zone', writers appropriate ways of using language (Mercer, 2000) as they work together. The word processor is particularly useful in this regard, encouraging a more playful multimodal orientation to writing and prompting considerable conversation as children make full use of the computer as a focus of their joint activity and are helped to use language as a tool for thinking together (Mercer *et al.*, 2003). Collaborative writing can help writers concentrate on the dialectical processes of composition, which Bereiter and Scardamalia (1985) describe as a debate between meaning and form which develops into some kind of synthesis. In collaborative writing, learners share possible ideas together and work to commit these to paper, as Cliff Hodges (2002) so artfully documents in working with student teachers.

The tension between the initial thoughts in their heads about what they want to write individually and how the whole story will eventually work is similar to the tension which arises as a result of the solitary synthesis between internal thought and external print on the page; the difference is that they can discuss possible solutions with each other, rather than having to wrestle with them alone.

(Cliff Hodges, 2002: 9)

She also shows how learners in collaborative writing contexts engage aloud in the compositional process, and as creative participants build on one another's insights. Writing together can help children give voice to their ideas in safe spaces where assessment of their individual performance is no longer a concern; this encourages more reticent speakers to take part and provides further opportunities for reflection and evaluation through discussion. In his analysis of one child's literacy learning in an Australian classroom, Geekie claims that the child's 'mental processes were constituted by the talk and action involved in collaborative story writing' (2003: 170) and demonstrates again the potential of open-ended small group collaborative writing.

The production of this book for example, could not have occurred without multiple opportunities to talk ideas through, to share experiences, reflect upon the We're Writers project and listen to the voices of the children and their teachers. Further generative discussions and reflective opportunities took place in the company of other colleagues, as well as partners and friends in the profession and these have all contributed considerably to the final product. As we exchanged draft chapters, debated each others' perspectives, disagreed with positions adopted and sought to negotiate our way forward through conversation and critique, our relationships and our arguments were tested and strengthened. In the classroom too, the nature of the dialogic exchange in collaborative writing will necessarily alter according to the particular purpose and social relations of those involved, and will also differ at various stages in the writing process. Nonetheless, such interaction can be motivating and involving and emphasises again the value of the potent relationship between talk and writing.

Conclusion

Talk is both the foundation and the binding element of the children's learning so teachers must ensure they involve children interactively throughout their reading and writing journeys. Although as Dyson (2000: 46) suggests, the 'sea of talk' is not always a peaceful one, for their talk frequently flows over the breakwaters of official talk agendas and their interactions are shaped by the voices which they bring from home, from the media and local peer cultures (Brice Heath, 1983). They negotiate multiple social and textual worlds as they compose, but their writing, Dyson argues, may be channelled by ideological waves in ways that constrain their individuality, as members of particular social, cultural or gender groups. Creative approaches that encourage children to interactively engage and reflect with others, voicing their views, singing, imagining and playing their way forwards, also need to recognise that communication and expression may not always result in written composition, and contorting meaning into writing may distort, detract or even demean the author's original intention and reduce their voice and verve. The spoken word needs to be valued in its own right and not just as a support for writing. As we have seen, working in collaboration with one's peers and the teacher, can increase autonomy in writing, other issues also influence children's growing independence and it is to these we now turn.

Chapter 4

Choice and autonomy in writing

To develop creativity and voice in their writing, we believe children should not only be introduced to a rich range of existing expressive domains, but should also be given the time and space to explore these for themselves, making choices, taking risks, and developing their preferences and independence as writers. The importance of personal significance and purpose in writing was powerfully pointed out to us by the children who took part in the We're Writers survey; they voiced a clear desire to exercise increased agency in their schooled writing, demanded more scope to select their own subjects and forms and time to pursue their own options. Their teachers were surprised at the vehemence of their views and chose to make this a major strand of the project work, working to develop children's voice, choice and autonomy they sought to increase the relevance of writing to these young people.

> An intrinsic need should be aroused in them, writing should be incorporated into a task that is necessary and relevant for life. Only then can we be certain that it will develop not as a matter of hand and finger habits but as a really new and complex form of speech.
>
> (Vygotsky, 1978: 118)

In this chapter we share the children's views which influenced the project's agenda, arguing that writing needs to be cultivated rather than imposed (Vygotsky, 1978), and that this can only be achieved by fostering increased volition and involvement. This can be affected through creative and contextualised teaching, with choice built into activities, as well as through offering periods of self-sufficiency, separate opportunities for children to write for themselves. We describe how the teachers in the project made extensive use of writing journals and how in this 'privileged space' (Graham, 2004), the children began to exercise their autonomy and make full use of their expertise and experience of different semiotic forms. They proved that given the chance to choose their genre and content, they were eager to write, able to make connections and develop their work and their cultural identity using the tools of their 'cultural capital' (Bourdieu, 1986). This shifted the balance of power in the classroom, as in their journals they combined their social and cultural capital and wrote for themselves and for each other, finding increased purpose and pleasure in this more creative and open-ended writing context.

The invisible child: demanding to be seen and heard

Whilst teachers' views about the NLS have been recorded and respected (Dadds, 1999; Fisher and Lewis, 1999; English *et al.*, 2002), children's perspectives about literacy and learning have been noticeably absent, and even in the official evaluation reports on the NLS, no pupils' voices are heard (Earl *et al.*, 2000, 2001, 2003). Yet the literature on raising achievement continues to assert that establishing children's views can make a real difference (e.g. Macdonald *et al.*, 1999; Dobie and Macbeath, 1998). In the We're Writers research we sought to be open to multiple perspectives and explored children's attitudes to writing and their sense of themselves as writers through a survey and follow-up interviews. The first three girls and the first three boys on the register of each class took part in the survey which they completed independently, although the younger children were helped by classroom assistants, who in some cases scribed the children's responses. In order to build a picture of some of the children's thoughts, the initial question asked was 'When your teacher says "Now we are going to do some writing", what goes through your head?' (Talley, 2000). Later questions invited comments on likes and dislikes in writing and asked them to evaluate themselves as writers, as well as record others' perceptions of them. Each child was also asked to describe one piece of writing of which they were proud and to explain their choice. The last section of the survey focused on their confidence in generating ideas for writing and the perceived source of their ideas. No question focused on choice or autonomy in writing, but the children raised it constantly, demonstrating that this issue was a common denominator of considerable importance to them.

   A picture was built up of the children's attitudes to writing and an interesting contrast was revealed between the views of children 5–7 years old and the 7–11-year-olds. The younger children were markedly more enthusiastic than their older counterparts and had more positive views of themselves as writers. Their favourite writing predominantly had both purpose and audience, for example, Mother's Day cards, notes for the message board, postcards, letters to friends and fictional characters. Many voiced their pride in stories they had written and viewed writing with enthusiasm, interest and commitment. Much of their writing as infants was undertaken in playful contexts and was carried out for their own reasons which facilitated varying degrees of authenticity, audience and choice. This provided these young learners with a sense of authority and power, significant elements in the development of writers. However, their attitudes contrasted markedly with the 8–9-year-olds who reflected predominantly negative attitudes to writing, and voiced concerns about their competence; they commonly perceived writing as boring. In the later years, the views expressed were more mixed and significantly, these more mature writers were aware that their views on writing depended on certain issues, namely the form required, the freedom offered and their mood.

Previous studies have also suggested that children's attitudes to writing decline as they get older (Hogan, 1980; Wray, 1993), but of more concern were the small, but significant number of 9–11-year-olds who revealed a degree of ambivalence towards the act of writing. They appeared somewhat indifferent to it and reflected a detached disposition, for example, *There's nothing I like, nothing I dislike, I just do it, I can't say I mind – well I don't care if we do or we don't, I don't have a view about writing, I just do it when she says so, I don't think about it, I just get on with it* and *More writing? Who cares?* In the interviews, several seemed genuinely surprised to be even asked their views about writing, *Why do you ask, what difference does it make what I think? I don't have any choice do I?* The children had little sense of their own volition in the processes of teaching and learning and appeared to view themselves as pupils rather than learners, in line with previous research into attitudes to schooling (Duffield *et al.*, 2000). Did they also see themselves as perhaps their teachers did – as 'human becomings' rather than human beings, as pupils in an educational system designed for tomorrow (Lee, 2001)? Arguably, they appeared to feel somewhat invisible and inaudible to those responsible for their development. Was their 'childness' (Hollindale, 1997) – what it feels like to be a child inside their own heads – possibly unseen by their teachers, required as they are to turn children's achievements into measurable statistics?

'I hate being told what to do and how to do it'

The surveys showed that the majority of the 7–11-year-olds and some of the younger learners, experienced more pleasure in writing when some degree of choice was offered, equally many noted their dislike of set writing and its limitations. The nature of the restrictions recorded included: imposed content, having to follow a theme or genre, writing to a specific title, timed writing and completing literacy worksheets. A sample of their comments reveal the potency of their views, *I hate it when it's timed as I panic, I don't like having to write about a particular subject – I prefer to choose, I don't like being told what to write* and *I hate being told what to do and how to do it*. Seventy-four percent of the children aged 9–11 raised the issue of autonomy quite unprompted, as 11-year-old Lewis commented, *I hate it when we have to follow a theme in writing and you have to do what it says on the sheet. There's no freedom and my writing becomes narrow, I can't use my imagination.* Many voiced their enjoyment in writing when more creative space was offered, for example *I love it when you can write what you want and do it in your own style, I like a story when I'm allowed to make it all up and make it all mine, I like it when I can use my own ideas, I like it when we don't get told how to do it.* These older children appeared to be motivated by the relative freedom of writing opportunities in which they could employ their own ideas and where they felt they had more control over how their writing developed. Many also commented that they found a particular pleasure in narrative writing, in being able to generate ideas and create and shape their own imaginary worlds. This preference for story writing was expressed in various ways, for example: *I adore story writing, I like writing stories from scratch, then they're really mine, I like stories best, I can make them up, I like making up my own story worlds and inventing characters and weird new places.* Their comments indicate that they are already aware of the power of the written word, that they enjoy the imaginative freedom of story writing and perceive that imposed writing with a closed agenda limits their potential. The children's desire for autonomy resonates with Myhill's (2001: 17) findings with secondary school pupils, who asserted a preference for writing that allowed both 'voice and imaginative freedom'. As she acknowledges, writing involves both crafting and creating, but as we have already noted, the teachers in our study tended to profile the crafting elements with the older children, studying and analysing linguistic features at the relative expense of providing opportunities for creating, composing and completing whole texts. This no doubt influenced the children's desire for more creative independence and increased imaginative and personal involvement in their writing. As OfSTED observe, in underperforming schools, children have

> little notion of themselves as writers in control of the process, rather writing is seen as performing, the content, audience and purpose of which has been determined externally rather than internally
> (OfSTED, 2002: 146)

The legal requirement that 7–11-year-olds should choose their own form, content, audience and purpose in writing had arguably bypassed these and other busy professionals (DfEE, 1999). Driven by assessment and accountability, at the start of the We're Writers project the teachers retained a relatively tight rein on writing activities. Only one school offered an extended writing time, the remainder taught writing within the literacy hour frame, tending to practice discrete skills in a manner similar to those observed by Frater (2000). The backwash of assessment may reduce children's choice in writing (the tests in England have now removed all choice), and infringes upon their desire for volition, shaping their attitudes accordingly (Moss, 1994; Wiggins, 1993). This 'brutal, unceasing emphasis on testing and marking ... leads to a superficial way of working', Pullman (2003: 9) perceives, and results in a diminished sense of individual owner- ship in children's reading and writing. It was clear that some of the older children in the research were aware of this, they knew how the school system worked and felt the pressure of the national tests as well as the stress of the eleven plus regime. The pressure was and still is on them to perform, to succeed and to achieve within these narrow boundaries, but encouragingly, they still yearned for open spaces and creative freedom in writing. Sternberg (1997: 203) argues that as children move through school, their spontaneous creativity diminishes, 'it's not that older individuals lack creative intelligence, but rather that they have suppressed it'. These learners knew that to achieve the targets they had been set, they should stay on the straight and narrow paths of conditioned and measurable conformity, but when asked for their views they voiced a deep desire to direct their own journeys and use their own route maps. Today's teachers too, are beset with contradictory messages regarding entitlement and opportunity, and need to recognise the tension between the incessant drive for measurable standards on the one hand and the development of creative teaching and learning on the other. Reconciling these may be challenging, but is not impossible and will encompass elements of what conventionally have been perceived as progressive and traditional education, combining quality teaching in creative and engaging contexts with opportunities for self- direction and autonomy. It was for these reasons that teachers in the project decided to introduce periods of independent writing time, mostly through the introduction of writing journals. They believed that the children needed time and space for their own writing in order to rediscover the purpose of writing and experience the pleasure of being an author.

Purpose and pleasure: writing in the 'here and now'

Those who read for pleasure know that the desire to read almost seems to have a physical sensation with which it is associated. Readers feel like reading, they know the reading experience well and anticipate the pleasures it will bring. In the same way, writers can feel like writing and are aware of what writing can do for them; children need to experience the power and potential of writing as they put it to work in variety of real and imagined contexts. They need to know, for example, that writing about an experience can help one order it and come to terms with it, they need to know that writing can persuade and change the status quo and that it can delight, making its readers wonder, ponder and even cry. As humans, we use writing for a range of reasons: to think with and make sense of experience, to understand ourselves and others, to communicate and share information, to give us power and make a difference, as well as to take pleasure from playing with words and meanings.

However, in work undertaken by Packwood and Messenheimer (2003) children saw that the main purpose of writing was to demonstrate to their teacher what they had learnt, about persuasive texts or the Second World War, for example. As a Croydon teacher expressed it 'the children in my classroom were writing for me and for the curriculum, not for themselves' (Johnson, 2003: 5). The disaffected older writers in our research also appeared to see no personal purpose in writing, and were simply undertaking it as pawns in a system in which they felt they had little control. Frater (2004: 80) too, reflects that much writing in school is apt to be artificial and undertaken for 'the circular purpose of learning to write'. The endless instructional circle of teaching, targeting and testing, positions children as somewhat impotent and without a sense of voice or volition. Michael Rosen (1989) describes three characteristics that he perceives make writing meaningful and worthwhile. First, he argues it is a powerful way of preserving the past on the writer's own terms. In doing so, the writer is able to manipulate memories and experiences and develop some control over their past and their future, as well as preserve the oral tradition and elements of their culture and identity. Second, writing, Rosen suggests, is a way of reflecting on experience and ideas, and becoming both participants and observers of our lives and others. Even the common practice of writing a 'jobs list' can offer organisational relief and enables us to gain some distance from the tasks to be achieved. Third, he describes writing as a way of opening up conversations with others, since writers share their thoughts, stories and philosophies with others, in a variety of multimodal ways and expect a response to this communication. Through engaging with the writing of others, and their own work, children can become more aware of the impact and influence of writing, on both the reader and the author, and find meaning and purpose in what they write. They can experience language as 'meaningful, contextualised and in the broadest sense, social' (Halliday, 1973: 20). In the We're Writers survey, some of the younger children reflected such knowledge, but the older ones felt more coerced into writing in particular ways about subjects they had not chosen and did not necessarily care about.

Contemporary educational policy appears to view children as transitional beings, reflects society's recent fixation with conceiving children as 'sites of investment' and the potential means of creating and maintaining a healthy economy (Lee, 2001: 77). This often results in a 'back-to-basics' utilitarian curriculum which is oriented towards the creation of skills demanded by employers (David et al., 1999). Currently, in schools judged as failing to meet their targets, frequently in socially deprived areas, the NC is often slimmed down, the NLS delivered more prescriptively and the formal school curriculum is differentiated along social class lines

(Cole *et al.*, 2001). This reduces opportunities for critical thought and a more creative educational experience. Advocates of this form of utilitarianism fail to recognise that childhood is more than a stage on the way to citizenship and school is more than a 'filling station' which helps to fuel these aims. It is clear, academic qualifications are no longer enough and employers increasingly emphasise the need for powers of creativity, empathy and flexibility (NACCCE, 1999), yet still far too little time is spent allowing children to reflect on their lives as they live them, as children in the 'here and now' of living (James and Prout, 1997). The teachers in the We're Writers project, recognising these difficulties and eager to respond to the children's requests, agreed to sanction periods of author autonomy through the introduction of writing journals and also sought to increase choice and relevance in the literacy hour where the teaching of genres took precedence. A wide range of different genres are taught in the primary years, with an emphasis on teachers presenting models of these, which young learners are expected to explicitly mimic in terms of structure or style. We agree that deep immersion in texts, both literary and non-literary is vital and knowledge about language is essential and should be experienced, modelled and imitated, but we are also convinced that children need to be given real opportunities to write for themselves, choosing their subject matter and shaping their writing in response to their own intrinsic needs and interests.

> Of course techniques matter; without them nothing substantial can be achieved. But unless children experience the richer meanings that literacy can give them, they are unlikely to become literate in the sense of making their own active use of literacy outside school as well as in.
> (Dombey, 1998: 130)

Their work needs to be shared and given status, so that children can begin to feel part of the wider community of authors, poets and journalists that exist outside the confines of the classroom. By providing time for independent writing, when children choose their form, subject and audience, they are able to express themselves as people and a better balance is created between the teaching of writing and the actual production and creative use of it. Children's writing is unique, they are the only ones who can create genuine 'children's literature' – authored by children and for children. This kind of writing is not a rehearsal for a future life, it is purposeful, self-initiated and self-directed, informed by knowledge and experience, but driven by the desire to communicate with themselves and others. It is writing for real.

Writing journals

Following the opportunity to work alongside Lynda Graham, the teachers in the We're Writers project decided to utilise the idea of establishing writing journals (Graham and Johnson, 2003) and exercise books were given out to each child to customise. Many brought in images from magazines and comics, and pictures of soap stars, pop singers, mobile phones were crammed onto the covers of their journals. Others used photographs of their families or pets and many drew detailed diagrams or borrowed pictures from the media to reflect a sense of growing self and identity as 10-year-old Emily's journal cover indicates, see Figure 4.1. Inside their journals, the children were invited to write about what they chose and significantly, their teachers agreed to look at them only if they were invited to do so. The We're Writers project focus group reported that the children received this news with a mixture of delight and disbelief. Some of the

Figure 4.1 Emily's journal cover

older children in particular found it difficult to believe that the teacher was not in some way going to assess their work, nor set success criteria for each piece of writing. Many required constant reassurance and considerable support. They appeared bemused by the condition of autonomy in which they found themselves, so dependent had they become on their teacher setting the agenda and framing each piece of written work. To help the children, many of the teachers made suggestions and some offered lists of the forms of writing that had been taught in current and previous years. This was an interesting strategy to which we return later. The number of writing sessions varied from school to school and from class to class; some teachers made them a daily activity, others timetabled several short sessions, approximately 15–20 minutes two or three times a week. The teachers ensured that at the end of the sessions the children had the opportunity to hear examples of each others' writing; in this way, ideas and themes began to travel around the class and groups of writers began to form around common interests, thus prompting collaborative writing and much conversation.

Some teachers initially expressed concern about children drawing in their journals, rather than writing. Drawing, in this context, was seen to be a second-order activity although it is a valid form of expression which enables children to interpret and reflect upon reality. As noted in Chapter 3, the roots of writing lie in various forms of symbolising, including drawing and so it was not surprising to find children drawing upon their pleasure, knowledge and experience of this form to make story worlds, create characters, advertise products, design posters, web pages, and draw game cards for example. They seized upon the more open opportunity which journal writing represented and leant upon their knowledge and understanding, as 'thoroughly experienced makers of meaning, as experienced makers of signs in any medium that is at hand' (Kress, 1997: 8–9). The time and resources given to these autonomous meaning making sessions gave the children the chance to draw on the media that best suited their intentions and some of their work exploded with depictions of sound and movement as they playfully developed their own individual artistic styles. Cutting and pasting often made their work three-dimensional and rich in texture and pattern. Their talent and enthusiasm for mixing modes mirrored the semiotic world with which they were familiar, and reminded their teachers that they are children of the twenty-first century. Creatively, they were connecting their own 'school of knowing' with the 'school of expressing', which can, Malaguzzi (1998) suggests, open doors to the hundred languages of children. In using words and images playfully, their work reflected the changes happening outside school and the real world of multimodal communication, and exposed the rather archaic nature of contemporary literacy curricula which are dominated by the written word.

Shifts in responsibility and power

As the children began to take increased responsibility for their writing in the context of their journal work, they had to make a number of significant choices, namely what they were going to write about, what form the writing would take, who would read their writing and most significantly what they were trying to achieve through this writing. Their intentions were not always known to them at the outset, but through the collaborative nature of the sessions, reasons for writing began to reveal themselves and children formed groups to work on the publication of a newspaper for example, or raps to perform in class, others created information pamphlets on animals, poems about their families or football magazine pages for each other. Teachers on the project were surprised to find the children were eager to share their work, despite the fact that it was made clear they could chose whether to invite others into their writing worlds. As the young writers began to write *for* themselves and *to* themselves, they developed a sense of themselves as a valid audience for their writing, but also found extremely important audiences in each other. Camille for example, aged 6, believed rules were important and having written them, Figure 4.2, published these on the class notice board for all to follow. In sharing with friends during their writing, the children gradually became more aware of their reader's point of view, their reader's knowledge, or lack of it, and their reader's interests. As Graham (2001) found, the experience of receiving a genuine response from an interested reader makes a significant difference to reluctant writers, particularly boys, as does the satisfaction of having their work read aloud, shared and enjoyed. Their desire to participate and have their say, created what Dyson (1997) calls a pedagogy of responsibility. As authors, she suggests children must learn 'they can never "own" meaning, because meaning only exists in the meeting of voices' (Dyson, 1997: 180). The children in the project focus group classes appeared, through their journal work, not so much to be sharing their writing, as sharing something of themselves, their interests and obsessions, their fascinations and desires. Their writing was a part of this however, a midwife to their growing sense of self. Whilst their conversations about the writing did attend to the language used, their first discursive focus seemed to involve them in engaging with the content and responding to each other as writers.

In addition, the teachers noticed the children returning to earlier entries in their journals and redrafting and reshaping their writing for sharing in a wider forum, reinforcing Graves' (1983) view that owners of their work are considerably more likely to take care of their 'property' than those who merely 'rent' it from authority figures such as teachers. In this way some of the writing in school became less artificial as the children explored what mattered to them in their inner and outer worlds. During this time the teachers began to realise that their roles had begun to shift. The children were cultivating a writing culture in which they were the experts, since

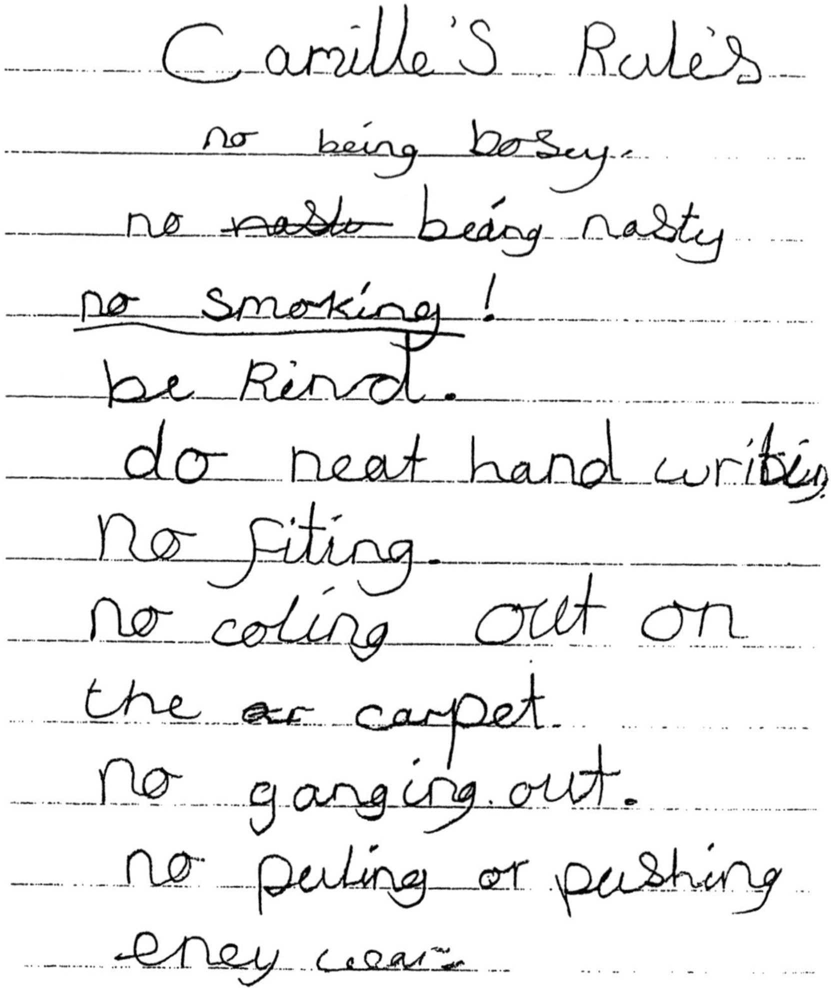

Camille'S Rule's

no being bossy.

no nasto being nasty

no Smoking !

be Kind.

do neat hand writing

no fiting.

no coling out on

the as carpet.

no ganging out.

no puting or pushing

eney ceear

Figure 4.2 Camille's rules

they set the pace and the agenda and they chose who to share their work with. In the process the children adopted a more creative stance towards writing, and in many of the classes it appeared to their teachers that the children invested more of themselves in the process of completing work. Persistence is an important element in teaching for creativity and the journals helped these youngsters both retain and develop their capacity to think for themselves and follow through their ideas. Most of the project focus teachers experienced their classes demanding more writing journal time, and many received complaints when time was unavoidably lost. One class of 7–8-year-olds, concerned to protect their journal time, even went so far as to ensure official information about this popular practice was produced, to be passed to visiting supply teachers.

The teachers were no longer in a position to lead from the front and direct all the writing undertaken, and they commented upon having more time to observe, to listen and to discuss work with their children. Arguably in this context, they were adopting Freire's (1972) conscientisation model and consulting the learners which in turn empowered these young people. Some found that children seized the opportunity through their writing to initiate private conversations with them, for example, Oliver, aged 7, wrote,

> 'Miss how I am doing do you think, with my behaviour '
> 'Tell me,' she replied, 'how do you feel about your progress with behaviour. Talk to me ... '
> 'I really feel good to be Oliver or in other words myself, because last term I was really, really going over the top with my fierce behaviour. I didn't really like what I was doing. But I had other things on my mind'

Oliver had taken the chance to secure the attention of his teacher, who felt he would never have initiated this conversation with her in person, the written word gave him and others the chance to reflect upon themselves and to write from the heart. Several of the teachers actually began their own journals and used some of the time to write for themselves and their own purposes too, as we document in Chapter 9. In contrast to their teaching in cross-curricular contexts, and in literacy when the focus was on knowledge about language forms and features, the teachers often had much less subject knowledge than the children in relation to the popular cultural icons or particular issues that the youngsters chose to explore. Leaning on Fairclough (1989, 1992), we perceive that in the context of writing journal time, the knowledge, social relations and social identities of those involved shifted. Knowledge in this environment was transferred from being the sole charge of the teachers, to being shared with, even owned by the children, as they employed knowledge from the home, from popular media and consumer texts, from their inner lives and outside school experiences. In addition, the social relations in the classroom changed as children exchanged their ideas with each other and valued each other as the first and sometimes only audience. They also took the initiative more and began to reveal to their teachers more about themselves as people – their interests and passions, persuasions and pastimes. This altered their social identities as these more powerful, independent individuals were recognised and celebrated in the classroom. Camen's amusing newspaper examples, Figures 4.3 to 4.5, shows how free this 10-year-old felt in the context of the journal environment. He drew his way forward into the David Beckham column which originated in his journal alongside a quick sketch of Maradonna. Later he chose to rework these initial visuals in the

World cup issue.

HAS SUPERSTAR STATUS GONE TO DAVID'S HEAD?

● He is the shining light of British football... But has superstardom gone to David's head... Literally Tomorrow as England turns out to face Argentina we shall ● See the answer for ourselves, because Beckham has allegedly been reported to be supporting his new latest hair-style.

starman

hair Today gone Tomorrow

The last of the Mohicans

Figure 4.3 Superstar status

context of a group of friends who were producing a World Cup broadsheet. Focused on a subject which he is passionate about, Camen took delight in playing with his idols and creating these humorous entries that experiment with words and ideas, drawing on his knowledge, not just of football, but of the world in which he lives. In his football alphabet, he shares his knowledge of the discourse around the game, and intelligently adds Zico for the challenging 26th letter. In all these examples, Camen's work is carried effectively through a measured presentation of both words and images,

Maradonna or
Kebab'a'donna!
THE SECRET OF
MY SUCCESS

England fans were
Surprised and -
intrigued at the way
the world's greatest
footballer prepares for
the clash against
England tomorrow-
The secret recipe?
6 doner Kebabs and
4 portions of chips,
with 3 Large Coca-
cola! The little man
was Spotted outside
a Local take-away
chomping away to
his hearts content.
When asked what
he thought of the
whole affair, he-
answered..."Yummy!!-
-but Just a little
bit more chilli
Sauce please??"

Kebab u'Like

Reported by Cameron.B

Figure 4.4 Maradonna or Kebab'a'donna!

although the latter is dominant in each, drawing the reader in via the headline and the visuals and tempting us to read the accompanying written column. He addresses the reader directly, asks rhetorical questions and employs appropriate language and a strong sense of the tabloid form. In the production of these stylish texts, he has shaped and reshaped ideas, experience and text knowledge. His texts have cohesion and coherence and his creative voice emerges with verve, as he demonstrates his existing capital which interacts with text knowledge introduced into the classroom.

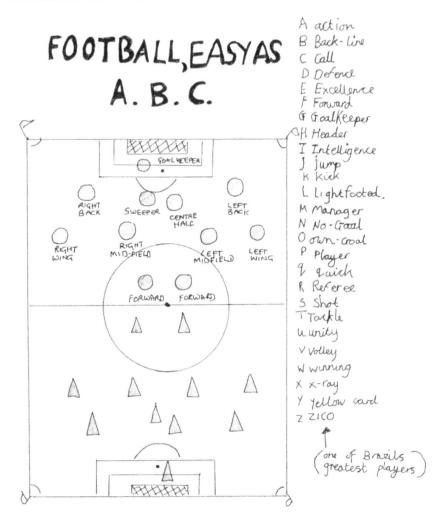

Figure 4.5 Football, easy as A.B.C.

Combining social and cultural capital

Giving children the time to choose their content and form enabled them to draw on the resources they possessed, intellectually, socially and culturally. They began to use writing for their own devices, making the process more satisfying and taking control of their experiences as they communicated them to others. They recognised the autonomy they were offered, and started to introduce into the classroom, practices that formed a part of their own social capital (Bourdieu, 1986). Children, like adults, are part of a complex network of relationships and acquaintances which make them part of a group, joined in culturally meaningful ways. Particular social groupings of children, like groupings of adults, have a collectively owned capital manifested within the material and symbolic exchanges that are integral to the group's perceptions and conceptions of their collective situation. Teachers in the We're Writers project, like the Croydon teachers before them, began to see this appearing in the choices being made (Graham and Johnson, 2003). As Camen's examples from his group's World Cup broadsheet shows, the young writers began to use characters, events and situations found in the texts from their social world. Children's current interests in music, toys, foods, computer games and other merchandise were drafted in and contemporary forms such as rap and hip hop were reflected in their writing. They often carefully recorded the voices of others in their journals, and wrote out song lyrics, chants, advertising slogans and catchphrases, which were frequently decorated and shared with friends or sung/read together. In this way, the children enthusiastically displayed their social and cultural capital that marked them out as members of various groupings. In one class of 10–11-year-olds, the children, having just completed their national tests, were given an open option time for the twenty minutes before lunch. Their teacher noticed that all but three members of the class took out their writing journals, such was the enthusiasm of the youngsters for this, their own literacy practice, and many continued earlier work with friends. The writing undertaken is listed below and shows the personal and cultural resources which the children explored. It also highlights some of their personal concerns and their connections to the popular end of term production 'Ali Baba'. The range of forms they employed in this work was considerable, it was not form led, but content led and oriented around personal and familial concerns, popular cultural interests and more school-based passions and engagements. Their work included some powerful pieces, for as Graves (1983) observed, when an author makes a good choice of subject their voice 'booms through'. Their selections, connections and decisions appeared to make a significant difference to the degree of commitment, interest and perseverance which young authors demonstrate.

Content Choices Made in a Single Session

What 6A will do when they are older

The future, my future

Poem about the end of SATS

Birthday present list

Who I want to be with on the school trip

My family

My auntie

My grandma and grandpa
My best friends
Favourite pop groups
Scripts for Ali Baba
Lyrics from Ali Baba
Raps for Ali Baba
Football teams
Cartoon of Power Puff Girls
Script for drama club
A story: The Wizard
A story: My dream
A story: The big fall out
Description of a place (Imagined holiday scene to come)
Editing a letter from Billy (literacy hour work from 'The Wreck of the Zanzibar'
by Michael Morpurgo)

In a younger class, Jodie, aged 8, made a list of her journal entries across
a month, which included: work essentials, an idiots art gallery, chat page,
other chat pages, class nicknames, a rap, Top of the Toons, tongue twisters,
a lurve page and a mobile phone page. The sheer volume of writing and
drawing recorded in her journal in this time is a testament to her commitment and labour, and was not atypical in this and many other classrooms.
Journals gave the children the chance to practice their writing, not through
skills worksheets, but through the process of whole-text production which
motivated and involved them. Jodie's intentionality, individuality and sense
of freedom is evident; she selected themes of interest and pursued them,
exploring and applying her understanding of written language and
drawing on objects and media from her world that give her social capital –
the power of functioning within a network. As well as being embodied in
material objects, cultural capital can also be found in the person themselves
(Bourdieu, 1986). Like a suntan, it is acquired over a sustained period of
time in a particular environment – cultural surroundings – and becomes
part of the recipient. Immersion in the texts and practices that make up
this cultural capital, leads over time to a total absorption of that way of
life. However, not all cultural and social capital is the same, or indeed
equal; different social environments produce different manifestations, some
with more power than others. As Bourdieu (1986) argues, school highlights
a particular form of cultural capital, institutionalised into educational
qualifications and based upon the absorption of particular texts and
practices associated with this form of capital. Bearne too, in commenting
on the journal work in Croydon observes:

The classroom can be seen as a site for overlapping domains of social and intellectual experience or 'capital'. In particular the journal work has made their literacy capital very visible. For some time it has been clear that children's home and school domains need to be seen much more as overlapping than as separate.

(Bearne, 2003b: 37)

The children chose to bring in elements of their cultural capital, and often mixed these with the cultural capital of the school, thus exploring the interplay between them, for example, Jade chose to write a diary, see Figure 4.6. A traditional textual form, its content connects to some of her experiences both inside and outside school as an 11-year-old and includes what she imagines/hopes will encompass the social life of a 15-year-old teenager. Her fictional entries, only a few of which are shown here, are packed with references to the network of interests, people and artefacts that form her real and imagined social worlds and, significantly, she appears relaxed in both and manipulates them to meet her desired ends. The images Jade draws depict objects associated with popular culture and these form part of the hybrid of cultural capitals that her journal entries represent, her

June 27th 1998   18:02

I am in love. I Knew it. Well there is this new guy at school called Josh Bennet, and I love him. I think I could have a chance with too because he came to sit with me at lunch fancy that! ME! Thats not all, he blew me a kiss in English and gave me a wink in Science! Wow, being in love feels so .. so sweet. Hang on gotta go, Vanessa's strangling the cat again!

                                                                 18:38

I saved the cat. I don't know why I did, I mean no-one likes Truffle. I guess I just didn't think it was fair my little sister should get to kill him, I'm the oldest, I should get the privilege. Know! I'm so tired. I'm going to bed now. I better hide Truffles in the broom cupboard so my sis can't get him.

Figure 4.6a Example from a fictional diary

(b)

June 28th 1998

I had a lie in and I feel much better. I got Truffles out the cupboard and she bit me. Oh well! Today I'm going to Suzannes birthday party. trampolining and then to Macdonalds, yum! I took this diary to breakfast and dad says I should get rid of it but I would never do that, I love writing and can write anything in here, all my secrets, my problems, everything. I am really excited about seeing Josh at the park. I'll get dressed up specially for me because he might ask me out. I'm going to wear my bright pink, mega baggy trousers with my strappy top the white one, with the silver belt I got for christmas. Oh, I'm really excited. Its nearly time to go I better get changed now.

June 28th 1998

(c)

17:23 pm

the new watch

J.B

the $20 there is hardly any chips left we brought something with it

the medallion all of us had at the party.

J.B + I B 4 EVER

the trampolin

Suzannes party was so cool. Josh asked me out and I said yes and he kissed me on the cheek. Then I two games and the prizes were a cool new watch and $20. Her family must be rich I mean to give away that amount of money! I'm glad I won it though. I can't wait to go and spend it. Then I met this really nice girl called Liz. She is the daughter of one of Suzannes mums friends, Sally. She's my age; 15 and she's really nice. I'm seeing her again tomorrow, perhaps we'll go shopping and I'll spend my prize money I don't know. We will have to wait and see I guess. I've got the watch on it's comfy. I can hardly feel it. Guess what, Mum has just told me that I'm allowed my room to be redecorated. Something must be going on, Mum would never let me out of the blue. We don't have the time or money. I'm going to ask Mum, though, I'm not gonna complain this could be my only chance. You will not believe it

Figures 4.6b and 4.6c More examples from a fictional diary

hopes and dreams are voiced as she confidently spills words onto paper, conversing with herself, yet keen to share her work with both her peers and her teacher.

Whilst the autonomy offered to the children through journal time created a window through which light from their world was seen in school, these independent writing times were, and still are, only a small concession to the cultural foundation of normal school practice. The basic fabric of school remained relatively untouched. The challenge of releasing time for journals and handing it over to the children was considerable and many teachers initially felt they had to offer guidance and give a range of set options for the children to chose from; some even felt compelled to list the established genre inside the front cover of the journals. They were undoubtedly trying to help, but this may have served to remind their young learners what schooled writing apparently 'is' – defining it from a specific cultural position and introducing a form of closure. As Giroux comments:

> Schools play a particularly important role in legitimising and reproducing dominant cultural capital. They tend to legitimise certain forms of knowledge, ways of speaking, and ways of relating to the world that capitalise on the type of familiarity and skills that only certain students have received from their family backgrounds and class relations. Students whose families have only tenuous connections to the dominant cultural capital are at a decided disadvantage.
>
> (Giroux, 1983: 268)

Journal writing does allow children to bring in texts and literacy practices that lie outside the more powerful cultural practices of society, although ultimately the literacy curriculum, supported by the state, its laws, policies and curricula, remains. National testing regimes also uphold dominant forms of social capital and the culture transmitted in school environments often 'confirms, values and validates' this situation (Hill, 2001: 102). Their journals did however show the nature and extent of their interaction with literacies not necessarily reflected in the curriculum, provided evidence of the resources children can draw upon to communicate and make meanings, and created a more inclusive culture in the classroom. Their own cultural capital was valued and this brought evident pleasure and satisfaction to the learners, who felt safe in incorporating subject matter from their own lives, as well as borrowing the forms and structures from out-of-school texts.

Conclusion

In order to understand children's dispositions, attitudes and insights, their views and voices need to be heard, since their emotions, perceptions and self-esteem as writers are very influential in their development as text makers. In appealing for a 'pedagogy of voices', Van Oers (2003) suggests that there should be a balance between the meanings and motives of children and the educational objectives set by society; certainly a more negotiated curriculum was developed in the We're Writers schools, and the children are now more regularly consulted and involved in the process of shaping their literacy curriculum in action. The experience of offering choice and fostering independence through writing journals highlighted the importance of providing time and space for children to decide for themselves what and how they might choose to write, and helped them develop a richer sense of audience and readership for their writing. Independent writing was also nurtured by negotiating options within other literacy activities and through their creative engagement in drama and storytelling, for example. Encouragingly, both the interim and summative surveys carried out across the two years of the project indicated the children's increasing enthusiasm for writing. The older children in particular, loudly and clearly voiced their pleasure in writing journals and continued to request that more time was allocated to this practice. Now more intrinsically motivated, these young writers seized the opportunities which journal time offered to write for themselves and for others. In doing so they borrowed from a range of semiotic sources, provided their teachers with a more holistic view of their differences and preferences as writers, and created classrooms which resounded with the voices of interested and individual young writers.

Chapter 5

Artistic voices

Literature

In an age that is creating more technology than some of us know how to handle and that demands new forms of reading, questions about the value of literature and how it supports young readers and writers deserve our reconsideration. Can we assume that literature still has a powerful role to play in children's personal growth and literacy development? For this to hold true we need to be convinced that good literature both mirrors and reflects our lives, provokes a response and has the potential to takes us forward in some way or another. Teachers know that literature excites, stimulates, informs and expands the horizons of readers, it also provokes and consoles, although its value in teaching writing is perhaps still not fully understood, explicitly valued or developed.

Literature helps us reflect upon and interpret the world as it is seen and constructed by others. The author Margaret Mahy suggests that children's imaginations are initially colonised by images from their immediate world, although this desire for familiarity may not last long since they rapidly develop an appetite to believe and take delight in fantasy and marvels. Convinced of the need for story in our lives, she claims that 'stories enable us first to give form to, and then to take possession of, a variety of truths both literal and figurative. Once we have part of the truth caught up in a story, we can begin to recognize it and get some sort of power over it' (Mahy, 1996: 140). From a very early age, children learn to manipulate language for both functional and storying purposes (Fox, 1988; Hall, 1995) and over time they learn to use writing for these dual purposes too.

> We all use language in (both) these ways, to get things done in the outer world and to manipulate the inner world. Action and decision belong to the former use; freedom from them in the latter enables us to attend to other things – to the forms of language, the patterns of events, the feelings. We take up as it were the role of spectators: spectators of our own past lives, our imagined futures, other men's lives, impossible events. When we *speak* this language, the nearest name I can give it is 'gossip'; when we *write* it, it is literature.
>
> (Britton, 1977: 111)

This chapter explores the power of written literature to shape children's imaginative experience and influence their writing. We highlight the significance of investigating high quality children's fiction in the classroom and describe the initially limited parameters of reading–writing practice documented in the We're Writers project. We then document more flexible and meaning focused practices which the teachers' adopted. Their changing pedagogy and personal involvement began to challenge and extend children's affective involvement in texts on their journeys as readers and writers. In tune with the rest of the book, we examine the generation of ideas and the role of literature in this and in developing knowledge about composition. We also highlight the importance of discussing literary texts and helping children make connections between reading and writing.

Literature matters

We are convinced of the value of stories for children, stories told to them, stories read to them and the stories they read for themselves. It is through story as well as through drama and other forms of creative work that children grope for the meaning of the experiences that have already overtaken them, savour again their pleasures and reconcile themselves to their own inconsistencies and those of others. As they 'try on' first one storybook character, then another, imagination and sympathy, the power to enter into another personality and situation, which is a characteristic of childhood and a fundamental condition for good social relationships, is preserved and nurtured. It is also through literature that children feel forward to the experiences, the hopes and fears that await them in adult life.

(Plowden, 1967: 216–20)

The tone and language of the Plowden Report may sound unfamiliar to us now, particularly in the wake of more prescriptively oriented documents, yet much of the strength of its underpinning philosophy can be found in classrooms which still celebrate the power of story in children's constructions of the world. Chambers reminds us that 'it is in literature that we find the best expression of the human imagination and the most useful means by which we come to grips with ideas about ourselves and what we are' (Chambers, 1993: 16). As humans we need to represent our experiences through writing; there is a real sense of triangulation between life, literature and writing. When 6-year-old Sheena writes, *Long, long ago lived a beatiful princess. Her face as white as the snow and her lips and cheeks were as red as cherries*, we know that she has been immersed in the language and patterns of traditional tales. But when she adds, *The queen quietly went over to her dorters bed. she had fallan out of bed the queen carefully picked her up. she did not move at all. Then she put the dovay over her, then she creaped out of her room then tiredly she went back to her own bedroom*, it becomes clear that the world of traditional tales and her own knowledge and understanding of life have become entwined.

The idea that children use writing, as they use literature, to make sense of their world is taken further by Kress (2000: 69) who argues that 'drawing the world and writing the world are much the same thing for a child; both are recordings, transcriptions, translations, "spellings" of aspects of the world of the child'. Reading, writing and other forms of symbolic representation can help to create or narratise our world and in the process shape our developing sense of self and awareness of our own and others' lives. Story matters in learning and in life, and children deserve to be supported in inhabiting story worlds and experiencing characters' perspectives to see if they fit their own life experiences and aspirations. Immersion in and exploration of stories in the ways suggested by Plowden are critical if we are to support the development of young readers and writers. The quality of the text and the connections it makes with the reader will influence any later writing, as will the classroom approaches employed to explore it; what we must avoid, however, is the endless dissection of narrative for specific language ends. Graham Greene proffers us insight as he remembers the very day that he found his way into books and stories, in describing his journey into reading and writing back in 1947.

> I remember distinctly the suddenness with which a key turned in a lock and I found I could read – not just the sentences in a reading book with the syllables coupled like railway carriages, but a real book ...
>
> But when I took Miss Marjorie Bowen's *The Viper of Milan* from the library shelf, the future for better or worse really struck. From that moment I began to write. All the other possible futures slid away; the potential civil servant, the don, the clerk had to look for other incarnations. Imitation after imitation of Miss Bowen's magnificent novel went into exercise books ... I think it was Miss Bowen's apparent zest that made me want to write. One could not read her without believing that to write was to live and to enjoy.
>
> (Greene quoted in Gross, 1991: 518)

More than half a century later, other texts matter to children in their literacy development although their impact could probably be similarly described. It is to the texts themselves that we turn first.

Quality texts

From conversations in our project focus group about their own early literacy experiences, it seems that for many of the teachers, Enid Blyton was encountered early and held a particular pleasure, with *The Faraway Tree*, the Famous Five and the Secret Seven stories feeding into their repertoires as writers. The work of Eve Garnett and Eleanor Brent Dyer as well as classics writers such as Louisa M. Alcott were also frequently mentioned in their childhood reading histories. Since these publications the range, style and quality of children's fiction has increased dramatically, offering vast and varied worlds for children to inhabit and many more literary voices for them to echo and engage with. 'In the stories children compose themselves we see what they have learnt as a result of having stories read and told to them' (Martin and Leather, 1994: 28–9). The breadth and variety of textual forms supports this process with picture fiction, graphic novels, magazines, comics, television and film offering different models of reading and writing. Figure 5.1 is the opening extract from a long story composed at home by a 9-year-old, and shows clearly the shaping influence of the

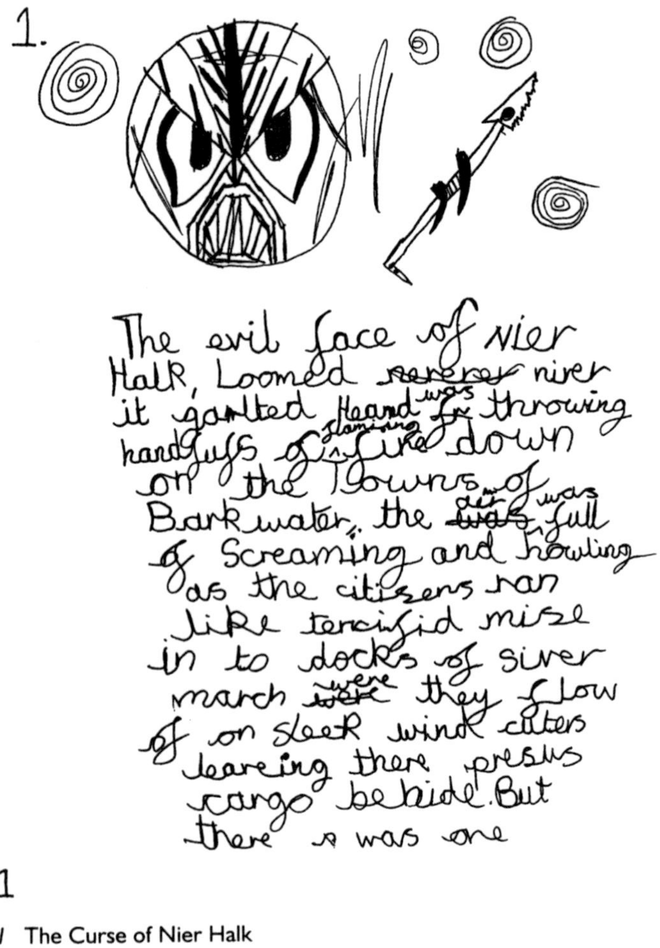

Figure 5.1   The Curse of Nier Halk

world of fantasy novels on this young writer at that time. Patrick had just completed the collection entitled *The Edge Chronicles* by Paul Stewart and Chris Riddell, six books in the Tolkien/Pratchett tradition and he chose to write a story based in the same fantasy genre. He may also have been influenced by *The Wind on Fire* trilogy by William Nicholson and Philip Reeve's *Mortal Engines* which he'd recently devoured with delight. His opening mirrors Stewart's style closely and borrows some elements from the series whilst inventing many others.

> The evil face of Nier Halk loomed nearer its galted hand was throwing handfuls of fire flaming down on the towns of Barkwater. The air was full of screaming and howling as the citizens ran like terrified mice into docks of Silver March, where they flew off on sleek wind cutters leaving their precious cargo behind. But there was one man left. Falcon ...

His full narrative encompasses some 970 words, all written in his own time over a period of a fortnight. Falcon, the young hero, travels through a time warp and becomes tangled in an adventure which takes him into several worlds. In Chapter 3, he is captured and imprisoned with the infamous Marcus Bittersflow and then rescued by a team of 'helpers', who are introduced in the following manner.

> First, there was the Captain with five steel teeth and an eye patch. Then there came Grands, the bards master with a face full of scars, but he was cheerful. He was followed by Sagro, the harpoon man, he was thin, his face had but one eye. Then there was Mela, whose other name was Tenso, he was the sail master with amazing senses. And last but not least was the hooker whose name was Silas Snatch. He was sly and quick to anger. Unlike the others he had only four fingers and two thumbs.

In the dreadful battle that follows their release, Marcus, the ship's scout, is fatally wounded when hit in the eye by an eagle crossbow. When Falcon, who is also injured, recovers, he asks after his friend and is told, '*He has danced with death and joined the souls of thousands of brave men*'. *Falcon went silent.* At the close of the tale, the young author uses a time slip to reveal to the reader that Falcon is an orphan and we are left assuming that our young hero will eventually take Marcus's place as the leading explorer, adventuring into uncharted terrain for the sake of his people. Patrick's desire to write this epic and his determination to complete it emerged from his deep fascination and pleasure in the series and the opportunity to try his hand at creating such a tale. The actions, descriptions and names of the characters, the dramatic events of the story, shaped by the different worlds that Falcon enters, and the language chosen throughout are all heavily influenced by the genre, demonstrating that the extended experience of reading narrative offers children one of the most powerful and effective ways of mastering the language of story or 'book language'. He also drew half a dozen visuals which help to tell his tale, mirroring the use of Chris Riddell's illustrations in the series. This young author goes beyond 'combinational creativity', and demonstrates 'exploratory creativity' (Boden, 2001), as he leans heavily and consciously upon his reading, shows that he has learnt some of the rules of the form, but also uses his writing as a means of exploring possibilities, themes and ideas that are particular to him. He elaborates his ideas, expresses his own individuality and creativity and conveys his story with fluency and flair.

In a recent research project with 9–10-year-olds, Barrs and Cork (2001) found that the kinds of texts that were most supportive to children as writers were: traditional tales, stories containing 'poeticised speech' and emotionally powerful texts. *The Edge Chronicles* has certainly taken this young reader on an emotionally charged journey and many such texts exist in schools, but as teachers we need to make careful choices in response to our learners and their particular interests and preferences. We also need to ensure that the text's meaning is profiled and investigated prior to any focused discussion of particular prosodic features. Different forms offer alternative access points, and as Graham (2000) has argued, provocative picture books, for example, can provide a reverberating space in which the creativity of readers finds expression. Picture books can also increase our opportunities to fill the gaps left by the text (Iser, 1974), multiply the ambiguities offered and extend our powers of empathy and identification. As such they can be used to stimulate creative and critical thinking, for such texts also bring the creative faculties of adults into play and make reading for all 'a distinctive kind of imaginative looking' (Meek, 1991: 116). They also provide excellent models of short stories, which are the most frequent form of narrative that children are invited to write. As Heaney (1980) observes, the voices of others significantly influence writers, both young and old.

> In practice you hear it coming from somebody else, you hear something in another writer's sounds that flow in through your ear and enters the echo chambers of your head and delight your whole nervous system in such a way that your reaction will be 'ah, I wish I had said that in that particular way'. This other writer in fact has spoken something you recognise instinctively as a true sounding of yourself and your experience. And your first steps as a writer will be to imitate,

consciously or unconsciously, those sounds that flowed in that influence.

(Heaney, 1980: 4)

Of course the texts encountered, enjoyed and imitated by children will not always take the form of literature traditionally recognised as worthwhile, those which act as 'touchstones of moral values' (Marsh and Millard, 2000). The Power Puff Girls, the Simpsons, Dennis the Menace and many more characters from the world of popular culture all carry narratives and artifacts highly attractive to children, so in school they 'need discursive space, sympathy and imaginative and moral challenges ... in order for them to integrate what they watch, hear and read' (Hilton, 1996: 2). Although this issue of the influence of popular culture is discussed more fully in Chapters 2 and 3, it is important to note that children are encountering narratives and literature in many forms both inside and outside school, all of which contribute to their personal repertoire, the store into which they dip when called to write fiction themselves. Children need to have stories read to them with skill and dedication, for when stories are read well, children are invited in as participants in the narrative, to share in the layers of meanings and the intertextual references. Whilst the influence of reading on writing may be evident, literature must never become a tool only to serve other masters. It is salutatory to note that in a recent international study (Mullis *et al.*, 2003), the UK children performed very well in the SAT-like comprehension tests, but fared very poorly in terms of independent reading for pleasure. Making explicit the satisfaction to be found in literacy practices and engaging with literature as a pleasurable activity and an end in itself is an essential element of literacy teaching. As Britton has observed, a sense of literary form grows 'from within, it is the legacy of past satisfactions' (Britton, 1977: 108) and comprehension should emerge naturally from interested exploration and sensitive consideration of the text.

Such satisfactions should be given higher profile by both teachers and policy makers. If satisfying children as readers and writers became a primary aim, then pleasure and playfulness would naturally inhabit the spaces between the written texts shared, explored and enjoyed and the child as a writer. To increase their satisfaction in stories, response to text activities are needed to allow them to interpret and reconstruct narratives as well as to increase their awareness of how the author has crafted the text. Such attention to the construction of text needs to be integrated into the children's creative encounters with texts, so their response is foregrounded, and their appreciation of the skills demonstrated do not mar their pleasure in the meanings and connections made. Indeed, as Meek carefully explains, 'having a voice in writing and working out how it will be heard are extensions of an early important reading lesson: how to become both the teller and the told. These and other literary competences are rarely taught deliberately' (Meek, 2001: 17). Quality texts regularly read and sensitively mediated by involved adults, can both lure the children into a position of increased understanding and influence their later writing. For 'reading is an integral part of the composition of text, with the writer interacting (as a reader) with the text as it is being produced' (Corden, 2001: 37).

Having selected a range of compelling narratives which invite specula- tion and interpretation, teachers can read these aloud and plan open-ended activities, including for example, drama, discussion, storytelling and explo- ratory poetic performances as part of the extended process of composition. Through the children's deep intellectual and emotional engagement in these activities, new insights may be harnessed, new ideas for writing generated and new knowledge about the art of composition embedded. Some of these energetic and poetic voices will remain with them, as Beverley Naidoo (2003) observed about the writing of the young Anne Frank 'I still feel connected to her voice forty years on'. As readers we often sense the textual voice of the writer which is complemented by the writer's sense of audience and this can 'create a potent textual bond' (Benton and Fox, 1985). Bakhtin (1981) suggests it is the writer's inner speech that we ourselves give voice to, even when we read silently and Barrs (2000) notes 'it's the very personal nature of this communication, direct from mind to mind, that makes reading such an act of intimacy'.

From reading to writing: analysis of texts for instructional purposes

Primary teachers' knowledge about children's literature and significant authors was arguably positively influenced by the introduction of the NLS in England, although some teachers we met were apparently astonished by the requirement that they should be familiar with such literature. Back in 1998, many schools, with pressured professionals and additional finance to spend in a very short time were tempted by the plethora of publishers' resources which flooded the market. As teachers sought to cope with the demands of timing and the structure and expectations of the literacy hour, these materials, created in response to 'perceived, rather than actual needs' (Goodwin and Routh, 2000), appeared to offer real support. But the endless files and photocopiables produced, purportedly encompassing every literary technique, offered bite-sized extracts and highly imitative and tightly framed writing practices. The schools in the We're Writers project, like many others, had bought into the various schemes for teaching writing within the literacy hour, although they tried to supplement these by reading and studying other fiction and by creating regular opportunities for the children to practise the skills of story writing. This last practice frequently took the form of timed pieces undertaken in preparation for assessment tests and to consolidate the forms and features of writing learnt for this purpose. Our initial survey of the children's writing revealed that in addition to leaning on schemes to provide extracts and the activities to go with them, the construction of story narrative formed the bulk of writing practice across the primary years. Children were regularly asked to re-write a favourite story, to contribute an ending, to write in the style of the text or were provided with a title. The single common feature across the sample of over 120 children was that the shape and general idea for the story was fixed by their teachers, as it is also fixed by those who determine the nature of national assessment tests.

On examining the context of these sessions more closely, we found that the majority of the 65 teachers started them with a story extract and then required the children to complete what they heard, often in the style of the author. In some cases, teachers were not familiar with the book or the rest of the story from which the extract they were using to prompt or study writing was drawn. When asked if the children were given any specific teaching before they began to write, most listed particular technical or linguistic features which they had profiled prior to the independent writing. Many also noted that they had listed the success criteria linked to the assessment requirements on the board as a reminder. These activities need to be understood in the climate of Spring 2001, and were, we believe, oriented towards fulfilling the perceived requirements for writing and the assessment of writing. For the purpose of developing writers, however, such limited practice in relation to independent writing is woefully inadequate. In addition, with the very best of intentions, many of these teachers also made extensive use of extracts in shared reading, treating the texts, like many of their colleagues across the rest of England 'as geological sites from which words and phrases must be quarried in a laborious process' (Dombey, 1998: 129). They were effectively sending children off on the road to writing with the songs of how to fulfil measurable technical requirements ringing in their ears, drowning perhaps any sense of the text's tune and meaning or the author's voice or intention.

It would seem that story reading and writing in schools can become a sterile and formulaic activity if practices such as the identification and reproduction of linguistic forms dominate, and if literary texts are given high status predominantly for the purposes of writing instruction. The disaffection that some children feel for this kind of schooled comprehension and templated composition relate to its lack of ownership, engagement, authenticity and purpose. As a result, many of the young learners in our project felt somewhat detached from the creative processes of reading and writing, perhaps because 'the desire to write has been sublimated by an induction into the structures of privileged forms' (Robinson and Ellis, 2000: 74). These youngsters were not alone in expressing their dissatisfaction. In recent years, professional authors too have voiced their concerns about the 'analysis paralysis approach to fiction' which makes books little more than objects for writing instruction. A group, including Chris Powling, Bernard Ashley, Philip Pullman, Anne Fine and Jamaila Gavin, all met with the Education Secretary in 2003 and expressed their concerns that constant comprehension exercises based on short excerpts were exacting a toll on reading and writing. 'What's at stake ... is nothing less than the integrity of the novel, the story, the poem ... valued for its own sake and on its own terms' (Powling, 2003: 3). In the company of gifted authors, poets, illustrators and designers, children can travel far and it may be that some, like the young Graham Greene, will find their way from powerful literature to the creation of their own texts, but most will need guidance and important conversations on the journey. The form that this guidance and its attendant talk takes during the extended process of composition is critical and it is to this that we now turn, guided ourselves by the teachers who transformed their practice and explored new by-roads and avenues in partnership with their children.

From reading to writing: engagement, reflection and response

The teachers' challenge was to move away from responding only to the perceived requirements of national assessment criteria and to move towards a more integrated and creative interpretation of current curricula. Their practice needed to encompass more dynamic, collaborative and engaging activities that allowed the children to draw on the intertextual threads between their own culturally defined literacy practices and literacy events in school (Dyson, 2001). Crucially, the teachers also needed time to read, research and reflect upon their practice, alone and in the company of others, and to dare to innovate, transforming some of the more limited literacy events on offer in their schools. In addition, in order to motivate their young writers and enable them to develop as autonomous and creative authors, our colleagues in the project focus group needed to develop their professional knowledge, understanding and independence. Their growth as more assured language artists and as teachers is documented more fully in Chapters 9 and 10, here we attend to their changing patterns of practice in relation to literature and explore more fully the relationship between reading and writing.

Development in reading and writing is undoubtedly reciprocal and it is essential that we lean on literature to help children enrich their writing. Writers are magpies, collecting ideas from the texts of their own lives and the narratives invented by others, and young authors can develop the craft of writing through increased awareness of the literary models that surround them. It is widely recognised that literature can influence young writers (e.g. Fox, 1993; Mallet, 1997; Barrs and Cork, 2001) and that rich reading offers a veritable storehouse of possibilities for writers. The Teaching Reading and Writing Links (TRAWL) project has also shown that critical reading and investigation of texts is an integral part of the writing process, and children's metacognitive development and awareness of the reader can be enhanced through thoughtful teaching about literary language and features of texts (Corden, 2003). The teaching on the TRAWL project however, despite its emphasis on literary devices, was not at the expense of the meaning or purpose of the text, and children were provided with opportunities to work on sustained pieces of writing in which they could make use of their new knowledge and skills in context. In this significant research, the children's growing text knowledge was coupled with an emerging understanding of authorship, and they were clearly involved in knowledge transforming not simply knowledge telling (Bereiter and Scardamalia, 1987). The learners in this research became more aware of the way in which authors choose to structure, use and manipulate language to achieve particular effects and were able, over time, to reflect upon the choices they themselves had made in a piece of writing. Having had their attention drawn to specific literary devices in context, they were able 'to discuss and critically evaluate texts, and to transfer the knowledge and insights gained to their own writing' (Corden, 2000: 153).

Conversation about texts is central to the enterprise of making connections between reading and writing, both conversations about books written by professional authors and talk about the texts composed by the children, since 'booktalk is the pumping of blood through literary veins' (Chambers, 1993). In the following example a group of 9–10-year-olds are discussing the picture book *Beauty and the Beast* by Geraldine McCaughrean, evocatively illustrated by Gary Blythe.

AMY: *Can we talk about the beginning, because I really thought it was effective?*
NAOMI: *Yeah, I'd like to. You know that bit, 'Under him the horse trembled with terror'? Well, I think that was good, cos the author doesn't actually say Gregor is frightened, he uses the horse to tell us that.*
AMY: *I like the words, the images, the similes best. I think it makes the text more poetic.*
SHANE: *It seems more real doesn't it? I feel drawn into it, like I'm Gregor.*
AMY: *Which one do you think is best? I like 'like the fingers of ghosts' – spooky!*
OLIN: *Do you, I like that one too, though I would have put more ghostly stuff in.*

Through focused discussion, explicit teaching in context and a variety of collaborative activities undertaken as part of the extended process of composition, this class shared understandings about language and debated the choices writers make. It was evident that over time such conversations contributed to the written work they produced as the brief extract from Naomi's writing indicates.

Beauty's name describes her very well, for she has a glowing complexion and is as beautiful as the beast is ugly. She is petite, small boned and frail, a doll like figure with eyes like deep pools of chocolate and a soft and dreamy look about her. Her hands are fine and delicate and her long silky tresses are as black as jet, swirling around her face. By nature Beauty is kind and generous, she finds good in everyone, and makes friends easily. Perhaps she is too trusting though, naïve even ...

Individual creativity is undoubtedly affected by dialogue with others (NACCCE, 1999) and frequent, planned and focused opportunities for talk about texts are a prerequisite for developing writers, alongside more spontaneous and open-ended engagements with powerful narratives. Such work, like most effective learning, is messy, does not fit neatly into timed spaces or linear learning trajectories. Instead, it requires time and space for talk, for genuine interaction with texts which are themselves sometimes chosen by the children, and many opportunities to revisit, revise and reshape writing through collaboration. For a literate community to flourish it is critical. Wells argues that there should be:

> frequent and rewarding opportunities for its members to have conversations with each other about what they are doing, and why and about how the texts they are engaging with are helping them to better understand themselves and their purposes.
>
> (Wells, 2003: 192)

Through close readings of powerful and resonant texts and through personal and affective responses and reflective discussions, children begin to notice the ways, means, manners and modes of different writers. Such attention to the text must encompass considerable reading aloud in order to profile the tunes and rhythms of texts, for this influences children's writing. Based on their research, Barrs and Cork insightfully recognise that emphasis needs to be given to reading and re-reading and on 'the way a story is told, the communications of meaning, the development of an ear for written language, and on the interaction between the writer and the reader' (Barrs and Cork, 2001: 43). The classroom approaches to literature which they found to be significantly supportive to young writers include reading aloud, response to text and drama work, as well as the practice of reading the children's work aloud to them during the writing process giving voice to the author's own tenor and tune.

Children develop their explicit and implicit knowledge about language through a range of such whole-text activities and are supported in the process of writing. Focusing on the whole text, its meaning, purpose and content is important, since as Gillian Cross observes 'I tend to concentrate on my language more when I've got the shape of the story right. The hang up I used to have as a child and teenage writer was that you had to get the language right first time' (Cross, 1999: 136). It is not that the technical features are unimportant, but that the overall text coherence, shape and meaning need to be attended to first. In referring to the materials used to introduce children to reading and writing after the First World War, Bruner notes that the 'three ancient maxims of phonics, lexis and grammar' were used and 'somehow the text and context got lost in the details' (Bruner, 1984: 199). Perhaps history has once again repeated itself. Have we allowed our concern with apparently pre-ordained genres and their attendant linguistic features to dominate our teaching of writing? This was certainly the view of the teachers in the We're Writers project who needed support to develop a more creative, responsive and exploratory attitude to teaching writing, one which increased the children's engagement, reflection and response.

In one class the children regularly created their own narratives, often through the role play area and with the help of story boxes and storybags. Katie, aged 6, having retold the story of Martin Waddell's *Owl Babies* with the help of some toy owls, worked to create an alternative ending (Figure 5.2). She was determined to make it a happy one, so borrowed a magical character from the world of folk and fairy tales with which she was well aquainted. Her fairy, like many before her, came to the rescue in the situation and, guided by the mother owl, restored order and synchrony to the owl babies' world. Katie borrows the verb 'huddled' directly from the text and integrates her surprise ending with her sad one, so whilst the problem of the tree falling is created it is also solved. As the DfES (2001) materials on teaching writing acknowledge, 'much of what children need to learn about writing, from story structure to written language features and punctuation, can be gained from storytelling, shared reading and the oral interaction stimulated by them'. In such playful and imaginative contexts, children like Katie can create new fictions, find the language to convey their meanings and use reading and writing in context. If the role play area and story boxes are based on familiar literature, the changes made, the scenes revisited and transformed will contribute to their emerging sense of authorship and ownership as they weave threads of their lives into the known stories and make intertextual links. One child's imaginative offerings in play may appear to govern and drive the group, but the imaginings of others will draw strength and gather pace as a result, as Paley's (1981)

OWL BABIES   Katie

Martin Waddell

Beginning: **3 Baby owls wake up and find their owl mummy gone**

Middle: **They come out of their house**
They sit in the trees in the dark
They talk and huddle together on one branch
The 3 baby owls wish and wish mummy would come home

End: **The Happy Ending**

Their owl mother returns and they are delighted

A Sad Ending
But then the flor started to crack and the tree staeed to fall the baby owls huddceald together as the tree fell down woods and theyr muther was not ther to help them. the b babies were sad

A Surprise Ending
But then their mother came she had a Fary with her. she told the Fary wate to do and the flor sbrted to go back together and the tree sbrted to rise

Figure 5.2 Owl babies revisited

observations of young Wally and his classmates show. Working on such affectively involving classroom practice can help us create a community of literacy learners who are engaged in the pursuit of meaning and who shape novel ideas and understandings as they draw on a range of potent texts.

From reading to writing: explorations in literature-based classrooms

From an early age, children actively play with language and subvert known texts, injecting their own interpretations, their own voices into stories, songs or rhymes (Grainger and Goouch, 1999). If there are few official opportunities for such playful practice in school then their creativity may go underground and may be prevented from surfacing in their writing. Opportunities to step inside stories, try on the characters and 'do their voices' are formative steps on the road to becoming story writers as they encourage awareness of sequence and structure, characterisation and dialogue and demonstrate the potential for transformation. As children respond to their reading in diverse ways, a rich store for use in later writing is created. Anna's delightful version of Michael Rosen's *We're Going on a Bear Hunt*, Figure 5.3, is an example of this. She composed this piece in free

Figure 5.3 Fairy hunt

choice time, a couple of weeks after the class had been on their own Bear Hunt in the hall and made up their own Caretaker Hunt travelling around the school. The rhythms, repetitions and patterns of the text have been recalled and applied by this 6-year-old with apparent ease and pleasure. She spent some considerable time completing her detailed drawings and added her verses, then read her work to the class, mirroring the intonation of the children's original rendition of Rosen's text. Anna too focused on her interest in fairies, prompted perhaps by the loss of a tooth and her interest in the reality or otherwise of the tooth fairy. She had also recently enjoyed the wordless picture book *The Tooth Fairy* by Peter Collington with some of her friends. Through such playful transformations, contextualised by powerful literature, Anna and her classmates were able to create their own authorial spaces. That is, they were able to spontaneously borrow ideas, temporarily invest them into their play, their play writing and their writing and drawing in play.

In another class of younger children, where the focus had been upon traditional tales for several weeks, a culture of stories was also evident as the teacher read and told many tales, traditional and modern versions. Reading and responding to literature in this class of 4–5-year-olds was a complex and engaging business. It involved the extensive use of reading aloud, frequent 'book zips', during which the children were able to predict the narrative of an unknown text based on the cover alone (Grainger *et al.*, 2004b), hot seating, questioning the text together, challenging the versions read, talking about the pictures and entering some of the imaginary worlds through drama. The class regularly discussed play opportunities based on well-known stories, deciding which story elements could be changed, and they were encouraged to create new versions on the playground as well. They made big books together of course, and used this opportunity to create unusual combinations, drawing on the stories they knew, for example, with gingerbread men, little pigs and Goldilocks all inhabiting the same adventure. They also regularly planned their role play area, discussing and voting together; for a while it was a house made of sweets in a gingerbread forest, although just a few weeks later it was transformed into a castle, complete with turrets and thrones. These areas were given shape and form by the adults, but the children worked on them and in them, for example, the castle was bedecked with pictures and portraits, and signs and symbols that represented the different knights the children had constructed in their play.

However, the really interesting transformations occurred as the children gained in knowledge and took more control. On one occasion, the story *Do Knights take Naps?* by Janet Tucker and Nick Sharratt (1996) was read to the class; the text's subversive and humorous nature invites children to play and their teacher gave them the opportunity to have their faces painted, to help them, in his words, *create a physical bridge between the story and their own characterization.* Those children with symbols on their faces of the Black Knight did in fact become both fierce and powerful! Any clothes with sparkles or sequins on them were seized and used imaginatively, draped over shoulders and around waists. Some children, without any costumes or props, imaginatively declared that their armour was pink, their horse had feathers or their powers were magic. As the children moved between the castle, the writing area, the book corner and the big block area, they drew, re-enacted the tale and transformed the text, creating new adventures together. When they wrote stories, their 'writing' was transcribed by adults. One child with a knight's green shield painted on his face, a leopard's costume on his body and a jewelled crown on his head composed the sentence *The Green Dragon Knight fights leopards.* Another, pausing briefly before 'flying' quickly onwards, wrote *It was a sparkly world. A little bird was flying around. Suddenly it saw a sparkly castle.* A third, who was coming to terms with the arrival of a baby brother, wrote *I am a princess knight, saving daddy from Timmy.* A fourth borrowed his identity from a popular cultural narrative and wrote *I am a Power Ranger Knight. I fight the bad prince.* In the process of their play, these children were combining and reinterpreting their thinking and making connections between ideas, objects and actions. They were also beginning to 'learn to make experience concrete in writing and freeze the flow of experience so it could be examined' (Geekie *et al.*, 1999: 140). They were clearly in control.

The creative practices with books and stories evident in this community of learners were planned, in the words of their teacher, in order for the children to have *the freedom to shape what they want to do and influence their own learning.* This teacher led by following and negotiated the agendas with the class, helping them enter and examine stories in order to consider possibilities and alternatives, extending their imaginative thinking in the process. This practice also enabled these 4-year-olds to begin to 'absorb the characteristic tunes and patterns' of well-known stories (Barrs, 2000: 55) and demonstrated their teacher's trust in them. The literature-based contexts encouraged exploration, investigation and transformation and reinforced their teacher's view that children are not consumers, but producers of text, actively constructing meaning in the company of authors, illustrators and each other. Their playful involvement in a number of core texts enabled these very young learners to revisit, retell and reinvent as they made discoveries, and transformed forms and meanings on their journey towards writing. As Vygotsky (1978: 116) has argued 'make believe play, drawing and writing can be viewed as different moments in an essentially unified process of development of written language'; this was borne out in this classroom and in many others in the early years as literature was explored more playfully with the children.

Developing a range of experiential encounters with literature and opportunities for response and related writing must be paramount in classrooms of any age, and with older children, whilst the activities may vary, the core issue of creative engagement remains. Reading journals for instance, which are in essence a conversation on paper about the meaning of the text, can play a valuable role in prompting reflection and can help develop an awareness of language and provide a record of powerful quotes which can be borrowed and adapted. Opportunities to discuss literature and the author's craft in shared and guided reading and writing and in literature circles can also pay dividends as these help writers make connections between reading and writing, and can prompt significant conversations about book language which may profile issues such as authorial independence, style and purpose. Teachers who ask open-ended questions about literature will encourage more authentic responses and create reflective discussions, oriented in the first instance to the text's layered meaning and message, later attending to its crafted construction. In this kind of socially supportive environment, reading and response, not comprehension and criticism will predominate as young readers draw upon their knowledge and experience to create insights and forge new meanings. Active experiences of literature must be encompassed, for as Gardner (1999) argues, our brains learn best when we are physically and intellectually involved. So the continued use of drama, storytelling and other interactive activities which mirror, support or demonstrate, explicitly or implicitly, the reading–writing connection also remain important.

Conclusion

If 'creative thinking is a break with habitual patterns of thought' (Robinson, 2001: 135), then new thinking may be required to enable some teachers of literacy to appreciate the complexity of the many literary texts and contexts which support young writers. The teachers in the We're Writers project demonstrated that they had taken steps towards creating bridges between the literature read, discussed and lived in their classrooms and the children's writing. Their steps were initially small and tentative, but in the climate of accountability these were genuine moves towards a new kind of subject knowledge and a more open and playful pedagogy. The development of these exploratory meaning-centred practices cannot be seen in isolation, the role of the teacher was also transformed, from instructor and mediator of the selected literature, to artistic collaborator in the process of engagement, reflection and response. As teachers, our knowledge of literature and its significance in developing writers is clearly of considerable importance; we need to be able to select potent texts for our classes and use such texts imaginatively to develop the reader in each young writer.

Chapter 6

Artistic voices

Drama

Drama, the art form of social encounters, is a powerful tool for investigating and exploring texts and developing children's voice and verve. On the learning continuum of drama, with free play at one end and scripted performance at the other, drama in education is situated centrally. Such drama, often called process drama (O'Neill, 1995), story drama (Booth, 1996) or classroom drama (Cremin and Grainger, 2001), employs elements of both free-flow play and theatre, and involves the creation of shared fictitious worlds which materialise through the imaginations of both the children and their teacher. Children learn from living inside these worlds and making connections to their own world. Language is an important component of this symbolic and dramatic play, in which, through the use of teacher in role and other drama conventions, ideas about the text are spun into existence and alternatives voiced and heard. In this way, drama can help children dig down into the substrata of the text, increase their involvement and insight and enhance their related written work, often undertaken in role.

Writing is an integral part of process drama, complementing talk and improvisation and adding to the multiplicity of meanings created. Drama can provide authentic and motivating contexts in which writing is a natural response to a social dilemma and in turn, writing or drawing in role can provide the opportunity to reflect on the drama. Such writing helps children build belief and deepens their involvement in the fictional context, since as they improvise and write in role they explore the motivational states, values and emotions of the characters. The quality of the writing produced in role will depend in part on the strength of the children's engagement in the drama, the role perspective they have chosen to adopt and the nature of the percolation afforded by the fictional encounter. The frameset of a traditional writing classroom, with direct instruction and the exposition of skills is therefore set to one side during drama, as the class work collaboratively to process and represent their understanding, using writing where appropriate as a tool on the journey.

This chapter explores the mutually supportive relationship between drama and writing and focuses on the contribution that extended imaginative play can make to the compositional process. We argue that writing in role can help children develop a clearer than usual sense of perspective and a strong voice. We highlight various connecting threads, in particular: the bridges between drama and writing in specific genres; perspectival learning; the role of tension in narrative; the incubation of ideas; and the significance of both affective engagement in, and detachment from, the dramatic encounter. Examples from the classroom demonstrate how, through creating and reflecting upon imaginary worlds, children can be encouraged to write empathetically in role and adopt a variety of role perspectives and different voices. Such writing often shows heightened sensitivity, passion, power and understanding. First however, we explore research into the reinforcing relationship between drama and writing and discuss various forms of writing in role.

Drama enriching writing

Relatively few researchers have examined the effect of drama on writing. However, Pelligrini (1984) did find that dramatic play was highly related to total word writing fluency, although this is only shown through single dictated words which limits the implications of his work. Neelands *et al.* (1993) concluded that drama and writing have a complimentary, interactive and mutually reinforcing relationship and others have also found that role play and other drama conventions are more effective than discussion in contributing to writing (Booth and Neelands, 1998; Wagner, 1998). More recently, McNaughton (1997) too has observed that children who engage in drama before writing, write more effectively and at greater length than who those engage in discussion alone. In particular, she noted that the drama enriched the vocabulary chosen, which contained more emotive and expressive insights and more natural speech patterns; she also perceived that the children's writing reflected a better understanding of the issues and had a clearer sense of voice. In her work the term 'voice' is used to describe 'writing-in-role where the writer appears to be able to "get under the skin" of the character and identify with him/her on an affective as well as cognitive level' (McNaughton, 1997: 79). A cross-case analysis, drawing upon five small-scale studies of process drama and writing, also found children's written work had more depth and detail and their understanding of the narrative was enriched by the multiple interpretations and transactions of drama (Crumpler and Schneider, 2002). Drama can, these researchers suggest, help us imagine new dramatic spaces within which writing can be taught with real relevance and focus, since it offers tools for kinaesthetically planning and generating ideas for writing. There are various kinds of writing in role, including:

Writing in role: This is undertaken during the imaginative action, and can serve to shape the unfolding drama and is written from inside the lived experience.

Writing alongside role: This is undertaken after the dramatic action, and can serve to reflect upon the drama, it may be written from a distance.

Working 'as if' in role: This is undertaken without any drama experience and may be undertaken cold or following in-depth discussion of the text.

The beneficial effects of writing in role are particularly clear when integrated approaches are adopted and the literary language of the text is revisited during the writing (Bearne *et al.*, 2004i; Barrs and Cork, 2001). Such writing in role emerges most easily in the context of an extended drama session when children are fully inside the narrative, cognitively and affectively. Writing from inside the imagined experience can help 'script' the unfolding drama and contribute to the class's meaning making. Writing alongside role often takes place at the close of an extended drama session, when the physical imaginary action is over, but the drama is still alive and fresh in the minds of the learners. At such moments, however, several children may still be writing in role and the edges between these types of perspectival writing will be blurred.

Writing alongside role may also be undertaken after a time lapse and may be more distanced and detached from the experiential process. Arguably, this incubation period can enrich the writing, as ideas are percolated both through the drama and through the extended period of reflection. Britton (1993) refers to this as the incubatory period necessary to produce literature and others too have commented upon the need for a time lapse, not to wait for the muse to descend, but for the writing to be internalised and reflected upon, both consciously and unconsciously. 'As for my next book I'm going to hold from writing it until I have it impending in me: grown heavy in my mind like a ripe plum' (Virginia Woolf, quoted in Calkins, 1983: 29). The teachers in the We're Writers project found that many children chose to return to drama themes in their writing journals, to try on alternative perspectives, revisit others' voices and re-examine their earlier insights and understanding. They noticed that when such opportunities were seized the children seemed to offer many more details which clarified the writer's stance and voice.

An example of such writing alongside role, or in this case drawing alongside role, is shown in Figure 6.1. In this, Abby, aged 9, recreates a significant object from an earlier drama investigation based upon Michael Morpurgo's *Blodin the Beast* (Morpurgo, 1995). In the narrative, all the villagers, except old Shanga and young Hosea, become Blodin's slaves. Shanga refuses to submit to Blodin, believing he must fulfil his life's work and complete his precious carpet which means more to him than life itself. In the drama, a

Figure 6.1   Old Shanga's carpet

month before, Abby had worked in a group drawing symbols, pictures and patterns to create an imagined version of the carpet, for as Shanga says 'there is more than wool in this carpet my son'. Time had been short and after each group had shared their designs, the drama had continued apace using the book as a guide. Three weeks later the story was read again to the class, which re-invigorated Abby's interest in its layers of meaning and in her journal she recreated the carpet.

Her depiction reflects the past, the present and the future of the community. Allegorical connections and intertextual links are woven into the tree of hope and the snake of temptation, whilst the benign figure of Shanga, represented as the sun, watches from the sky in a manner not dissimilar to old Mufasa in *The Lion King*. Shanga is a God-like father figure to Hosea who watches over him. Abby's group's drawing of the carpet was based on hypotheses generated from the text, and she includes some of these possibilities, like earth, wind and fire to help Hosea on his journey and fruit to nourish him. Her new drawing also included a symbolic representation of the wheel of life which her group created as a piece of group sculpture, and she conveys a sense of new life shown through the growing flower. Through the drama, the classroom had been transformed metaphorically into another world which the children had imagined both individually and collectively, and in the original visual Abby and her friends had more effectively captured this sense of another place, another time and another world. Returning through choice to this representation, her new drawing benefited from incubation and breathing space, as Beverley Naidoo (2003) has commented, 'occasionally I need to put the narrative away, to allow myself time to breathe, then I can see it more clearly'. Abby's first work was more literal in nature and showed the actual narrative events, her later carpet was visually simpler yet more complex, operating both metaphorically and symbolically.

Bridging between drama and specific genres

In contrast to the extended meaning making of process drama, drama conventions can also be employed in shorter textual encounters and may form an intermediate activity between reading and writing in the literacy hour, for example as a precursor to shared, guided or independent writing. In this case, the class may use two or three drama conventions to examine a moment or character in the text and then record their insights written in role. Evidence from the teachers on the We're Writers project suggests that even such brief forays into imagined worlds can serve to interest and engage the children, supporting OfSTED's (2003) view that drama is one of the most motivating tools in the curriculum. However, the quality of the writing produced in this context will depend upon a number of factors, in particular the teacher's ability to build bridges between the drama and the specific genre of writing chosen. In the literacy hour, if the teacher is foregrounding the teaching of writing, then careful selection of appropriate drama conventions will be necessary to prepare the ground, so learners are explicitly supported towards communicating in this genre. For example, if persuasive writing is selected, then persuasive role play in pairs, groups or the whole class can usefully be improvised and reflected upon. Initially the class's shared text, whether fiction or non-fiction, may be used to capture interest and then drama conventions can be employed to motivate, generate and share ideas. Some explicit teaching of writing may also be interspersed into this time, before the final piece of drama is undertaken. This operates as an oral rehearsal of the tune of the text type and helps to move the children closer towards the written form. Parallels can be drawn with the spoken word here since, as Bearne (2004) asserts, the spoken word may be closer to the written, particularly at the level of whole text structures than has commonly been assumed. The forms of talk which Bearne (2004) identifies, namely generative, informative, performative and evaluative talk, can be used to create a trajectory between drama and specific forms of writing, as shown in Figure 6.2.

An example may help to highlight the particular nature of this tailored journey. In a class of 6–7-year-olds, a teacher from the We're Writers project wanted to support her learners in writing a diary entry, so the drama activities were planned with this end in mind. The class had kept their own corporate diary the previous week and on the following Monday, the book *This is the Bear and the Scary Night* by Sarah Hayes and Helen Craig (Hayes ans Craig, 1991) was read to the class. In small groups the children made freeze frames of the story, creating a physical storyboard of the narrative; the book was then re-read to accompany the visual pictures. Each group then discussed what the bear was thinking at their moment in the narrative, for example, one group showed him floating in the pond and called plaintively *Help I'm soaking wet, I'm going to drown*. The story had captured their interest and together they'd been involved in generative talk in order to create their freeze frames and agree a phrase which captured the bear's feelings; this made an effective summary of the tale. In creating the text the class were involved in informative talk, sharing ideas with one another. Their teacher showed them the picture of the bear alone at nightfall with the ironic speech bubble 'I'm not scared', re-read the lines 'This is the bear alone in the park and these are the eyes which glowed in the dark' and invited the class to adopt the bear's rigid and afraid posture. Together they prepared to begin individual interior monologues and the class thought out loud in role as the bear. To prepare for their writing, the children were reflecting upon the situation and the bear's fears and were in effect rehearsing the pattern and tune of diary writing through their simultaneous performative talk. Their voices were subdued, not only because they were muttering under their breath, but also because of the bear's unfortunate situation. Their teacher then suggested that the bear might have kept a diary and wondered aloud what he might have written when he returned home the next day, would he remember how he felt on that scary night, the loneliness, the fear and the sense of abandonment? The class settled to the writing unusually quickly,

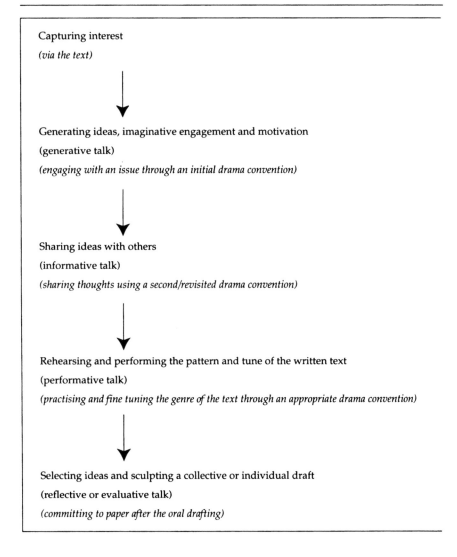

Capturing interest

(via the text)

Generating ideas, imaginative engagement and motivation

(generative talk)

(engaging with an issue through an initial drama convention)

Sharing ideas with others

(informative talk)

(sharing thoughts using a second/revisited drama convention)

Rehearsing and performing the pattern and tune of the written text

(performative talk)

(practising and fine tuning the genre of the text through an appropriate drama convention)

Selecting ideas and sculpting a collective or individual draft

(reflective or evaluative talk)

(committing to paper after the oral drafting)

Figure 6.2 Travelling towards specific forms of writing via drama

having been prepared for this inner voice writing through the adroit use of particular drama conventions.

Taddea's diary entry (Figure 6.3) voices with considerable vividness the bear's night time adventure and she successfully conveys his sense of disquiet, particularly through her use of the ellipsis. She was in the group who had depicted the lines, 'these are the claws which couldn't hold on and this is the bear who fell into the pond', so perhaps she was pinched

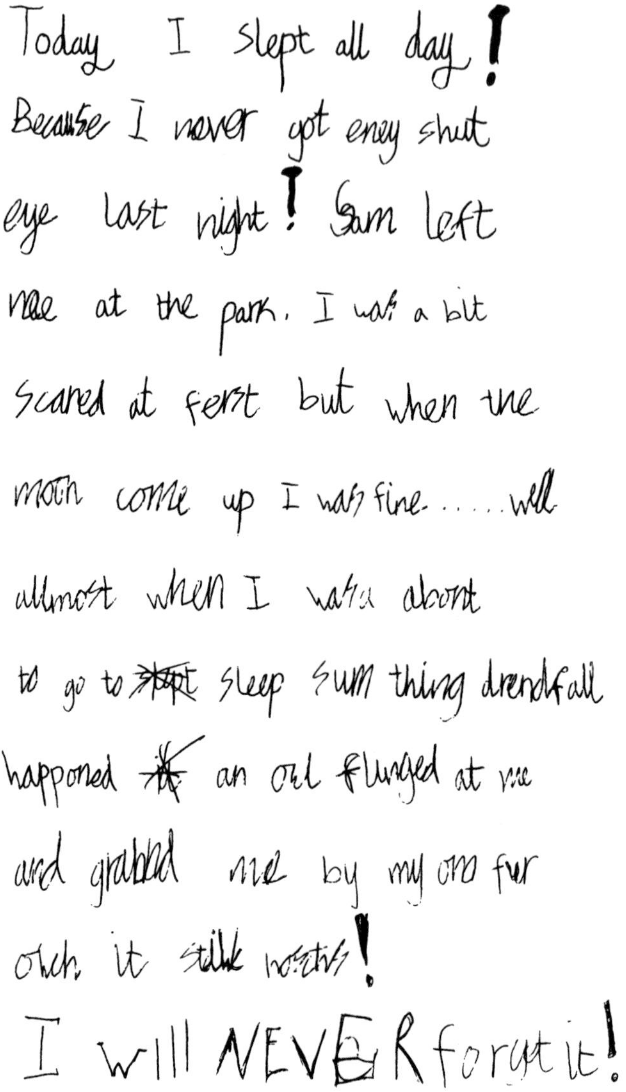

Today I slept all day!
Because I never got eney shut
eye last night! Sam left
mae at the park. I wa' a bit
scared at fert but when the
moth come up I wa' fine......well
allmost when I wa'a abowt
to go to ~~stet~~ sleep sum thing drendfall
happoned ~~it~~ an owl flunged at me
and grabed me by my oro fur
owch it still hrts!
I will NEVER forgt it!

Figure 6.3 Bear's diary entry

inadvertently by a friend in the process. She expresses the pain of the owl's claws clearly and finishes with the clear invective, written in upper case for emphasis *I will NEVER forget it!* The lived experience of the drama seemed to become a kind of oral thinking frame which helped her sculpt the content, structure and perspective of this writing, aided by the process of consciously bridging between the drama conventions and the specific form of writing. A variety of activities exist which can be employed at the final stage of the journey when the class are moving from the drama into the writing. These include teacher modelling, joint composition, burst writing on whiteboards and the use of post-it notes. The teacher may summarise the knowledge gained about a character, create a literal writing frame to record the pros and cons of a situation examined or use other shared writing supports. Such activities can record the children's ideas generated, creating raw material for later use, or their ideas can be written in the chosen genre as an example for them to imitate and extend upon. In the context of role play areas too, the teaching of particular text types can be highlighted, so that children are prepared to write in a particular genre and make use of these forms through writing in role in 'real' contexts (Cook, 1999, 2002).

In contrast to the planned use of drama to elicit particular forms of writing, writing in role during an extended process drama session is likely to be more spontaneous, with the teacher remaining open to seize moments in the drama when writing seems both appropriate and necessary. In such contexts, the drama, not the writing, will take precedence and any written work in the form of maps, diagrams, charts, notes, letters and so on will be an integral part of the exploratory process contributing to the unfolding fiction. In such extended sessions, the journey between the drama and any writing is likely to be much less explicitly framed, since the teacher will be responding to the children's ideas and interests, not working towards a particular genre (Grainger, 2003a, 2003b, 2004). We now turn to the connecting threads between such extended process drama and more authentically positioned writing.

Perspective, voice and choice

Drama develops children's insider knowledge and understanding of texts as Taddea's writing shows, and critical to this learning is the adoption of multiple role perspectives, since in process drama many characters' voices will be heard, questioned, challenged and evaluated. Perspectival learning is the essence of learning through drama, the imaginary worlds that are created are metaphors to link personal experiences with the unknown or outer social world (Henry, 2000). Part of drama's raison d'etre is to open up new ways of looking at the world which reflect the complexity of living and ensure alternative positions and different views are examined. To write in role from a particular perspective during process drama, seems to provide the learner with an extended opportunity to examine and develop that stance as they reflect upon the events of the fiction. In the process they may become 'part of a dialogue with the text and with the author, entering the world of the story, and taking on a narrator's voice and role' (Barrs and Cork, 2001: 209). Another example from the classroom may serve to illuminate the significance of perspective and choice.

In a drama based on Michael Rosen's short story 'The Bakerloo Flea' from his short story collection *Nasty* (Puffin, 1976), a class of 6–7-year-olds adopted various roles. These included nightshift workers on the London Underground, police officers and the management. The story was unknown to the class, but the teacher used the first part of the tale to guide their investigation and the class established clear roles for themselves as cleaners. They descended the endless flights of stairs, collected rubbish, scrubbed the platforms, pasted up posters and found, for example, dead rats, cans, empty crisp bags, apple cores, loose change and bags of clothes belonging to the homeless. Despite their different views about what to do with the £20 note, a camera and a carrier bag of clothing, all of which were imaginary, when a mutant flea was sighted the class quickly decided to fight it. Later, having constructed the giant flea's body and discussed the possible dangers, the cleaners voted to place their problem in the hands of 'them upstairs'. Their difficult discussions with the management indicated that their boss was reluctant to accept their story, complaints were voiced, one child resigned, deputations were sent down the tunnels, the flea was heard and sighted again and a solution was sought. Various ideas were constructed through freeze frames, some more humane than others, the police were drafted in and some of the class worked as police officers interviewing cleaners and the management and planning how to destroy the flea before the impending morning rush hour. After a genuine mid-morning break, their teacher, in role as one of the management, requested urgent written suggestions about how to deal with this creature. The children, writing in self-chosen roles offered ideas which in essence sought to capture and kill the dangerous creature. Anthony, however, had a different view. A quiet boy, who often avoided writing, he wrote quickly and purposefully, then marched to where his teacher was sitting with a group, interrupted her and slapped his writing (Figure 6.4) defiantly down, saying stoutly *You're not being fair, I want the flea to live.*

Figure 6.4 Antony's in-role writing

Through this writing, Anthony voices the view of the imaginary person he was both being and becoming. His stance is clear, he was in role, not as a cleaner, manager or police officer, but as a rat catcher, a specialist in the field of fleas. As such he did not share the others' views that the flea should be destroyed. His writing gave him the opportunity to portray this alternative perspective, one with which he felt more at home. Through discussion with his teacher, in which he remained in role, it became clear he needed to voice his views further and he quickly recorded these, speaking authoritatively and determinedly into the tape recorder.

> I am the rat catcher. I won't let that flea be killed. He is not a harmful creature, he's a nice animal. He'll feed on all the rats and dead mice, so chuck them down the hole and he will LIVE. Nobody can kill him, I won't let them. He lives down that tunnel and he can stay there, its his home and we must stop thinking of ways to get rid of him and let him live.
>
> Don't keep talking about ideas to trap him, we'll just have to take up the train track and when the track and the trains are out of the way, then we'll drain the electricity and give it to somebody who is poor and then they'll have enough for ... 20 years.
>
> This is Professor Anthony talking, and I'll tell you something. I work as a rat catcher and if you have rat problems, tell me about them and I'll get rid of them for you by giving them to the flea. Rats eat cheese, they spread poison and disease around and they also ... cause a lot of trouble. So we need that flea, we really do.

Anthony appears to have used this chance to shape his ideas and extend and clarify his argument. His voice on the tape is unusually strident and expressive and is in marked contrast to his normal register. His words are offered almost as a speech and his authority, expertise and authorial voice are clear, influenced by the professorial stance he has adopted. He sought to develop a role/job for the flea, closely aligned to his role as a rat catcher, and his work reminds us that the complexity of children's symbolic and dramatic play depends in part at least on the context of the play situation and the potential for possible positions within it (Umek and Musek, 2001). He has determinedly avoided his teacher's implied linearity in terms of the narrative's likely resolution, and has remained open to other possibilities, making an original contribution to the class's drama. In adopting the role of a rat catcher Anthony has found an alignment, akin to a foothold in the text from which he can negotiate meaning more readily. Within this fictional world, his personal narrative is full of 'stance and scenario' (Bruner, 1984: 198) and his autonomy and choice of perspective is significant, demonstrating that the imposition of a particular stance or role position does not sit comfortably within the context of drama. Drama helps learners like Anthony to stand in the shoes of others, see the world from their perspective and experience alternative ways of being and knowing. If writing is integrated into such examinations of difference then increased assurance, fluency and a more authentic sense of voice can be expected. The children will have journeyed through the open door of the text, wearing the shoes of various characters who have different views and perspectives. In the process they will use and inhabit their voices.

> Writing in the first person, when the voice is not your own, requires the writer to be able to view events from another perspective and to use language that is appropriate for both the implied writer and the genre.
>
> (Steele, 1999: 183)

In the fictional world of the London Underground, through both speech and writing, Anthony demonstrates how closely his sense of stance is allied to his imaginative ownership of the drama. His teacher, in celebrating his unusual degree of involvement and innovative contribution, was reminded that the world of drama needs to be owned and directed by the children. Later that day the young Professor was back in role. This time he proposed that a special flea enclosure at London Zoo should be created and that the flea should be fed on an exclusive diet of London rats, thus reducing the rodent population. This was voted upon, a humane capture was undertaken and Michael Rosen's very different version of the narrative was finally read to the class. A central component of this process drama was that the children chose the direction of their world making play, albeit with their teacher facilitating the examination of the consequences of their actions. In such contexts we may find, as we did in Anthony's case, that 'analogous relationships exist between interpretative/dramatic moves of young learners engaged in process drama and interpretative/rhetorical moves of young learners engaged in writing' (Crumpler and Schneider, 2002: 78).

Narrative tension, fluency and flow

The role of narrative in learning is widely recognised (e.g. Moffett, 1968; Bruner, 1986; Rosen, 1988) for children think through story and 'shape the world in narrative structures' (Bruner, 1999). Such narrative thought is not only supported by literature-based classrooms however, but also by artistic engagement in imaginative play, storytelling and drama. In these contexts narratives are created, investigated, shaped, shared and valued. In drama in particular, the desire to create narrative action and construct past, present and future scenarios is very strong, so if literature is used as a basis for drama, then the narrative hook draws the children imaginatively into the tale and encourages them to fill the gaps in the text as they negotiate and construct meaning together (Iser, 1978). As co-authors of a new text, they will be reflecting upon their own and others' stories and writing from inside the fiction.

> To the triad of reader–text–transaction (Rosenblatt, 1978), drama adds two other layers – drama and writing. Reconstructed as reader–text–drama–writing–transaction, drama becomes a conduit that facilitates a flow of imagination between process and product.
>
> (Crumpler and Schneider, 2002: 77)

Drama can achieve more than this however, since it is potentially more transformative than this metaphor of a connecting conduit implies. An example may demonstrate this process of text interrogation and the value of using literature as a pre-text to frame the dramatic action (O'Neill, 1995). In a class of 10–11-year-olds, the novel *Holes* by Louis Sachar (1998) had been selected for a unit of work. The teacher read the first two chapters in which it is implied that the young Stanley Yelnats has committed a crime. The judge offers him a choice, 'you may go to jail, or you may go to Camp Green Lake'. The children, working in groups, created flashbacks to indicate the possible incidents which might have led to Stanley's court appearance. Some chose freeze frames, others chose group improvisations which were also frozen to take photographs for the local 'Texas Herald'. Their teacher read on through Chapters 3 and 4, revealing Stanley's innocence and arrival at Camp Green Lake Juvenile Correction Facility. Stanley finds the place is barren, Mr Sir, the man in charge, is unpleasant and he is bizarrely required to dig five-foot square holes on a daily basis. The class hung on to every word, no doubt peering forward into the many open spaces left by this 'writerly' text (Barthes, 1999).

Their teacher, enriching the text with additional action, informed them that even as Stanley was marched to his tent, a bus-load of journalists were rumbling down the long dry road to the Camp. Some children's rights campaigners had also joined them, having heard rumours about the strange practice of making prisoners dig holes in the hot sun and they intended to demand a press conference. This was set up as a formal meeting with their teacher as the Warden and others in role as Mr Sir, journalists, campaigners or visiting parents. The tension evident in the text, in the threat posed by the yellow spotted lizards, in the forced labour of the inmates and in Stanley's innocence, acted here as an 'animating current' in the drama, inviting the children to speculate their way forwards (Taylor, 1995). The Warden's ingratiating welcome was impatiently interrupted by a child in role as a journalist and a multitude of questions and challenges poured forth. Health care, living conditions, food and leisure pursuits were all raised as the clearly suspicious visitors responded to the gaps in the narrative and demanded knowledge and justice for the inmates. The press conference was at times confrontational and moved quickly and unpredictably generating interest, electricity and tension. Through their imaginative involvement the children identified questions and further holes in their understanding as they engaged in possibility thinking together (Craft, 2000). Finally, the Warden, declaring herself affronted by the insinuating nature of their questioning, withdrew and the conference was summarily closed. A heated discussion spontaneously ensued, this time out of role, about the truth of the answers given, the strange practice of digging holes and the moral order of the Camp. Writing seemed a natural response to the uncertain dilemma and the class settled to their chosen forms very quickly. In the leader columns, diaries, letters and Camp records produced, the children's total engagement in the process of possibilisation was evident. This two-part process of imaginative thinking establishes a question in the mind and then responds to it emotionally, socially, physically or cognitively, thus generating ideas for writing, widening options and offering alternative insights (Cremin, 2004). The apparent ease with which their pens committed to paper, testified to the generative power of the drama and indicated that the children and their teacher, also writing, were still inside the 'flow' of the learning experience. Flow is 'the holistic sensation present when we act with total involvement ... we experience it as a unified flowing from one moment to the next' (Cziksentmihalyi, 2002: 55). Teachers in the We're Writers research project commented upon the speed with which children often moved from drama into writing, as one noted *they seem to plunge into writing almost without realising it*. This enhanced ability to flow thinking into written words has also been observed in drama by Wagner (1994) and is influenced by the flow of creative energy and generated by the problem creating and problem-solving nature of the drama. Through the drama, the children began to formulate possibilities and discover what they wanted to say, although the literal act of writing in role also involved them in reflecting upon the dramatic action and continuing to shape their views. In the 'no penalty zone' of drama (Heathcote, 1980), where ideas and improvisations are honoured as imaginative alternatives, self-confidence can grow quickly and this may tacitly be transferred into the act of writing as Alex's example from the Holes drama shows (Figure 6.5).

In Alex's entry in Mr Sir's diary, it is clear he is using the writing to make his thinking visible and shape his emerging understanding of the events and issues surrounding the camp. Still in role, his writing has become

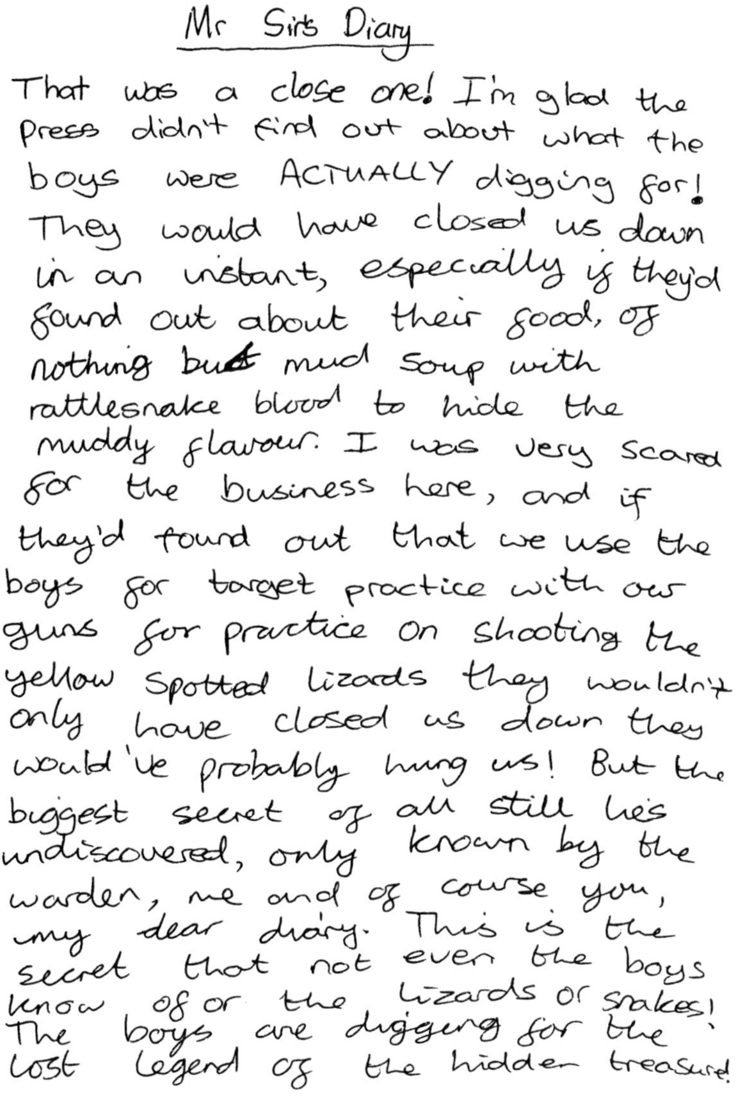

Mr Sir's Diary

That was a close one! I'm glad the press didn't find out about what the boys were ACTUALLY digging for! They would have closed us down in an instant, especially if they'd found out about their food, of nothing but mud soup with rattlesnake blood to hide the muddy flavour. I was very scared for the business here, and if they'd found out that we use the boys for target practice with our guns for practice on shooting the yellow spotted lizards they wouldn't only have closed us down they would've probably hung us! But the biggest secret of all still lies undiscovered, only known by the warden, me and of course you, my dear diary. This is the secret that not even the boys know of or the lizards or snakes! The boys are digging for the lost legend of the hidden treasure!

Figure 6.5 Mr Sir's diary

itself an act of contemplation, revealing a more coherent understanding of the storyline from the perspective of one of those in authority in the camp. Like the majority of his peers, he chose to adopt the stance of those 'in the know', the powerful Mr Sir or the Warden, perhaps because the children wanted to solve the mystery of the reason why the teenage inmates were forced to dig holes in the hot sun. Alex has in fact identified the reason given by Louis Sachar, although at this point he was unaware of it. The imaginative predicament of the drama, imbued with ambiguity and tension, encouraged the children's personal and affective involvement and created considerable speculation which they sought to close through their writing. Using writing in this way to effect closure and solve the scenario has also been observed in other contexts (Grainger, 2003c) in which children handle the uncertainty of the unknown, the 'ambiguity of play' (Sutton-Smith, 1997).The open-ended ethos and problem-solving nature of drama invite such creative and imaginative responses which are not additional elements, but are central to the symbolic and communicative nature of the activity, encouraging empathy and insight. In such contexts, children search for meaning, employing the intentionality of their minds to imagine, create and solve the situations and dilemmas in which they find themselves.

Emotional engagement

Writing whilst in role, Booth argues, enables children to 'enter a new sphere of attitudes and feelings' as they seek to gain an understanding of what is happening in the drama (Booth, 1996: 123). Their affective engagement will be most marked when the teacher attempts to plan and structure the work based on their interests and responses. Through the imagined experience of the drama, various feelings will be engendered, imaginative empathy may be developed and different views and attitudes examined. At times the children will be 'living through' the drama and will experience it as real (Bolton, 1984). This parallels Rosenblatt's (1978) aesthetic reading of literature, which enables readers to engage experientially with the text and become attentive to the meanings and sounds and patterns of the language. We believe that the affective involvement of the learners in the drama world of a literary text, enables them to draw more insightfully upon the unfolding narrative as a source of ideas for writing and if the text is revisited discursively and re-read aloud several times the writing may also be influenced by the language patterns of the text. If teachers draw attention to the style and structure, feeling and content of a text through both drama *and* a focus on the text's language then, as Barrs and Cork (2001) have shown, powerful emotive writing may result. Their work centred on Kevin Crossley-Holland's *The Green Children* (Oxford, 1994) and included examples of children's writing in role which combined both the emotions explored in the drama and the speech rhythms and language of the text. They also observed an increase in the use of mental state verbs in the writing. The children, having experienced or imagined the emotional state of characters, often made more explicit the characters' views, thoughts and feelings in their written work. The teachers we worked with in the We're Writers project also noticed this 'passion on the page' (Grainger, 2001a, 2001b, 2004) and observed that the children's emotional engagement in the drama frequently surfaced in their writing in role giving a clearer sense of voice, stance and sensitivity. In a class of 9–10-year-olds, *Almaz and the Lion* by Jane Kurtz (Puffin, 1995) had been investigated through an extended drama. In this picture book tale, the young orphan Almaz finds it hard to accept her new stepmother, Kibret. The tale is told from Almaz's perspective and voices the injustice and alienation she feels. In contrast, Kibret's stance as a young woman taken to marry a stranger is both unknown and unarticulated. Much of the children's writing in role was written from Kibret's perspective and echoed the language of the text, conveying a real sense of her situation, as Eliot's fairly typical piece indicates.

> I was led away from my past life to be wed to a strange man. I liked him, but I had only known him a couple of days. We went to his town, to his house and sung, danced and feasted on food that I did not make. It was strange to feast so. I had always helped out with food at home. As time passed I became worried about Almaz. She was going out alone, running off to the caves. I had been told there were lions there. I loved Almaz, but when she spoke I couldn't answer. I showed her how to weave. She was good at it and fast. She had complimented me on my injera before, but she definitely respected me, by saying my fingers were lovely. I loved her more than ever. A week later she came home and played a song of triumph that used to be played at my old home. I offered to braid her hair and she hugged me and danced around me. 'Family' I thought.

Through the drama, Eliot had been helped to move out of his personal language register and he effectively reflects the viewpoint of the role he had adopted; the literary language of the text is also echoed in his writing. This uncertainty about Kibret's new life is voiced in his opening line *I was led away from my past life to be wed to a strange man* and reinforced through the repetition *we went to his town, his house and sung, danced and feasted on food that I did not make. It was strange to feast so.* The melody of his writing mirrors the author's tune and captures the reflective mood of the text reinforced through the interior monologues and decision alleys undertaken to build insight and empathy in the drama. As Meek has observed 'if we want to see what lessons have been learned from the texts children read, we have to look for them in what they write' (Meek, 1988: 48). Strong emotive texts like this and quality classroom drama can work together as potent partners to empower empathetic writing in first person; in such contexts children learn that 'to write as someone else is to accomplish a kind of reflexivity, me yet not me, peculiar to authors' (Barrs and Cork, 2001: 12). Other children's writing also demonstrated that the slow speed of the drama, the use of ritual and the time given to exploring characters' inner thoughts and feelings, enabled them to write from within the role with increased understanding. Georgie for example, conveyed a sense of losing some part of herself as she looked back towards her old home and indicated, like Eliot, a sense of reflective deliberation rather than immediacy and spontaneity.

> I rode silently on the donkey looking back all the while. I felt as if that my old village was a mirage, perhaps it had never existed. All I could see was a sandy plain, as though all my memories had been lost in a storm at sea. I closed my eyes and saw, in my twisting mind, my village – my old village – my home … my birthplace

Kibret's plight as she is escorted to her impending marriage is plaintively recreated here, no doubt enriched by both the drama and the regular re-reading of passages from the text. By stepping inside Kibret's mind, and voicing her thoughts as well as listening to their peers pondering similarly in role, the children were able to find the words to express her feelings, as they thought their way forwards and examined an issue they had perhaps not yet experienced. They were making 'productive' connections based on the drama rather then 'reproductive' connections drawing on what was already known (Kearney, 1991). Writing in role offers children the chance of exploring new voices and views through their engagement in imaginative play. The strength of their first person engagement in the drama and the reflective strategies employed appear to influence their writing, enriching their emotive evocation of the character's perspective and their ability to write from inside, to express another's voice, an inner voice.

Conclusion

Drama develops children's imagination through action, interaction and reflection, providing further lived experience which they can draw upon as a basis for writing. Through inhabiting a fictional world and responding to the conflicts and tensions experienced in it, children are involved in generating ideas, expressing and constructing meaning in a variety of ways and reflecting upon their insights. It would appear that whether their ideas are spontaneously generated and recorded, or incubated and revisited, the affective and cognitive engagement of the drama offers young writers a significant and supportive form of percolation. This process of percolation encompasses everything that happens to the writer apart from the actual setting of marks on paper, and may therefore include incubating, contemplating or rehearsing the experiences and ideas expressed in writing. Through percolating, the writer begins to discover what they want to say and through engaging in various perspectives in the drama, children enrich their voices with others' stances, adopt others' registers and others' words. In the extended process of composition, the percolation offered through the symbolic and transformative nature of drama clearly supports young writers on their journey towards communicating creatively and effectively, with voice and verve.

Chapter 7

Artistic voices

Storytelling

> The roots of story are internalised through the circle of reading,
> listening, telling and writing.
>
> (David Almond, 2001)

The social act of telling stories, Almond suggests, plays an integral part in
developing an understanding of the nature of narrative and although
children are offered frequent opportunities to read, write and listen to
stories in school, they also need to tell and retell tales or the circle of
understanding will be broken. Despite the wealth of tales that children
bring to school, including family stories, gossip, anecdotes, hopes, dreams,
televisual tales and others read, heard, experienced or created, the children
in the We're Writers schools initially experienced relatively few
opportunities to tell and retell these orally. The absence of speaking and
listening objectives in the influential NLS (DfEE, 1998a), and the pressure
of written tests and targets have mitigated against planned opportunities
to develop children's talk (Haworth, 2001; Grainger, 2000) as the teachers
in the project acknowledged. In addition, the focus on textual features and
the organisation of texts has sidelined the essential purpose of story, to
create imaginary worlds which engage, entertain and make us wonder.
Stories are a 'culture's coin and currency' (Bruner 2002: 15), a way of
mapping ourselves into the world and connecting us to one another, so
children need to give voice to their stories and those of others, to rehearse
the fluency and flow, feel the structure first hand and shape the meanings
in their own words. As Harold Rosen observes, 'stories are part of an
essential process, the creation and recreation of a collective identity' (1984:
16). Oral stories deserve a higher profile in the primary classroom.

In this chapter, we consider the creative practice of storytelling, both in
its informal conversational and more consciously sculpted forms, and argue
that it is a powerful tool which can be capitalised upon in school to enrich
the quality of writing and in particular narrative writing. The nature of
this contribution is complex, but some of the many connecting threads
which we examine include: investigating identity through leaning on life;

developing a sense of the audience and reader through the experience of storytelling; internalising the structure and shape of narrative; echoing the language and cadences of traditional tales and creatively transforming tales whilst still retaining their essence. Once again, we highlight the importance of children and teachers engaging artistically through the extended process of composition and developing their authorial voices through full involvement. First however, we seek to explore the relation of storytelling to literacy and examine the value and nature of narrative as means of organising and representing experience.

Storytelling: a learning tradition

It is widely accepted that story is a 'fundamental structure of human experience' (Clandinin and Connelly, 1990: 2), a 'primary act of mind trans-ferred to art from life' (Hardy, 1977: 12) and as longitudinal research into early home and school language indicates, stories provide a major route to understanding for the young child (Wells, 1986). Different cultures and communities make different use of stories (Brice Heath, 1983; Gregory and Williams, 2000), but children's own stories need to be recognised and not pushed off the agenda in favour of the teacher's chosen texts. Children manipulate both the form and content of stories for their own purposes, learning to be literate through their encounters with different story voices. As humans we all engage in inner and outer storytelling and through the process we build our experience of living, shape our identity, give order to chaos and make sense of both lived and vicarious experience. As Harold Rosen (1984) notes, narrative is an 'irrepressible genre' and a major means of thinking, communicating and making meaning right across the cur-riculum. Children with a wealth of experience of story, show considerable implicit knowledge about narrative conventions, plot lines and linguistic styles in their oral retellings (Fox, 1993), so the classroom needs to celebrate literature in all its forms. In reworking and retelling personal and traditional tales, as well as more overtly literary stories, children can become the official storytellers, interacting with their audience and reshaping their chosen tales through the creative social process. Their tales may be scribed by an adult, recorded onto tape or played out imaginatively, so the process of composition, whether oral or written, is supported from the outset (Burgess-Macey, 1999). Bilingual stories and storytelling can affirm children's individual and social existences and encourage the creation of an inclusive culture in the classroom, in which children may switch languages comfortably (Romaine, 1989). Folktales have a particularly important role to play in providing a bridge from oracy to literacy since there is no absolute distinction between oral and written traditions. In retelling tales children are leaning on the voices of writers and oral storytellers; often, however, their retold tale will not need to be written as well as spoken, but the process and experience of telling, of bringing stories to life and regularly sharing them with interested others can, over time, make a marked contribution to their writing (Grainger, 1997, 2002).

Leaning on life

Personal tales and anecdotes deserve to be given higher status in the English curriculum, for retelling such tales can help children reflect upon and interpret their lives and can create natural writing frames of lived experience which can give structure and coherence to their writing. As they recall experiences and embellish and play with the events they share something of themselves with others and 'tap into the human intention to make sense of experience' which Britton sees as 'genuine authoring' (Britton, 1982: 101). Teachers' own tales and literature links can trigger memories that return with vividness and in revisiting and unpacking these events, quite ordinary experiences are made extraordinary and invested with meaning and personal significance. Such memories are not merely recalled and reported upon, but are carefully and unconsciously selected and recreated in the process of telling. In sharing tales of lived experience with trusted friends, children explore their growing sense of self and reflect upon their identity. As Calkins (1986: 21) observes about children's personal narratives, 'we need to say to others, "This is me, my story, my life, my truth." We need to be heard'. Through reflecting on their individual and social histories, children examine the impact of particular events, make connections and nourish their inner worlds. No child need be a prisoner of his own autobiography (Sachs, 1985) and as the authors of their own lives, whether in oral or written form, they can exercise choice over the text and its meanings and participate in 'the continual process of re-inventing, [and] rewriting, one's world' (Dyson, 1997: 185).

The storytelling might take the form of re-enactment in the role play area or be verbalised in table-top role play or as part of a conversational reminiscence. In a classroom culture which values autobiographical tales, children develop a strong sense of agency as they share their lived experience, learn to listen to and learn from others, respect both individuality and difference and celebrate their own uniqueness. Stories are 'the ground that humans hold in common, not what divides them' (Crossley-Holland, 2000: 10) and through sharing personal tales, young authors can revisit their lives, learn to see themselves and voice their experience of living. As they put into words the pieces of their lives, that for whatever mysterious or unconscious reason matter to them, they often recapture their personal involvement and convey with relative ease a sense of themselves and their social identity.

The writer Berlie Doherty (2001) sees 'fiction as a combination of I remember and let's pretend' and children should be encouraged to draw upon characters, settings, events and episodes from everyday living in their writing. In the We're Writers project, the teachers were surprised that the children were apparently unaware that they could use their lives or observations as a source of ideas. Only 21 per cent of the 390 writers were aware of making connections and borrowing events from life to fictionalise. They were conscious of borrowing ideas from literature, from television and from their teachers but appeared in the initial stages of the project to devalue their life experiences and memories as a resource. Some of the older children voiced the view that to borrow from real life was to cheat or to conflate different genres *You have to make it up or it's not a real story, You mustn't mix up autobiography and fictional writing, that's wrong* and *Miss doesn't like it if we bring our own stuff into stories, although we do a unit on autobiography, its okay then.* However, a few explained that they did let members of their family inhabit their stories, disguising their identity, but leaning on their characteristics, for example, *I use my dad a lot in my writing, he's funny and quirky, he's often the fall guy and good for a laugh* and *My mum is often in my stories, I give her different names and roles, but she's always my mum really.* Their lives and homes are full of stories, places and people that can enrich their fictional and descriptive writing, but it seemed that they were not usually encouraged to borrow from or develop such stories, except perhaps in the autumn term in line with the genre recommendations of the NLS. Unstructured free writing, particularly personal narrative in the form of diaries and journals, Hillocks (1995) argues, is a tap root of further develop-ment and deserves to have a central place in the ongoing curriculum. This needs to be supported, however, by the opportunity to tell tales, to engage creatively in the shaping of memory and to develop a sense of their own voice.

Children must be in the driving seat in sharing personal tales, their choices must be respected, their privacy respected and safe supports for introspection provided. Memories and anecdotes can be triggered in various ways including: teachers telling their own tales; personal timelines; interviewing relatives; precious possessions; photographs; postcards and pamphlets from places visited; personal storyboxes and literature links. The emotive thrust of personal tales are often stronger than in invented narratives, since echoes of the remembered experience, and the feelings and thoughts associated with it are likely to surface, especially if sufficient time to tell and retell, dwell and reflect is integrated into the extended process of composition. In one class, the children had been sharing anecdotes about family and friends, the classroom was full of laughter and camaraderie with small groups of children huddled together talking and listening to one another. Luke, aged 8, a disaffected writer who often committed no more than a sentence or two to paper, reflected upon someone he loved, and two days later in journal writing, leant upon his life and wrote at length about his nan, see Figure 7.1. Initially, he sets the scene and

MY NAN

My Nan is special to me because she gives me Kinder eggs comics books, and she gives me all my toys when I left them round there she gave me sweets she took me out shopping, and gave me her love, when I was in trouble she gave me a house and tried to stay out of trouble and my nan had her lg with yellow stuss on one day st was really ill and I had to go round the town to crokon to get a doctor and they called a ambulance out and got her in bed we got her to the Hospital and they were looking at her lg and she got some after surgery. She came out and went home about 15 mins later she had to go back and then 3 weeks later found out that she had cancer of the bowel and we went home the next morning I had to go to school but the Hospital my dad she was dying rapidly So mum said I'm not going to school and went to the Hospital we were sad when I was told that she might not make it to bye bye but she was well enough to talk and she was living there untill she died.
When we went to see her in the room I couldn't help it and I just felt

So upset I burst out cying & crying.

Figure 7.1 My nan

reminds himself of her generosity and then turns to address his main theme, her illness and death and his feelings about it, showing that 'the craft of the storyteller is not in the events of the story. It is in the path taken through the story by the soul of the storyteller' (Pullman, 2002). In this work, of which he was exceptionally proud, and in which he took a step forward as a writer, providing detail and working at length, Luke is the subject of his own curriculum, satisfying personal needs and finding his voice, albeit tentatively, through using writing to reflect upon his nan's demise.

As Fox found in the stories children tell, 'knowledge is maximally personal, related to their inner affective existences and to their external and social experience' (Fox, 1993: 32). The opportunity to tell or write such stories can invest children's lives with meaning and give them strength to face life's difficult moments as well as help connect them to one another, In telling his poignant tale, Luke was in a position to transform his perspective and that of his listeners, since personal stories enable us to adopt particular stances, forms of agency and ways of being in the world, and are a constant act of self-discovery. Following this writing, his attitude to work, and in particular to literacy began to shift, albeit subtly, suggesting that this is an example of what Woods calls 'creative literacy – literacy that brings about personal change, and that empowers and enriches' (Woods, 2001: 65). Through telling personal tales children can voice their emotional, imaginative and interpersonal awareness which can motivate them to use language for intrinsic means, not external schemes, and investigate their identity in the process.

Developing a sense of the audience/reader

In observing children working together to retell an oral story for an audience, the dramatic aspects of the story often come to the fore, as they explore the use of voice and body to convey the tale with conviction. Both speech and writing involve negotiation with an active audience (Bakhtin, 1986) and exploring this process can help make connections between these language modes. In effect, the oral storyteller straddles two worlds, living inside the narrative yet remaining aware of their audience. Barry, aged 7, at the close of a storytelling afternoon told his teacher that his audience had laughed at his story. *What did you do?* his anxious teacher enquired. *Oh, I added more funny bits, to make them laugh more* Barry explained with evident satisfaction. As Crossley-Holland notes, 'the storyteller must enter a tale and allow it to enter them, when this happens the process of creating begins' (Crossley-Holland, 2000: 22). In this context, Barry had experienced the very real pleasure of being the spell binder, of entrancing and engaging his audience, and had spontaneously created ideas and integrated them into the tale as he told it. Motivated by his peers' involvement in his story, Barry had exerted power over language and had flexibly manipulated his story in response to his audience's emerging interests. Storytelling, in its communicative power, engagement with the audience and exploration of the human condition, enables learners like Barry to exercise a degree of creative control over their language and over their listeners. The intimacy and immediacy of telling often evokes a creative experience, albeit a temporary one, which teases out the imaginative and linguistic potential of both tellers and told.

A storyteller's sense of audience and the need to tailor the tale for them is paralleled in the written mode by the writer's developing sense of their likely readership, since all writing involves the author imagining their audience. As Bearne (2002: 99) observes, 'lessons learned through face to face engagement, through the use of spoken voice can then be directed towards developing a secure written voice'. Matthew, aged 10, had told and retold several tales about accidents and mishaps to friends in his class, no doubt transforming and adapting these stories as he did so. Following the storybuzz in which members of the class moved around the room alternately listening and telling, Matthew chose this particular incident to retell for the class's collection of autobiographical tales.

The Day I Cracked my Head Open (I'm exaggerating a little bit)

Years ago when I was six or seven, I was playing outside with my friends, we were playing on the yellow lines and leaping about. It was the middle of summer and I was getting hot so I ran to the water fountain to get a drink.

I was so thirsty I rushed in and tripped over the first step and my head went CRACK in to the spiky handle! Blood was everywhere, dripping down from my head onto my coat and I was screaming in pain. Luckily Simon, from class 2 now class 3, saw me and took me straight to Mrs Browning, she put a bandage on it and called my house immediately. My mum was out but my dad was still there. He was just leaving for London when the phone rang. When Mrs Browning told him what had happened he raced to the school and since my mum had the car, he had to come on the motorbike! When he arrived I got on the back of the bike and we rode home! I had to wear his old helmet, which rubbed on my bandage and hurt even more.

At home I felt relieved but shaken up. Dad let me watch TV with a warm drink and then he took me to the doctor. We weren't kept waiting, I expect they'd seen the blood coming through. The doctor put three stitches in my head. At first I was terrified because I thought that they were going to use a needle and thread and sew into my skull! After that dad took me home for the rest of the day. Since then I've NEVER run to get a drink.

In this retelling, Matthew shares his memory with pace and humour as the events surrounding his head injury are brought to life drawing on 'the unique alloy of memory and imagination' (Rosen, 1998: 188). His final affirmation that he will never run to get a drink again, is suggestive both of the moral closure common to fables and of a direct address to the reader/audience. It adds coherence to the tale, connecting as it does to the introduction and echoing the rhetorical device of speaking directly to the audience. As the storyteller, Matthew has made choices; giving particular emphasis to his own fears and feelings, he has taken what he told from his experience and in turn made it the experience of those who listened to his tale. Their responses will undoubtedly have influenced his written narrative. The smiles and sounds of interest, surprise, shock or laughter in the time of telling, will have operated as immediate, if implicit, feedback and will have subtly influenced his selection of words and the nature, speed and intimacy of his later writing. In this way the telling becomes a form of oral drafting and in actually committing his tale to paper, Matthew will no doubt have honed and crafted this narrative still further. Such opportunities can be used to help Matthew and his peers consider the reader's point of view in planning and writing, for 'it is often through the liveliness of story-telling that children first come to appreciate the full dramatic texture of language in use' (Grugeon and Gardner, 2000: 105). The interpersonal involvement of the storyteller and their audience and the ways in which this qualitatively influences the telling, can be explored through sharing the same tales at home and school and comparing the differences, the minor shifts in slant and alternative choices made. Discussion of these can lead to an increased awareness of the ways in which authors draw readers in and shape their work for particular audiences.

Internalising narrative structure

Traditional tales are widely recognised as robust vehicles for storytelling and as quality models for story writing, they have always served to bring people together and to stimulate imagination, and in schools in which the standards of literacy are high, such literature is extensively used to scaffold understanding about narrative structure (Frater, 2001). By nature and origin, these tales address themselves to the ear rather than the eye and structurally are often highly patterned, with repetitive sequences, interchangeable story elements and overt shapes which make them a valuable resource to lean upon and extend. Research has shown that traditional tales are particularly supportive to children's development as writers (Barrs and Cork, 2001), as they examine human nature, often dealing with powerful emotional experiences and many are told in a poetic and literary manner. Storytellers from yesteryear, however, built upon their repertoire of tales through hearing and telling them, not through close analysis of their story grammars, and today's young tellers also need the chance to examine the overall shape and pattern of narratives through voicing stories and capturing their shape, essence and meaning. As storytellers sharing tales, children inhabit the story and experience its emotional rhythms, feel the protagonist's pain and participate in the sense of tension. The emotional temperature of a tale is intimately related to its overarching shape and if it is lived through and brought to life with voice and flavour, an implicit and felt sense of the narrative structure will develop, for as Rosenblatt (1978: 20) observed, 'form is felt on the pulse first of all'.

In the We're Writers project classrooms, where storytelling was given priority, the structures and shapes of traditional stories began to be internalised and made available for creative use, this made a marked difference to children's assurance as writers. In preparation for telling tales to others and committing the tale to their story memory, the children in these classrooms considered the structure of the stories in a variety of ways. These included story seeds, mountains or plates (Grainger, 1997), sequential freeze frames making a physical storyboard (Grainger *et al.*, 2004b) story mapping (Benton and Fox, 1985) and block graphs (Lewis, 1999). However, identifying the story's structure was not enough, the young people also needed to tell and retell the tales and parts of them, and travel on a complex pattern of pathways before they were able to use these shapes for themselves. Their journeys involved them in revisiting their chosen tales and experimenting with supportive prompts for retelling as well as the chance to tell to others who did not know their chosen tale. As their repertoire of story shapes and possible resolutions expanded, the children actively combined elements and created new shapes which leant on the known. For example, one class transformed texts through drama and then retold their new tales, others created stepping stones for their stories and then retold these to younger children in a festival of voice and choice. The act of retelling allowed these children to use and become familiar with the overall organisation and big shapes that carry a tale's meaning, and the oral rehearsal of whole-text structures that storytelling provided, enabled them to gain a clearer sense of the grammar of story.

Echoing the tunes, rhythms and language

Traditional tales represent a rich resource of markedly musical stories with strong patterns and potent lyrics which are often echoed in oral retellings and absorbed and transformed into written forms. The inhabited voice of the child storyteller sings such music into existence and in the process children become more creatively engaged in their own learning, for storytelling does not require accurate recall of the words, but invites a playful approach, enabling the teller to make their own choices and discover the pleasure of making language do what they want. Fox's (1993) research highlighted the markedly original and inventive use of language employed by young storytellers as they play with words, rhythms and meanings, and she showed that returning to favourite tales and texts gave children the chance to explore and enjoy language and take risks with it.

The repetitive and rhythmic language of traditional tales often demarcates the tale's structure, and alongside any accompanying actions operates as a mnemonic device; rhythmic structure is a potent facilitator of verbal memory (Neisser, 1967). Recording and discussing the literary language of tales, and their evocative words or lyrical phrases can help develop children's awareness of the role of language as a shaping force in the story; they could, for example, make notes of common phrases, runs, repetitions or songs which contribute to the effect of the tale. However, the opportunity to use this language through joining in tales and in their own oral storytelling is also important. Over time, as they experience, employ and reflect upon the language of tale telling, some of the tunes and patterns, words and phrases will be tacitly transferred into children's writing and echo through their work. As language artists in storytelling mode, children lean on the imagined world of the known narrative, and in order to evoke it and share it with others, they need to recreate it in the immediacy of the telling, and select language which effectively achieves this goal. In writing too, they will be involved as artists in generating alternatives and selecting from among them.

> When children hear stories, they do not simply listen to what happens, but store up the rhythms and cadence of the language, which they draw on in their own stories.
>
> (Barrs and Cork, 2001: 173)

Through discussion which considers the voice and verve of a tale, children can be helped to discover its dominant style. It may, for example, have an immediate and humorous appeal as in the American 'Big Wide Mouthed Toad Frog' or be more lyrical in nature as in the African tale 'The Children of Wax'. With multiple retellings on the market it can also be interesting to examine how different authors' versions shape and influence the style of the tale and the manner of its telling. In the We're Writers project we noticed that children who experienced rich opportunities for hearing, telling and retelling tales began not only to voice stories more confidently and flexibly, but also made use of the highly patterned introductions common in folklore, and the rhetorical device of appealing directly to the audience in words and gestures. Some of the learners employed a variety of 'traditional' opening clauses and sentences in their written work, including:

> In a time before our time began ...
>
> In the place where North meets South and West meets East ...
>
> Once upon a time, it wasn't in my time and it wasn't in your time, but it was in ... time, ...
>
> Once, many paper thin moons ago, there lived ...
>
> In a time when beasts could sing, birds could talk and insects did chew tobacco ...
>
> This is a tale of two friends, who weren't always friends, in fact once they were enemies, read on and let me tell you.
>
> My tale begins in a time of wonder, a time of mystery and magic, listen and you will hear.

The youngsters' use of stock phrases from oral literature and their ability to adapt these, demonstrates that the material of traditional folklore is accessible to all and shows that the opportunity to read, hear and voice these opening sentences can influence later writing. In a class of 7–8-year-olds in the project, the teacher recorded the following written examples of writers appealing directly to the reader in their stories; these mirror the conversational appeal of an oral telling.

> ... And Little Turtle cried and cried, like you would if you'd lost your mummy ...
>
> It was a great party, didn't I see you there?
>
> He was hot, very hot, can you feel how hot he was?
>
> Everyone laughed at the Raja's big ears, can I hear you laughing too?
>
> He was afraid, as we all are sometimes, frightened and afraid...

These young writers were seeking the reader's involvement through talking directly to them and writing with increased immediacy and style as a consequence. It can be interesting to identify these and other forms of metanarrative asides, when tellers step out of the tale to appeal to the reader or to comment on their narrative, since this is one way in which writers continue to borrow from the oral tradition. Glassie (1986: 8) has argued that 'all printed texts of folk tales are compromises between the written and the spoken word, between writers and storytellers' and through taking part in the oral tradition of tale telling, children can widen their linguistic repertoire, borrowing features from this genre and employing them appropriately to enrich their writing.

Retelling known tales enables children to rely upon the given framework of events and frees them to develop the characters and their motives, to work on the physical landscape or the emotional tenor of the tale. They can use their knowledge of the overall shape and direction of the narrative, but are free to play their way forward; finding the language to do so and drawing on the literary language of stories they have heard, voiced and imbibed over time. Such opportunities offer elements of constraint and freedom, that critical combination needed to develop creativity in action. One such activity, 'telling down' provides an opportunity to focus in this way on the language of the tale (Grainger *et al.*, 2004c). After a tale has been told, children identify significant images or moments in the narrative which they saw clearly in their mind's eye and either share these conversationally or draw them. Then each child selects one to 'tell down' and flesh out more fully in the class storybuzz. Damon, aged 10, elaborated on an event in the Chinese tale 'The Weaving of a Dream'. His teacher in her oral retelling had not expanded on this moment, but had merely noted that as the youngest son, Lejé, rode across Flame Mountain, he did not cry out for he knew he'd be burnt to ashes. Damon had evidently imagined this moment vividly and seized upon it immediately, digging down into the substrata of the text and embellishing it as he told it to others. Later he chose to rewrite it as an extract from the tale.

Flame Mountain

As Lejé sped towards Flame Mountain, he sensed the surging heat before him. He saw the fire reaching to the heavens trying to grasp hold of God. He had heard tales of the flames trying to torture God, and now he too would have to endure them. As he came nearer, he could see the fire whips lashing out at him, he braced himself for the worst. Plunging in he felt the searing heat bellow forth, it seemed as if the fire was burning him inside and out. It was like drinking a goblet of fire, blisters were appearing everywhere, even on his tongue. But he did not scream. After half a day of agony, his horse broke through the surface of the flames and when the wind brushed his burning body his bleeding blisters disappeared. He had survived the flames of the mountain of hell.

Through the storytelling process Damon has evocatively recreated both the physical setting and a sense of Lejé's anticipation, pain and bravery as he travels through Flame Mountain. In this powerfully imagined experience of the flames of hell, Damon takes risks with words and phrases, expanding the scope of what he is usually able to make them achieve. His idea of the fire trying to grasp hold of God builds up the tension, as Lejé too will have to endure this torture. He uses his senses effectively; feeling the searing heat, seeing the fire whips lashing out and employing the intertextual simile 'like drinking a goblet of fire'. This possible connection to Harry Potter is extended by the blisters on his tongue which are finally removed in the alliterative run, 'when the wind brushed his burning body his bleeding blisters disappeared'. As Damon wrote this descriptive passage, he was observed reading it aloud to himself, attending to the aural rhythm of his writing and appreciating perhaps the impact of the short sentence 'But he did not scream'. This serves to emphasise that Lejé had heeded the old crone's warning and gives the reader hope. Without the opportunity to voice this visual, to describe and re-describe it through the storybuzz, we believe Damon's writing would have lacked its creative edge. In the telling he will have begun to generate ideas, try them out, experiment with images and tunes and feel their impact on his audience, for 'the meaning is in the music; it is in the language: not phonetics, grammar or syntax, but pitch and cadence, and the colour of the word' (Alan Garner, 1984).

Through reflective discussions and storytelling conferences, we can develop children's awareness of how their creative voice play and choice of paralinguistic features engage their audience's imagination and evoke a felt response. Gesture, intonation, emphasis, tone, volume and use of pace and pause all create additional layers of meaning which, as writers, they may want to convey in words or accompanying visuals. As Olson (1996: 42) notes, the challenge for the writer is to covey the 'illocutionary force' of an utterance and express the features of spoken language. Through thoughtful consideration of the differences between oral and written retellings, both teachers and children can explore the affordances possible in each mode and begin to identify ways in which writers demarcate emphasis, build tension or convey a character's intonation or physical demeanour.

Creatively transforming tales

Every storytelling is unique and involves some degree of creative reworking. Historically, both adult's and children's authors have reworked narratives of all kinds, and traditional tales in particular have been replaced, parodied, modernised and retold from different perspectives. As the story-teller, Hugh Lupton (2001: 32) observes, such tales are not the creation of any one person, but are 'everyone's creation and everyone's property … a shared cultural invention'. Storytellers experiment with tales and frequently play with the characters and the language even if, structurally, the reworking is similar to an earlier version; in this way new meanings and insights emerge through subtle alterations. The children in the project also experimented with tales, creatively transforming them in a variety of ways. To demonstrate this, some written reworkings of the story of Little River Turtle are examined. In essence, the tale tells of Little River Turtle's adventures when, forgetting his mother's advice, he follows a beautiful butterfly into the desert. There, sobbing and alone, he encounters Coyote who desires to learn to sing like Little River Turtle. He cannot teach Coyote to sing however, because as he explains, he is not singing, but crying. Eventually the brave little turtle is returned to the river and Coyote slinks off, practicing his 'song' and howling at the moon from that day to this. This explains how Coyote got his 'song' (for a full retelling see Grainger *et al.*, 2004b).

In one class of 6–7-year-olds, the teacher initially told only the opening elements which Anvita's story path (Figure 7.2) effectively depicts. In working across the page from left to right she shows Little River Turtle's river-bed home and the fronds of grass he nibbled, the face he drew in the sand and the beautiful butterfly he followed. Through the economic use of visuals, Anvita conveys Little Turtle's clown-like laughter in the short grass, his roaring like a lion in the long grass, the little pebbles which he traversed as a ballerina and the long smooth pebbles he slid across like a famous ice skater. At this point as difficulties arise for Little Turtle, her story path descends and symbolically she shows the pain of the hot sun through the zigzag lines on his back. Her experience of this climactic moment and sense of suspense was emphasised through taking the story path home to tell the beginning of the tale to parents and siblings. The class then created further adventures for Little Turtle through drama and brought him safely home before their teacher shared the end of the version she knew.

In the same school a class of 10–11-year-olds also selected different ways to represent and transform the story of Little River Turtle. Some groups created emotions graphs to map out his journey and then retold the tale from Little Turtle's perspective to a younger class, two groups turned to the media and improvised their own TV interview with the now famous Little Turtle and others chose to create story skeletons, taking these home to retell. No one was asked to rewrite the tale, although in their journals over the following weeks a number of versions of Little Turtle were committed to paper, showing different elements of voice and verve and various degrees of transformation and subversion. For example:

I sat on my bed, bored of all my toys. I'd played all my computer games, I worn out my mechanical newt and read all my books. A-ha, here's an idea! I'd do some yoga! I sat down, but no matter how hard I tried I could not get my little legs into the yoga thinking position. So ... I had another idea! I'd go swimming! Perfect!

I opened my drawers excitedly and pulled out my trunks and grabbed a towel.

'Mum' I shouted

'Yes love?'

'Can I go swimming?'

'Yes, but don't go too far!'

Figure 7.2   Anvita's story path

In this humorous opening extract from Anastasia's first person narrative, she conjures up an amusing picture of Little Turtle trying yoga and uses a direct style, as if the turtle is talking to himself. Later in her tale, she includes a measure of authorial commentary when referring to Coyote: *Boy did he have a short fuse! He was a real mean one that wolf* and ends by tentatively promising herself that one day she'll tell her mum the truth, *I will, I will, one day, I will ... yeah one day, maybe ... one day.* The voice of the character rings through on these and other occasions, no doubt influenced by her earlier retelling, which helped Anastasia identify with Little Turtle, transform the rhythms of speech into writing, and maintain pace. Anastasia found her stance through her group's emotions graph and voices her story from the inside out with evident skill and pleasure. In contrast, Katie's narrative is a more straightforward retelling from a more detached and omniscient third person narrator. She makes extensive use of adjectives and adverbs and frames the tale in a more overtly literary manner, perhaps conforming to schooled expectations about introducing main characters and describing the setting. She begins in the following manner:

> Far, far away in the warm lands where dolphins dive in the beautiful oceans, there lived two turtles. One of them was a very young one and the other was slightly older. The young turtle had brown smooth skin with a shell that was elaborately patterned like a hard tea cosy, and the other had wrinkled, grey, skin with a slightly less 'embroidered' shell. Both these turtles lived in a cave right next to a deep blue river fairly near the shore. The mother turtle would always say to the baby turtle, ' Remember little one never stay in the sun too long, otherwise your shell will crack'.
>
> Our story starts one fine July morning, the sun had just risen and only the birds were up and about. Little turtle awoke, feeling ready to greet whatever adventure awaited him ...
>
> When he reached the river, the water was so enticing that all doubts were wiped clean from his mind. He jumped in. The sensation was wonderful. I could stay here all day he thought to himself.

In the second paragraph however, having set the scene, she appears to find her own voice when she deliberately steps into storytelling mode with the metanarrative aside *our story starts one fine July morning* ... Whilst Katie does not sustain this sense of immediacy and a number of arguably redundant adjectives creep back in, in places she begins to inhabit the tale and share it with conviction. For example, when Little Turtle finds himself lost, alone and with a drying shell she comments, *Little Turtle remembered his mother's words, but pushed them to the back of his mind – he was in enough trouble without feeling guilty as well.* In this way she relates to the reader and is both the teller and the told, the speaker and the hearer of her own writing. Other writers in the class explored alternative voices in their writing, Mahdi for example adopted the style of an interviewer in the Ricky Lake Show, which emerged through some animated role play with friends, see Figure 7.3. When the writing was finished, Mahdi and two friends performed the interview for the class, using his writing as a play script and enjoying the amused reaction of their classmates.

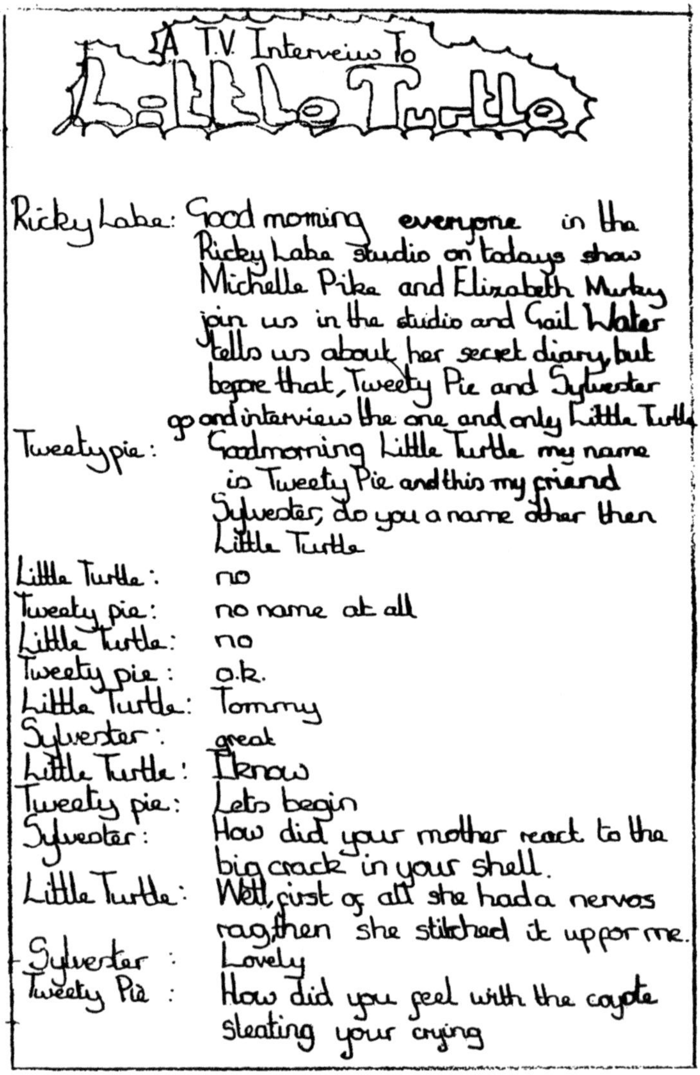

A T.V. Interview To Little Turtle

Ricky Lake: Good morning everyone in the Ricky Lake studio on todays show Michelle Pike and Elizabeth Murky join us in the studio and Gail Water tells us about her secret diary but before that, Tweety Pie and Sylvester go and interview the one and only Little Turtle

Tweety pie: Good morning Little Turtle my name is Tweety Pie and this my friend Sylvester, do you a name other then Little Turtle

Little Turtle: no
Tweety pie: no name at all
Little Turtle: no
Tweety pie: o.k.
Little Turtle: Tommy
Sylvester: great
Little Turtle: I know
Tweety pie: Lets begin
Sylvester: How did your mother react to the big crack in your shell.
Little Turtle: Well, first of all she had a nervos rag, then she stitched it up for me.
Sylvester: Lovely
Tweety Pie: How did you feel with the coyote sleating your crying

Figure 7.3 Extract from the Ricky Lake Show

The word play in the names of Gail Water, Michelle Pike and Elisabeth Murky create an amusing start and the light-hearted interchange between Sweety Pie and Sylvester is both slightly zany and quick fire as the interviewer becomes increasingly impatient with Little Turtle's brief and direct answers. The comic irrelevance of his designer swimming trunks, which he says are *'illuminous Pink Speedos'* was also well received by the class, connecting as it does the world of the story with their world of designer clothing. Through orally telling and retelling the tale of Little Turtle and through the use of drama activities, the children were given the chance to rehearse their verbal artistry and voice their ideas, some of which they chose to recreate and polish through writing. Their evident pleasure in this playful process should not be underestimated, reflecting as it does their involvement and delight in transforming and subverting tales in diverse and creative ways.

Conclusion

Through retelling tales, whether personal or traditional, children widen the number of tunes and structures in their repertoires and feel the flow of language as they stretch their voices in spontaneously recreating and transforming stories. They lean upon life and the tradition of oral literature and focus on the relationship between the audience and the reader as they shape, draft and polish their work. They also experience the power over language that such opportunities bring and expand their awareness of the features and styles of stories, making inter-textual links as they give them voice and shape, feeling and form. Ted Hughes (1976) has observed that stories represent units of the imagination, which, once they are well known can be possessed and revisited at will, so it is, we believe, with storytelling which is a missing link in story writing and a potent tool in extending children's voice and verve.

Chapter 8

Artistic voices
Poetry

Poetry is a multimodal form of communication. This has been recognised by poets across the ages and by those readers who have become devotees. Children who play with language, its sense and savour, rhythms and rhymes also implicitly understand this. The intrinsic pulse of poetry incites physical movement from the lips to the limbs and demands that poetry is read with voice and verve. Its multimodality means that poetry does not live easily on the page, and needs to be ignited by all available means to allow readers to engage with its complexity and release its potential. Readers deserve to see, hear, taste and feel the patterns of poetry, and writers too may use all their senses in composing and animating meaning.

Research and inspection evidence has shown that children, as they grow older, often demonstrate an antipathy towards poetry at school (O'Brian, 1985; Dias and Heyhoe 1988; OfSTED, 1993; QCA, 1998). This may be because schools tend to operate in a mono-semiotic system, basing much, if not all their poetic practice, in the logic of the written word. Children meeting poetry in such an environment are unlikely to perceive it as having life outside this single mode of communication, and will construct their own theories of poetry based upon such limited practice (Fleming, 1992). Outside the classroom however, children engage in a rich world of language play, through playground rhymes, songs, chants, jingles, jokes and lyrics although they may not recognise these as poetic experiences (Grainger, 1997). If the poetry they meet in school is studied, read and written in a manner which profiles form and technique at the expense of playful exploration, thoughtful contemplation and pleasure, then its multimodality, accessibility and voice may be reduced.

In this chapter we examine children's experience of poetry, its nature and sensory appeal, and reflect upon children's playful and poetic voices, which, from an early age, resonate with others' tunes and rhythms. We discuss ways to draw on poetry's diverse properties and explore how poets draw on the voices of others to enrich their own work by transformative means. We also consider how other modes of communication can be used transductively in composing poetry, the importance of musically and physically engaging with poetry and the significance of choice, as well as approaches that profile form, freedom and creative engagement.

Children's experience of poetry and its modes of sensation

From an early age children delight in sound play and in their babblings as infants they investigate noise levels, intonation patterns, rhythm and repetition. Their first encounters with language are frequently poetic in nature, as caregivers playfully interact with them repeating words and phrases and using marked intonation patterns. Young children's outcrops of 'singing' are full of feeling, often enriched by experience of shared word play, nursery rhyme, rhythm and song. Their later speech play will be widened through their acquaintance with the world of books, the lore and language of the playground and other forms of poetry in the world. The culture of childhood reverberates with poetry and music: with football chants, youth club songs, hymns, adverts, pop music, jingles, signature tunes and others' language, all of which bring word play, pattern and rhythm to their ears. Yet it appears that this pleasure in language play gradually fades in the context of school as poetry is studied, tested and taught (e.g. Benton, 1984; HMI, 1987; QCA, 1998).

It is possible, however, to help children recognise that, for example, their jokes, rhymes, banter and rap are all poetic forms that heighten the ordinary use of language, and that they already experiment with the rhythmic heartbeat of poetry running through their favourite pop songs, games and chants. In the classroom we can nurture their affinity with rhythm and beat and capitalise upon their pleasure in poetic language. Many will never have seen the Smurfs' song, Steps' latest single or a popular chant written down, but they will know the words, the pauses, the tune, the beat and the actions which often accompany contemporary lyrics. The existence of poetry in everyday life needs to be made visible in the classroom and its democratic and accessible nature celebrated and affirmed in action. We can widen their awareness of the voice of poetry in the world: in the media, the street and the community and include an emphasis on the physical, social, musical and performative nature of much of this poetry. Through reading, writing and discussing poetry as well as through experiencing, presenting and interpreting a wide range of such texts, children can build upon their pleasure and deepen their understanding of poetry's sounds and words, rhythms and resonance. The opportunity to integrate other visual and performing arts such as painting, sculpture, dance, drama and song into their experience of poetry can influence their pleasure, under-standing and production of it. Children also need the chance to compare poems that have been heralded by society as classics and those that are more modern, since it is important that children meet a variety of voices offering different cultural perspectives and a wide range of styles and forms. Such reception of language allows for greater productive language possibilities, although the youngsters themselves need to be in the driving seat in choosing poetry to read, re-read and explore in various ways. As the poet Gareth Owen (1988) observes, 'poems are often monologues of a sort and the breakthrough comes when I discover the speech rhythms of the persona I have temporarily occupied in order to voice the poem'. Such speech rhythms need to be heard, voiced and experimented with by children through a rich programme of read aloud, shared and guided work and independent reading, response and performance. Poetry can also be used as a form of play script with groups re-voicing the verse, perhaps using conversational verse by Alan Ahlberg, Kit Wright, Michael Rosen and Richard Brown for this purpose.

Historically, writers and critics have had serious difficulties trying to define poetry, perhaps because of its multimodal nature and the fact that, as with all forms of art, radically different examples exist and evolve over time. Some writers see poetry as a genre defined by its difference from prose, others perceive it is distinguished by its economic use of language and still others highlight presentational differences. Auden and Garrett famously defined poetry as 'memorable speech', and suggest it must move us emotionally or excite us intellectually, noting that the stimulus is 'the audible spoken word and cadence, to which in all its power of suggestion and incantation we must surrender, as we do when talking to an intimate friend' (Auden and Garrett, 1935: 2). Children know what they like, asserting humour and accessibility as criteria for their selection (Lambirth, 2004), but we can widen their pleasure and understanding of poetry if we bring it life through different modes of sensation and communication. It needs to be lifted off the page and experienced multimodally. Poetry is read with the eye: the way the poem is presented on the page, the length of line, the spaces between verses and words and the shape of the poem all carry significant meaning and poets exert a marked control over the visual appearance of their work. Poetry is also read with the ear, as the word patterns, inherent rhythms and rhymes are heard on the inner and outer ear and the sounds and savours of words and syntax are experienced aurally. Poetry is tasted on the tongue, and can be 'a diet of pleasure and a meal of words' (Grainger, 1998) for the mouth is 'a theatre in miniature in which we physically enact a poem in terms of sound' (Dias and Heyhoe, 1988: 11). Poetry is also felt: its pulse can make hands clap and toes tap and it may prompt gesture and other movement. Performance poetry in particular employs movement as central to its meaning making.

Mode shifting

Readers explore poems from multi-sensory and multi-dimensional perspectives, so opportunities to tap into poetry's multimodal potential and shift across modes need to be made available in the classroom. Ted Hughes explains how the inner qualities of poetry are borrowed from other forms of expression and are brought into being through the senses.

> [The poet] can be excited by countless varied feelings. And his inner singing and dancing fit the feelings. But because he is a poet, and full of words, his song-dance doesn't break into real song, as it would if he were a musician … it breaks into words. And the dance and the song come out somewhere in the words. The dance makes the words move in a pattern, which we call meter and versification. The song makes the sound of the lines rise and fall against each other, which we call the music of poetry or the cadence.
>
> (Ted Hughes, 1963: 11–12)

The written form of poetry, with its own multimodal possibilities, offers a dynamic harbour for the creative act of transduction (Kress, 2003); if a poem is responded to through other modes of communication, its meaning and theme will be reconfigured according to the affordances of the other modes. Examples of a conscious and deliberate shifting of modes may help to illuminate our argument. In interpreting Adrian Mitchell's poem 'Back in the Playground Blues' one class of 10–11-year-olds in the We're Writers project were invited to create group tableaux of the scenes this 'soul music' evokes. Having observed the group's freeze frames, the class then added words and phrases, which they chanted, shouted, whispered or crooned in repetitive refrains; some were borrowed from the poem, others were invented. Their words and images very effectively conveyed the mood and heightened Mitchell's message about the persistent power of bullies. The affordances of the physical and linguistic modes released new perspectives about the poem, enabling the children to become actively and imaginatively involved. In a younger class, the children interpreted poetry through dance and later small groups choreographed their way towards writing a poem based on a dance. As they travelled, they created and evaluated both their physical and their scribal compositions and discussed the way in which each interacted upon the one another (Pickard, 2004). Broadening the modes of response through different representational means needs to be encouraged, and can create opportunities for discussion about the locked-in potential of written poetry, which may help children recognise the importance of converting poetry from the logic of the written word to other modes. The playground poem 'Ma, ma, malade' for example, Figure 8.1, composed by a class of 8–9-year-olds demonstrates how such rhythmic poetry needs the support of other modes of representation.

Simply reading this poem is not enough, the affordance of the logic of writing cannot release its full poetic power. Such poems are prisoners of the page; like caged lions only some of their qualities, power and beauty can be viewed from a single perspective. Reading poetry frequently

ma   ma   malade
ma   ma   malade
gimme gimme with another head ding dong
gimme gimme with another head ding dong
ma ma malade
ma ma malade
gimme gimme with another hand clap clap
gimme gimme with another hand clap clap
ma ma malade
ma ma malade
gimme gimme with another feet stamp stamp
gimme gimme with another feet stamp stamp
ma ma malade
ma ma malade
gimme gimme with another hot dog
gimme gimme with another hot dog
put it altogether and what do you get
ding dong clap clap stamp stamp hot dog
put it backwards and what do you get
hot dog stamp stamp clap clap ding dong

Figure 8.1 A playground poem: *Ma ma malade*

demands the release of several modes of meaning. The children's playful construction of Ma Malade and the leaping and dancing which accompanied its construction, remind us of Adrian Mitchell's perception that poetry is 'the mind dancing to the drumbeat of your heart' (Mitchell, 1999: 30). Their verse was included in a popular class anthology of playground poems which, whenever it was read in school, appeared to prompt the children to translate the encoded rhythms into sound and movement. In effect, the young readers were applying restorative measures to resuscitate these rhymes and re-establish their multimodal potential.

A focus on form, technique and meaning

Poetry is an especially crafted form of language and poems draw attention to themselves through their shape, form and sculpted language. The influential NLS (DfEE, 1998) lists 37 different forms, for example, haiku, tanka, cinquain, riddles, tongue twisters, puns, and kennings. From our experience in the We're Writers project, these forms were often perceived as requirements and 'covered' accordingly as recipes for writing, which can markedly reduce the time spent on free verse, free choice writing and on the exploration of poetry chosen by the children themselves. Knowledge of form is central in the work of Brownjohn (1982, 1994) and Pirrie (1987), who both argue that children need to be introduced to specific forms and techniques and provided with examples of literary models which they can emulate in their writing. Their concern, mirrored by the NLS is to widen children's understanding of the craft, in order to equip them with control and knowledge, believing that freedom and the power of self-expression are gained through the experience of such boundaries. Although Pirrie (1987) does recognise that children's experiences are a significant source of inspiration, she is stringent in her insistence that canonical poetic language and an awareness of form releases an aesthetic outlook upon the world.

In contrast, Michael Rosen (1989), also concerned to liberate children's imagination and expressive potential, sees the imposition of form and technique as removing children's autonomy over the means to represent their first-hand experience. He perceives that such practice inevitably translates children's interactive experiences into apparently safe and arbitrary forms, and may stifle both what they want to say and how they wish to say it. Brownjohn and Pirrie appear to advocate, albeit implicitly, the power of transformative practice across the medium of poetry, such transformation is 'a resource for establishing links between categories, and for producing new resources out of existing ones' (Kress, 2003: 47). In this way children create new versions from an existing repertoire and emphasis is placed upon the teaching of form. Certainly young writers do find the shape and rhythms of others' poems supportive and take pleasure in creating their own versions of well-known rhymes and rhythms demonstrating the 'natural poetic art' of the young (Styles, 1992). The following imitative examples from a class of 5–6-year-olds indicate just this artistic capacity.

Red blood juice! Red blood juice!
When I feed it to my sister
Her bones go loose!
Daisy

Ice cream paint! Ice Cream paint!
When I feed it to my dad
It makes him faint!
Zach

> Twinkle twinkle strawberry cake
> That's what I like to make
> Flour and eggs put them in
> Bake it in a metal tin
> Poppy
>
>
> Humpty Dumpty sat in a castle
> Humpty Dumpty played pass the parcel
> All the king's horses and all the king's men
> Wouldn't play pass the parcel again
> Tammi

Working with rhyme and word play, nonsense verse and song, these children experienced language at its most physical, playing with words, sounds, tunes and rhythms as they might play with sand. With a little help from their teachers, these young learners, whose ears were tuned to the musicality of poetry, fitted their own words and ideas into the shapes offered and took considerable pleasure in repeating their rhymes over and over again. But how much time should be spent teaching about forms and techniques? The question of balance is again an issue here, since time also needs to be spent encouraging children to play, to experiment, to write, to communicate and to find and express their voices through this art form. In the We're Writers project we found that children were involved in dabbling with the forms and features of poetry for the unitary purpose of learning about them, and this appeared to fill many of the available classroom hours, particularly at Key Stage 2. The teachers acknowledged that most of the time they devoted to poetry was spent mirroring forms or generating lists of metaphors or similes for example, which they noted with concern, were not transferred permanently into the children's writing. Many of the teachers did immerse the children in poetry, but tended only to read aloud examples of the specific form under scrutiny and then followed this with mimic-writing. They believed this practice was what was expected of them and felt they were conscientiously responding to the NLS lists and requirements (DfEE, 1998). Such close attention to form and feature creates the danger that children's writing may be detached from their own purposes and disconnected from the potential affordances of the written word. If the writing of poetry is drained of the life-blood of one's creative and expressive purpose, then the voice and verve of the poet is likely to be absent.

The predominance of form and reification of formulaic strictures and structures may also inadvertently downgrade free verse and result in children's meanings being seen as subordinate to the form, rather than the other way round. The children in the project were expected to show that they could write poetry, but also needed to be encouraged to *want* to write poetry and to *experience* its transductive potential. Robert Frost (as cited in Styles, 1986) asserts that 'poetry begins in delight and ends in wisdom' and it is our challenge as professionals to support, maintain and extend children's delight in poetry and increase their pleasure, wisdom and insight in this opaque language over the years. If we leap in too soon with the intense analysis of poetic forms or spend too much time examining techniques, then we risk separating their experience of poetry in the world from that met in school. Meek perceptively comments that 'the magic of poetry should not be overwhelmed by too many earnest endeavours to earn its keep' (Meek, 1990: 31). Over-reliance on daily classroom objectives, which signpost the way for mirroring techniques and forms may reduce children's access to poetry and focus their insights solely on knowledge about such literary language. Children deserve opportunities to develop their preferences, to explore alternatives, meet a variety of forms, use their own language, extend their understanding of the craft and create their own poetic texts. Much of their work will result from playing with words seriously and finding meanings perhaps within the discipline of a chosen form, so both form and freedom may play a part in the final composition. Balanced provision is the key, with the guiding principle that their work should always involve making and communicating meaning. Utilising different response to text activities, children will be investigating, both implicitly and explicitly, how poets manipulate form and language to convey their chosen meanings. As children read, write and experience poetry, they encounter ways to convey their communicative content and their voices ring out more clearly, particularly if, as we explored in Chapter 2, they are encouraged to write expressively in the voice they already possess, their oral voice. Much of this work will be free verse written perhaps in the first person, allowing for the expression of feelings and ideas and retaining that sense of poetry as memorable speech. Such verse will be constructed out of contemplation and delight, and will be part of 'the voice of poetry in the conversation of mankind' (Oakeshott, 1959).

The conversational context: poetic voices at play

In avoiding an overly instructional frame and creating a conversational context in the classroom, we will be developing a playful attitude to language and poetry, widening the children's options and increasing their involvement in the process. Rosen observes that he sees 'each poem I write, each poem I read, each poem I hear as part of a conversation – a chat' (1989: 26) and since 'spoken creativity is more likely to occur in intimate and collaborative dialogic conditions' (Carter, 2004: 215), we need to focus on building a community of language artists in the classroom. In such a workshop-oriented environment, children can explore poetry, its forms, substance and meanings together. Evidence from such environments shows that children's conversation, captured on tape, is sprinkled with other people's words and voices: 'memorable speech' from home, the street, the media, the playground and the classroom (Grainger, 1999). The girls in particular in this research recalled and repeated significant dialogues and took considerable delight in revisiting the marked intonation patterns and memorable phrases of TV characters, enraged neighbours, furious parents and siblings. These 9–10-year-olds seized opportunities to 'do the voices' as a way of giving cognitive and emotional coherence to their experiences. When we reproduce the voice of others in conversation, as Bakhtin (1986) points out, it is often for the purposes of judgement and evaluation. This was certainly the case with Sasha, who shared with her teacher that she wanted to write about her father, but couldn't find the words. He had died from a heart attack two years before. Later, during a poetry workshop, Sasha was recorded sharing this emotive dialogue with her group.

> Yeah, some foods are bad for you. See my dad shouldn't have had salt, it was bad for him … and I said to her (Sasha's mother),
> 'You could've stopped him'
> and she goes 'No I couldn't'
> and I said 'You could've stopped him'
> and she goes 'If he wanted it, it's his own fault'
> and I said to her 'You should've stopped him , you should've stopped him'
> and she hit me.

The conversation moved on and Sasha appeared to relax, such was the emotive power of this poetic snippet. Some time later she told her teacher that the family had visited her father's grave, *I told my mum it wasn't her fault really, it couldn't just have been the salt, could it Miss?* Tannen (1985) argues that literary language has much in common with conversation because it depends for its effect on interpersonal involvement, although Carter sees literary language as a continuum and argues for the recognition of 'a cline of literariness in language use' (Carter, 2004: 69). For these children, the dramatic dialogues which patterned their informal talk appeared to be experienced in the same way that they experienced poetry: affectively, cognitively and physically as consciously sculpted sound and meaning patterns. In an environment which celebrates the musical properties of poetry, children also replay contemporary tunes and choruses and find themselves humming chants and ditties as they compose. The unofficial agenda and conversational context of such an environment will be full of their unadulterated enthusiasm for verbal experimentation, with children flexing their voices on words and phrases, repeatedly turning them over in their mouths and savouring their flavours. Toying with idioms, unusual words and catchphrases made popular by the media is a practice often observed in young children at play, and is one which deserves to given a higher profile. Children delight in uttering, muttering and subverting words and gain both kinaesthetic and musical pleasure from such verbal encounters. Sometimes such word play may be captured and shaped into written verse, as in 7-year-old Alisdair's Snowman poem

Hello Man
No man
Body man
Head man
Coal man
Carrot man
Hat man
Scarf man
Snowman
Hello Man!
Smile!

Alisdair played with the words, sounds and shapes, the raw materials of this art form to create his poem, which he read aloud with considerable panache and pleasure, making each word earn its keep as the figure of his snowman grows in the reader's mind's eye. His last two lines became a kind of ritual greeting in the classroom for a while, until replaced by other experimental wordplay. These examples indicate that children's creative conversations and tendency to play with words and tunes are full of poetic possibilities and show that their 'knowledge of poetry is not only grounded in all the poetry they've heard, but also in their everyday experiences, the conversations they've listened to and participated in, and the poetic games and songs they've played' (Grainger, 1999: 296). The voices of the young at play are full of interest, intonation, rhythm and colour, and their conversations bear a kind of poetic energy, derived from their culture and community which we need to help them recognise, value and develop. Such speech play is vital to the acquisition of a poetic discourse. In recognising the poetic resonance in children's voices we can release their potential as poets and support them as they explore the creative power of language, celebrating their informal dialogues, ditties, songs and word play in school and providing an environment of experimentation and discussion.

The rhythm of life is a powerful beat

Poetry offers remarkably rich material for encounters with explicit and pleasurable rhythms; in particular oral poetry such as nursery rhymes, playground lore, jingles, raps and popular songs, as well as the rhythmic verse of poets such as James Berry, John Agard and Grace Nichols. Rhythm and music often increase the emotional and aesthetic impact of poetry and when verse is read aloud, the pace of delivery and the sound and patterns of the language influence the meanings evoked. Rhythm plays a central role in this, connected as it is to our very being.

> Rhythm is fundamental to our very existence and to the way we experience life in our bodies. Our bodies work in rhythmic ways: our heartbeat, our breathing, the way we walk, run dance, swim ... jogging, swimming, and even walking becomes a pleasure only when we get into a rhythm.
>
> (Furniss and Bath, 1996: 25)

Even ordinary conversation can be set to a metronome, making rhythm as vital to talk as it is to poetry, music and oratory. Poetry has its origins in oral cultures, where ballads and narrative verse were composed and sung as ways of recording particular events. Folk songs, chants, plainsongs and singing games all celebrate the close relationship between music and poetry, and this oral inheritance is the spring from which much subsequent children's poetry has flowed. If we offer children the chance to play with the tunes of their popular culture and oral traditions, they learn to experiment with these rhythms in their own voices and discover new cadences and melodies to savour and remember. Children, as we have argued elsewhere, often read their work aloud as they compose, to hear its sounds and tunes, taking an artist's role in listening to the patterns which emerge and shaping them accordingly. Manipulating the music of their oral compositions, and adding instrumental or body percussion can help them feel the significant rhythms and build on the linguistic flexibility they encounter in the playground and the media. In developing their latent appreciation of sound and rhythm, we must acknowledge the interactive processes by which children's reading, listening and affective engagement influence the poetry they write.

In the We're Writers project, a multicultural class of 7–8-year-olds were given the opportunity to write poems and perform them. Their teacher drew on their own interest in rap, reggae and hip-hop music and brought in examples which they listened to, tapping their feet and hands as they did so. She sought to validate this avenue of their communicative and aesthetic repertoire and helped them explore its relationship to poetry. Their work extended beyond the use of pen and paper; they incorporated the spoken word, drew on slang and other examples of non-standard English, and made full use of body percussion and drum-like sound effects in their collaborative production of verse. They danced individually and in groups to the rhythms that they generated, and effectively combined a number of modes of communication to make and shape their poetry. The class clapped and cheered each group's poetic performance, repeating the choruses, some of which were 'sampled' from popular music as they engaged with the spatial and temporal experience of rhythm and image and responded physically and interpretively. During this work the atmosphere in the class was highly charged, and power was transferred from the teacher to the children, who pooled their resources to compose. The children, more experienced in this domain, used their knowledge of rhythm and beat while their teacher looked on with respect and enjoyment. It was impossible to capture their work fully in any single mode so their poetry remained unwritten in the conventional sense, although it was recorded for others to enjoy, such was the vitality and energy of their combined voice and verve.

Poetry in motion

Musical rhythms in poetry are often accompanied by physical movement and a felt engagement, which makes a marked contribution to poetic experience. David Beckham making that perfect pass to a team-mate for example, or Darcy Bussell pirouetting across the stage at Covent Garden are both seen as poetic and demonstrating 'poetry in motion'; reflecting both beauty and a distillation of experience (Andrews, 1991). As humans we capture and represent our world through the modes of communication available to us; through art, dance, drama, music and literature, and the content of these forms of aesthetic representation derive in part from our active physical interaction with the world. This is illustrated by George Orwell's poet, Gordon Comstock in *Keep the Aspidistra Flying* (1936; 1989: 13).

> Outside, the slimy street looked grey and drear. From somewhere round the corner came the clatter of hooves, a cold hollow sound. Caught by the wind, the dark columns of smoke from the chimneys veered over and rolled flatly down from the sloping roofs. Ah!
> Sharply the menacing wind sweeps over
> The bending poplars, newly bare,
> And the dark ribbons of the chimneys
> Veer downward tumty tumty (something
> Like murky) air.

In this extract, the depressed poet struggles to compress his thoughts and mood into poetic structure and draws on the sights, sounds and atmosphere in London's winter streets. The ontogenesis of his verse is found in Gordon's interaction with the world, which is translated into a rhythmic use of sound and words and is eventually stored on the page. The poetry of this moment, as described by Orwell, has undergone a journey via the human mind into written verse, although it remains poetic throughout. Such a transductive approach to writing poetry explores other modes to find the content and inspiration to write. Poetry that is born of physical experience, drama, dance, music or image carries a meaning that has been transducted from one or more of these modes into the logic of the written word. The meaning comes to rest in the words and lines of the poem, but like energy compounded into nuggets of coke, its power needs to be re-ignited by readers prepared to galvanise the same multimodal methods release it. The writing of poetry may well be the mode of communication where the act of transduction is most evident, for poetry like other forms of composition does not need to be literally transcribed to be defined as 'writing'. Oral compositions too need to be encouraged and recognised.

> Most of my poems start in my head with the rhythm … And I'll pace up and down the room as I'm saying it, and sometimes I'm actually kind of dancing … For me, one of the most important things about poems is how they're said. When they roll off the tongue nicely, that's when I know that they're ready for writing down. There's a difference between creating a poem and writing a poem. I create poems anywhere and everywhere – like when I'm jogging – but the actual writing happens here in the office.
>
> (Zephaniah, 2001: 18)

For Zephaniah, poetry may be stored in the form of writing, but it begins in movement, rhythm and spoken language. As Ong (1982) notes, bodily activity is natural and inevitable in oral communication and in the composition of poetry it may help to shape the verse and create the patterns. Seamus Heaney (1980) too, in commenting on Wordsworth's constant walking to and fro, up and down the gravel path, imagines that 'the swing of the poet's body contributed to the sway of his voice'. Zephaniah's oral creations are poems themselves, indeed in their pre-written form they may reflect his most vibrant 'writing'. Not all poets, however, explicitly begin composing in this way, some prefer to play the rhythm out internally as they write words and hear their pattern and tune emerging. Nonetheless today's children who are often physically active and full of energy, deserve to be given the chance to compose orally and physically, feeling the rhythms in their bones and moving their way forward into poetry. When children compose collaboratively their poetry may be shared as a literal dance with words, or as a drama or piece of music, it may never appear in written form, but is likely to remain on their tongues and in their memories as a living act of composition: the co-creation of memorable speech.

Enlivening poetic practice

Teachers working on the We're Writers project, having established more open ended classroom contexts, worked to play with the conversational, musical and physical nature of poetry and witnessed their children gradually using a wider range of resources to make meaning. The young people mixed modes, drawing and annotating their pictures with language and creating three-dimensional shapes, they also danced and sang poetry into existence. Such literacy events functioned beyond contemporary definitions of poetry practice and expanded the more conventional model of merely reading and writing written forms. The children's engagement reflected their multimodality in the real world of communication, as they drew on modes that best suited their purposes. Transformation and more critically transduction were at the heart of such creative acts, as groups of children represented chosen poems in various ways in order to feel their rhythms, communicate the messages and convey their essence. Such strategies are not merely interesting, engaging and motivating, but demand that the children reflect upon and reshape their understanding of the text with others. So, through the experiential process of living inside the text and reflecting upon it, the learners came to understand more of the theme, structure, style and meaning of the verse. Providing time to share their performances and reflect upon the insights gained was important, but in units of work on poetry this is possible as long as we profile the meaning first and attend to the form when the children have experienced it for themselves. A teacher's reading, however dramatic, can never replace the experience of children rolling the words over their tongues, feeling the rhythms in their blood and bones and evoking the meaning through creative collaboration. Together, groups of learners can experiment with possible ways of communicating the poem's essence. Control is, as we have argued earlier, a key feature of creative learning and contributes markedly to any written work that emerges later in the compositional process. In seeking to understand poetry, children need to experiment with language, interpretation and meaning in small group discussions, shared readings and performances and through experiencing the multimodal representations of others. Such exploration will necessitate being open to others' ideas and thoughts as well as being critically evaluative of their own developing interpretations. A poem's rhythm, structure and meaning can emerge through such involving endeavours. As 9-year-old Cameron observed having worked in this manner over several weeks, *When we do things with poems, its like wearing 3D glasses, they come off the page and I can see them more clearly.* Through exploring poetry in these and other open-ended ways, children are able to inhabit the voices of professional poets and find the tunes and patterns in their own voices when they come to write. There is no formula for creating poetic energy and voice, but over time and through rich experience of the genre in the extended process of composition, a playful and exploratory approach to poetry can make a significant contribution to children's written verse.

Choice and autonomy

Full immersion in the genre, accompanied by a range of opportunities to lift poetry off the page supports the growing independence of young writers, who also need to choose their own content and forms. For like all successful poets, children write better when the subject is something about which they are knowledgeable or about which they care deeply. Since the influential creative writing movement, influenced by Maybury (1967) and Marshall (1963) amongst others, the assumption that children need to be stimulated in order to write expressively has held sway. Young people have been required to write poems about natural subjects, which can be experienced first hand, for example snowflakes, autumn leaves, fruit, flowers and pastoral landscapes, reflecting perhaps the romantic conception of childhood that connects children with nature and innocence. Indeed, much published poetry written before the 1970s emphasised: 'the smallness and prettiness of children; their location in a rural setting, often an idyllic one; and the association of poetry with magic and music' (Styles, 1998: xviii). Teachers working with children today, however, know that their interests and leisure activities are very diverse, influenced by the rapid growth of new technologies and the power and potency of popular culture and that the content of their writing needs to connect to their lives and their interests and concerns, not merely to the changing seasons. Themes can be negotiated with children and choice must be provided so they can revisit the tunes and rhythms performed earlier, try out for themselves particular forms which the teacher has introduced to them and write about what matters to them in their own authentic voices.

Love
I love playing Tekkon 2
People getting hit by lightening fast attacks
Shouts of pain and distinctive battle losses
My heart beating 10 million times a second
Suddenly dropping
People talking in an unintelligible language

I'm saying to myself in hope
'Come on Come on'
I'm thinking if I win who will I be fighting next?
What will they say after the battle?
I love playing Tekkon 2

In this poem Sam, aged 9, explores his pleasure in the Play Station game Tekkon 2. Although his subject matter may not be described in a traditional sense as poetic, for Sam, the electric experience of the game is worth expressing. He voices his thoughts in a poetic manner, drawing on experience of the sounds, images and movements in the game. His own experience of playing it and often winning has contributed to this verse, his chosen vocabulary encompasses words associated with the technology of the game and his repetitive last line gives shape to his work. Not normally an experienced or a keen writer, Sam reminds us that children's poetry is unique and that we must not be over eager for youngsters to replicate the work of adults. Poetry can enable children to reflect on their present state of being and explore self chosen themes as they consider their emotions, their fascinations, their failures and successes. As Seamus Heaney observes:

> Finding a voice means that you can get your own feeling into your words and that your words have the feel of you about them; and I believe it may not even be a metaphor, for a poetic voice is probably very intimately connected with the poet's natural voice, the voice that he hears as the ideal speaker of the lines he is making up.
>
> (Heaney, 1980: 58)

In our last example, Lucy, aged 9, Figure 8.2, also finds her voice and gets her own feelings into her words, using her poem to reflect upon significant events in her life history. Through opportunities to tell and retell tales of lived experience in a unit on autobigraphy, she was reminded of particular events and anecdotes and was given the choice to explore one or more of these in whatever form she chose. Creating the metaphor of the wind as time passing, she mentions significant objects, such as the pram which was sold, the fireplace on which she cut her head, the blossom tree which had to be cut down and her beloved aunt Muriel who died. The structural repetition emphasises the passage of time, her chosen layout creates a reflective feel and the present tense of the last line, *I swallow the wind*, reminds the reader there is more of her life to come and she welcomes this. In her first draft she wrote *things have changed me*, but when she read her work through, changed this to *the wind has changed me*, unconsciously realising perhaps that the wind is the driving force in this work. Through

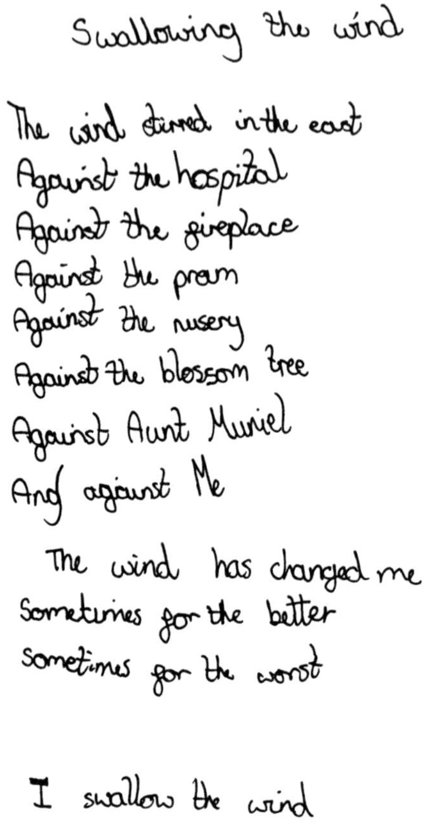

Swallowing the wind

The wind stirred in the east
Against the hospital
Against the fireplace
Against the pram
Against the nursery
Against the blossom tree
Against Aunt Muriel
And against Me

The wind has changed me
Sometimes for the better
Sometimes for the worst

I swallow the wind

Figure 8.2 Swallowing the wind

her experience as a writer she also knows that writing is a reflective tool, and in the comfortable environment of the classroom she feels secure enough to take risks with words and meanings. In addition, through her experience of poetry she knows how words can be sculpted, creating patterns and compressing meaning. When asked about the text she commented, *I just needed to write this, if we hadn't had writing time today then I would have written it at home, after our story sharing, I was thinking about things and the words 'swallowing the wind' came into my mind – a poem I thought.* Her pleasure and emotional involvement in this writing was evident in her quiet assurance, her ability to explain the trajectory of the piece and her desire to read it to the class. Her work reminds us of Wordworth's perception that poetry is the 'spontaneous overflow of powerful feelings' and that spaces need to be made available to children to express themselves, voice their thoughts, reflect on their lives and share their insights with others.

Conclusion

Poetry is language at play, a condensed form of meaning which we read with our ears as well as our eyes, taste on our tongues, feel in our bodies and respond to with our emotions. Children are not merely writers with pen and paper, but artists who draw on their oral inheritance, their natural physicality and their bodily engagement with language, to invent, create and perform poetry. Gradually, the teachers on the We're Writers project came to see the writing of poetry as a semiotic act, which, like other forms of composition, needs a rich diet of reading and reflection, engagement and experience, and real time and space for conversation and redrafting. In exploring the natural marriage between rhythm and poetry and experiencing many voices along the way, some of the teachers discovered, alongside their learners, that the rhythm of life is a powerful beat and in adopting more active and creative approaches to poetry, they began to recognise and develop the multimodal nature of poetry and celebrate children's poetic voices at play. They also began to value the opportunities that poetry, like story and other written forms provide for reliving experience, therapeutically even, when the author reflects upon and reformulates reality in order to create new insights.

Chapter 9

Teachers as artists

In recent years, pressured to prove their efficacy in a heavily monitored and inspected system, some teachers may have become detached or distanced from the art of teaching. As we highlighted in Chapter 1, accountability and control have reduced their creative engagement in the curriculum and affected teachers' perceptions of their role in the process: are we, as Mortimore (1999) asks, 'architects or bricklayers?' Are we developers of the curriculum in action working *with* children or technically competent deliverers of a prescribed package working *for* children? Teachers of writing do need secure knowledge about language to lay firm foundations, but we also need to be inspired designers, artistically involved in the process.

> Teaching kids to read and write should be an artistic event. Instead, many teachers transform these experiences into a technical event, into something without emotions, without creativity – but with repetition. Many teachers work bureaucratically when they should work artistically.
>
> (Freire, 1985: 79)

This chapter examines these views and discusses the importance of teachers engaging as artists in the writing classroom, personally and professionally involved as role models and collaborators. As Craft argues if 'the artistry of teaching is being undermined by a technicist view of pedagogy, teachers need creativity to respond to this situation' (Craft, 2001: 53).

We explore how, through their own imaginative involvement, teachers' creative potential can be released and their confidence, commitment and understanding of the artistic challenge of being a writer can grow. Through journeying alongside children, responding to texts, performing poems, becoming tale tellers and taking roles in drama, teachers can be empowered to model writing from inside the compositional process. We believe that teachers need to make full use of the language arts to create a rich environment for supporting and developing writing, and argue that as teachers we must recognise, nurture and develop our own creative potential by taking part in such generative practices and dwelling in the realms of possibility. If our aim is to create a community of writers then we should endeavour to perceive ourselves as learners, as language artists and as writers. Despite the fact that we all write: notes, cards, emails, lists, reports, diaries, poetry and plans for example, we rarely share these to show children we too are writers, stretching to find our own voices in diverse contexts. In taking part as real writers in the classroom, we will be able to see writing through both telephoto and wide angle lenses and appreciate the advantages of both proximity and breadth.

The artistic engagement of the profession

We have argued that effective teachers of literacy are also affectively involved, creative and reflective teachers, yet negligible time in initial training or in in-service is devoted to the affective domain or to developing our creativity. As Barnes (2003) highlights, student teachers transfer from an ITT curriculum dominated by 'The Standards' (TTA, 2003) and by detailed documentation and surveillance, into a profession where excessive paperwork and endless administration is recognised as one of the most frustrating aspects of the job (PriceWaterhouse Coopers, 2001). Teaching is undoubtedly an emotionally demanding and a stressful occupation and more time and energy needs to be given to the creative and emotional health of the teaching force. Research following continuing professional development courses with a strong practical, personal and creative focus (e.g. Woods, 2001) has consistently shown that 'teachers perceive and value the link between creative approaches and their own motivation and sense of pleasure in the job of teaching' (Barnes, 2003: 41). Yet English has been nudged to the margins in debates about arts education (Marshall, 2001) and the NLS training in England has tended to focus on raising teachers' subject knowledge through government packages on phonics and grammar for writing for example. Despite honourable intentions, the packages provided for the NLS consultants were initially delivered to the profession who were, in turn, obliged to attend and accept the perspectives offered. This may have contributed to a dependency culture in primary education. Yet as the OISE Report (DfES, 2003) has shown, many teachers have yet to understand the principles of such practice and as Frater (2001) and others have observed, some have become de-motivated and deskilled, pressured by the breadth of required curriculum coverage and dragged down by their own lack of autonomy in shaping children's learning. Engaging the profession creatively and artistically is not a panacea, a palliative cure for past practices and prescriptions, but it does represent a possible way to redress the balance between knowledge about language and creative language use and it can rejuvenate and empower teachers. It may also counteract the competency-based models in teacher education which fail to acknowledge the individual existential complexity of students. 'The experience and practice of the teacher-as-artist/composer is at the heart of the pedagogic activity' (Robinson and Ellis, 2000:75) and in other artistic domains, such as piano, ballet or sculpture for example, teachers are also practitioners in their field. This is not entirely the case in relation to writing.

> Far too many teachers are not writers in any but the most superficial sense. They have never struggled … with trying to express the inexpressible. They do not know about the drudgery of writing and the relief of getting the job finished. They do not know that writing, as much as music or art, exists in a tradition of its own which is a resource for generating meanings. They have never used writing as a way of exploring possibilities or reflecting upon their lives. They do not really understand what it means to be a writer.
>
> (Geekie *et al.*, 1999: 219)

Teachers of writing, who are professionally involved as individuals and as managers of the learning can also be involved as fellow artists/writers in the classroom. In this role, they are released from the more traditional patterns of interaction and are more personally involved, thinking and feeling their way through situations, taking risks, asking questions and profiling pedagogies and practices which help them develop their own and the children's creativity. As artists, teachers are not, however, just open to experience and reflectively engaged in different artistic practices, they are also involved in reflecting upon these experiences from a degree of distance and evaluating them critically. Teachers operating as artists in the language classroom are simultaneously reflective professionals. The challenge of developing our own and the children's imagination in action is an exacting one, but cannot be achieved unless we become fully involved as writers and readers, tale tellers, performers of poetry and role takers in the context of drama. This does not demand a profession of extroverts or performers in the flamboyant sense, but a creative profession actively involved in the artistic processes of teaching and learning.

Teachers as readers

Literature is a way of thinking and knowing about the world, a medium through which possibilities can be explored and personal responses evoked. Much will depend upon the chosen texts however, which need to provide a 'reverberating space' in which the creativity of the reader finds expression (J. Graham, 2000: 62). Teachers themselves need to find such space in the books they read at home and particularly those they share in school. Across the two years of the We're Writers project, at every project focus group meeting we read children's literature to our colleagues, to engage and move them, to discuss and debate issues and to create a common culture of shared experience. We were not surprised that the teachers began to purchase these and other books for themselves and for their schools, particularly the picture fiction, or that they developed a passion for literature and for 'performing' such texts to their classes. Many of them voiced the view that this simple act had made a marked difference to their attitude, receptivity and openness to learning.

> *Thank you for the glorious books, they've opened my eyes – they've so much potential, I never knew there were so many good kids/adult books before.*

> *I've become an avid reader of children's books again even though my own children have grown up and gone.*

> *I hadn't realised books were like songs and could be brought to life with so much impact.*

> *I didn't realise that the books themselves made so much difference, I won't let anyone else choose mine for me now.*

> *I used to use lots of extracts, now never, not unless I'm reading the book to the class, enjoying the whole story together makes all the difference.*

The initial audit showed clearly that decontextualised extracts held sway in many of the schools involved in the project, perhaps because the teachers had not fully appreciated the power of children's fiction as a tool for supporting reading and writing, and perhaps because they hadn't recognised or personally experienced the potency of such fiction for themselves. Yet as Rosenblatt (1995) has argued, readers, if they are going to call forth a work of art from a text, must attend to the personal associations, feelings and ideas being lived through during the reading, as well as the more public aspects of reading meaning. At the beginning of the research most of these busy teachers noted that they had neither the time nor the inclination to read regularly; at the close, they were planning units of work from a core collection of texts, were voracious purchasers of children's literature, and several observed they had begun to read for pleasure again. We discussed their roles as creative participants and spectators and Benton's assertion that spectatorship is a two-way activity which 'enables the collaboration that art demands if it is to be understood' (Benton, 2000: 202), and we agreed that their practice too needed to be collaborative and invitational in relation to literature. In 2004, the Arts Council, in response to a perceived lack of professional confidence, put the training of teachers in reading for pleasure at the centre of its strategy for children's literature.

The Council's concerns resonate with our findings that teachers need support and encouragement to read aesthetically for themselves, as well as for their learners.

Although many books to support the teaching of reading and writing may be well known to teachers, the 'firstness' of their encounters with some texts is of prime importance (Meek, 1991), so that their responses are genuinely exploratory and retain a ring of authenticity and personal engagement. In the Croydon Reading Project, teachers noticed that through sharing their emotional response to texts, they made it possible for older primary children to access and share their own affective responses and demonstrated that this is a legitimate part of reading (Graham, 1999). In the context of guided reading or literature circles, teachers who are reading with the group, reflecting upon the layers of meaning and sharing their own personal connections, are positioned differently, able to offer partial understandings and have these enriched through a more even-handed discussion and debate. In this situation, the power relations may shift subtly and a more equal frame of enquiry may be adopted as meaning is collectively constructed. Such discussions can also have an impact on children's growing capacity as writers, for example, a group may consider how the writer has achieved his effects and made the readers tense and uncertain through the creation of a threatening atmosphere or emotional conflict. In later work, children may also work to make their readers feel afraid, surprised or suspicious, using tension and cliff-hangers to evoke this.

> Unless teachers are concerned with how readers actually respond experimentally, emotionally and aesthetically to the texts they read, reading them may well be seen as a necessary chore rather than as a means of delight and exploration.
>
> (King, 2001: 35)

This also applies to teachers who, as readers, perceive literature as a rich source of possibility, a place for imaginative involvement and reflection, not merely a model or trigger for writing. Such teachers profile their own and the children's aesthetic and affective response to literature and teach the writing curriculum in creative and empowering ways, providing time to make connections and to interrogate views about the world as they bring their creative faculties into play.

Teachers as storytellers

In becoming oral storytellers and retelling tales, teachers can develop their verbal artistry, their ability to use language, pause, pace, intonation, gesture and feeling. Simultaneously, they also learn to interact with their audience and reshape their tales through this social process. Such artists engage with the narrative and the audience from the inside out, in participant mode, as well as from the outside looking in, in spectator mode (Benton, 2000). In retelling traditional tales, teachers release themselves from the written print and develop their potential to play with words and sounds, hear their own tunes, refine their skills and develop their communicative competence. Many teachers in the project focus group gained energy, satisfaction, confidence and pleasure from storytelling, particularly when they sang the tale creatively into existence and enticed their audience to wonder, feel and respond. Modelling this creative engagement needs to encompass a metacognitive layer, however, which may for example involve the teacher in reflecting upon the process of telling the tale or their awareness of vocabulary choices. As one colleague observed, *when I am stuck for an appropriate word or phrase and the story is not flowing freely, I find myself playing around in the moment waiting for the 'right words' to emerge.* Others also noted how storytelling had freed them to borrow lines and phrases, events and happenings from elsewhere, and observed that the act of sharing stories, particularly personal ones, had reminded their children of other life stories. Teachers can also explore how their own oral tales and paralinguistic gestures may be mirrored in writing. In creating atmosphere through words, voice, volume, gesture, pause and intonation, teachers creatively sculpt much more than words and may usefully invite the children to help convey the essence of their narrative in writing. In this way, the class can transform the dimensions of the multimodal nature of storytelling into writing, so the cadence, space and pace evident in the oral version are transferred into the written form.

Teachers in the project also made use of their new oral storytelling skills in other situations, when for example, the class need to be persuaded to clear their work away. In drama too, many found that the ability to retell the children's ideas, framed within the ongoing and unfolding narrative, offered invaluable support for the learners and increased the coherence of the dramatic text. In this context, the teachers were operating as oral artists, enriching the children's imagined experience as the story-teller of their co-authored narrative. Many of the teachers who expressed real delight in the art of storytelling felt their personal confidence had also increased as a result of feeling more assured as tellers of tales. Their words speak volumes:

> *I'd never felt able to tell tales before, I only ever read them – now it's almost the other way round. I just love the freedom to take the class with me on the journey of the story and add bits and pieces for particular individuals.*

> *In college years ago we were introduced to storytelling, but I never did it, I wish I had – it's so powerful, so involving.*

I love telling Dreamtime stories best, I collect them off the web, then try them out in class and if they pass muster I tell them in assembly – I'd never have thought I could, but I can and I love it.

Becoming a storyteller has made a huge difference to me, I feel more confident, not just in literacy and that, but in other situations too. When we were on the school trip, I was asked to tell stories at bedtime and the other staff really listened too – I reckon I was seen in a new light.

As these teachers developed their artistic capacity to tell and retell tales, flexibly selecting their language yet leaning on literature, they appeared to be repositioned and were viewed by their colleagues in school as language artists in their own right and as more creative professionals.

Teachers performing poetry and improvising in drama

As the previous chapter on poetry suggests, teachers working as artists in the classroom, modelling engagement and making meaning themselves, will want to participate in poetic explorations with their class, experimenting with the language, ideas and meaning of verse and seeking to explore possible ways to convey this to others. Such explorations necessitate being flexible and open to others' ideas and thoughts, as well as being critically evaluative of the emerging interpretation of the poem. Fox and Merrick (1987) observe that poetry must be experienced before it can be analysed and as teachers we too must take part in this experience, using percussion and performance or even ostinatos to highlight meaning. This can energise our own and the children's engagement and provoke multiple interpretations of the sense and savour of the words. It is possible to step inside the shape and pattern of the multimodal nature of poetry and explore a chosen poem's message, structure and rhythm, so together, as members of the classroom community, we flex our voices on the language of poetry and 'discern the colour, the life, the movement and drama of words' (Chambers, 1993: 56). Our own poetic compositions, whether written publicly through modelling writing or committed to paper individually, will be heavily influenced by tasting, feeling and hearing how words sound. As teachers we must ensure that we are not left outside, scribing children's words from a distance, but are composing from the inside, as genuine writers and poets and able to reflect upon our language, form, rhythm and cadence. The insights gained from our experiential encounters with poetic texts and those learnt through the demands of writing poetry ourselves enable us to be more effective teachers, fully involved in creating, crafting and evaluating writing.

If we are also involved in world-making play, we will take a variety of roles and genuinely join the class on an imaginary journey, prompting belief and commitment. Working in role can enable us to challenge the class to develop divergent thinking within the fictional context, draw us into the creative encounter and help us enrich our creative capacity through living in drama time. Drama in particular, can help teachers develop their confidence and competence in working creatively, although as research has shown, teachers and student teachers are wary of this medium, with its connotations of theatre and performance (Wright, 1999). The risk taking involved may also contribute to the primary profession's reluctance to embrace its potential. Some teachers lack the confidence to take up roles and may prefer the children to use drama conventions on their own in more tightly framed literacy sessions. Gradually however, the teachers we worked with came to trust the art form and felt more able to respond in open-ended scenarios, which enabled them to take small risks and experience the satisfying and energising nature of drama. Widening their experience of this tool for learning helped them live with the unpredictability and spontaneity of drama and appreciate its complexity. The openness which characterises much drama, contrasts markedly with a directive teaching culture and imaginatively involves the teacher, working both inside and outside the experience. 'Seeing the teacher as a fellow artist is the key to relationships in the drama classroom', Bolton (1992: 76) argues and displaces the skills of management and instruction by the pressing need to negotiate and re-negotiate the direction and content of the work in progress. While a lesson plan exists, the teacher must be feel free to release themselves from this and adapt it in order to respond to the needs and interests of the children, letting the drama venture into unknown imagined territory.

In such contexts, the project teachers found themselves raising possibilities rather than confirming probabilities and making the imagined reality more complex (Taylor, 2000), as during the drama they searched for conventions that might unsettle the status quo or open up new avenues for investigation. This obliged the learners to struggle with the contradictions, challenges and multiple perspectives they had created. Sternberg (1997) has argued that schools for the most part discourage risk taking, but in the safe fictional frame of classroom drama, this is encouraged, especially when the teacher is confident enough to live with the ambiguity inherent in it. In demonstrating their own belief and commitment to the imaginary situation, the teachers who were fully involved invited the children to engage with them, although in the early stages, some children, unsettled by this new experience and by their teacher's alternative perspective, laughed and giggled. This subsided, however, when they become emotively and intellectually involved in the drama themselves. With the teacher in role, the usual power relations in the room were altered, particularly when a less powerful role was adopted, this provided more space for children to take the initiative, to lead and shape their learning. These teachers described the complexity of operating at several levels at once, as they moved in and out of the lived experience and were clearly struck by the potential of this environment of possibility for transforming their own and the children's understanding.

Teachers as writers

If teachers of writing don't actually write – or even consciously talk creatively – in the way they expect children to do, then we believe, as Betty Rosen (1991) observes, that they will neither maximise their creative potential nor fully understand the challenge of being writers. So, as part of the We're Writers research, teachers' reflective journeys as writers were documented. The project focus group members responded to question-naires, took part in writing workshops, were interviewed and kept reflective journals about their own creativity and writing. The sessions provided regular opportunities for free choice writing, writing in role as part of a drama and structured opportunities for writing when the form and content were prescribed. In these sessions, all the group, including the authors of this book, took the time to write and we now examine the surprises and understandings gained from this part of our enquiry. The issues which emerged included: the tension between public and private writing; the need for a secure writing environment; the importance of re-reading writing at the point of composition; the significance of choice and autonomy and the potency of drama as a tool for percolating ideas and enabling writing in role. The consequences for classroom practice are also considered.

The tension between private and public writing

Initially, the teachers in the project focus group lacked confidence as writers, often voicing the view that they had not 'written anything' since school, they seemed to perceive narrative and poetic writing as 'real writing'. From the outset, most expressed concern and discomfort about writing alongside their peers, perhaps because they were more overtly than usual positioned as learners and felt vulnerable about this role shift in the domain of writing. In our sessions and in school, the teachers had taken part in drama, storytelling and response to literature with growing ease and confidence, but when it came to committing words to paper in the last eight months of the project, their levels of anxiety increased markedly. Their perceptions and comments about themselves as writers were frequently self-derogatory or self-effacing, for example, *Why am I so hopeless at this?*, *I have always been awful at writing, Help! I'm an awful speller.* In addition, a clear fear of comparison was in evidence, *I bet everyone else will have better ideas, It'll be embarrassing if we have to share, mine will be the worst.* This initial focus on the product and concern with others' value judgements inhibited their involvement and assurance in this mode of communication, despite the fact that these colleagues write for functional purposes every day of their lives. The questionnaire indicated that the teachers with the lowest levels of self-esteem wrote predominantly for functional purposes and undertook much less expressive writing than their more confident peers. Their own school experiences were also clearly influential.

> *My writing was never read as an example in school not ever. I hated writing then and I hate it now, I am just no good at it.*

> *I was always awful at writing, I never had any ideas for stories.*

> *I always got low grades at school, so writing evokes a sense of inferiority in me, I've never been any good at it.*

The difficulties of engaging in writing and its connection to their identity and sense of self inhibited these adults, and in the early workshops one teacher even tore her writing out of her folder in order to ensure her privacy. This fear of failure or possible exposure raised the issue of the ownership of their own writing. When the workshops began, members of the group had reasonably strong professional relationships with one another, but they still found it difficult to share their personal and expressive writing and commented that they were unused to engaging in such writing for themselves. Despite the supportive space, their growing friendships and professional expertise, they still found it difficult to speak about their writing and to listen to one another's work. They also felt unsure how to respond appropriately to each other. As one colleague commented, *I was glad we just shared in pairs or small groups, gradually I felt less threatened and have come to realise the value of others' comments, I liked it best when we wrote collaboratively.*

I didn't really make much effort in our early workshops, I treated the whole thing flippantly and distanced myself from it. Once I realised you weren't going to judge our work or make it public, then I felt safer and let myself get involved in my writing – I began to write for myself. In fact this teacher, Tracey, after several weeks of not sharing her work and avoiding becoming involved, was so pleased with her poem on pottery, see below, that she read it aloud to the group and gave her permission for us to include it in this text. None of the group knew that Tracey went to weekly pottery classes or that she gained considerable pleasure from this artistic endeavour.

Pottery

A pot
Smooth, shiny,
Thrown, stroked
And shaped as thought
A vessel for my therapy.
   Tracey

Yet the time of writing together remained a challenging space, it was a risk to share our writing selves and our identities, since we were in some senses facing our subjectivity in the company of others. The evaluative judgements of others and the sense of the personal were discussed at length and, as a consequence, the group decided that children's emotional security and right to privacy needed to be reconsidered, particularly when writing in the expressive or poetic mode (Britton, 1993). They worked to ensure children's ownership of their writing journals was respected and encouraged youngsters to adopt the practice of paper-clipping private pages together, and when some children chose not to share their work with their teachers this was honoured. Another connecting thread which emerged from the unsettling tension of sharing our writing was the need to more consciously create a secure writing environment in the classroom. This was achieved in various ways, including open class discussions, reducing the practice of grading writing and by establishing a more collegial working atmosphere with many more collaborative writing opportunities. Children's work was celebrated and critiqued by both the young authors and their peers, and the teachers began to put their own work on the overhead projector and sought advice and feedback from the children, reflecting a real concern to reshape or sharpen their writing. They also invited their classes to offer support to one another and established response partnerships to facilitate this. Reflection time, a trusting ethos and conversations of a constructive yet evaluative nature, were seen to be crucial in the growing confidence of us all as writers, regardless of age or experience.

Authentically modelling writing

The questionnaire indicated that the majority of the teachers rarely modelled writing spontaneously in front of the children, most assiduously prepared such writing at home and pretended to be thinking out loud in front of the children as they wrote, or wrote the opening paragraph of their story at home and allowed themselves to continue this composition 'authentically' in school. This practice of preparing writing was particularly marked with less confident teachers of writing, who expressed low self-esteem as writers, and who were understandably concerned about their ability to model specific literary features without a previously prepared version. Poetry was perceived as the hardest form of writing to model and was always pre-written at home by teachers of the older classes prior to classroom modelling, reflecting an uncertainty which Luce-Kapler *et al.* (2001) also found in work with ITE students. Yet the demand to create similes or metaphors with immediacy or invent a tanka or cinquain to order is exactly what these teachers were expecting of their children, and in effect they were seizing the opportunity to incubate and stretch their own ideas, but were not offering their novice writers the same experience. The teachers felt most assured in modelling non-fiction writing, which they perceived was due to their knowledge of the features of procedural or persuasive texts, for example. Such knowledge gave them the security and the confidence to verbalise the process, but they were not as comfortable with writing poetry and narrative.

Yet young learners need to be apprenticed to real writers, who are genuinely thinking through the process as they write and are tentatively and authentically exploring ways of conveying their emerging argument or narrative. As teachers, we need to demonstrate to the class that writing is a problem-solving activity (Bereiter and Scardamalia, 1987), a process of thinking and evaluating which involves us in conversations with ourselves. Modelled writing should involve us in sharing our own creative processes and may expose our false starts, blank spots, and uncertainties. Through this process, we will be reflecting upon the purpose of writing and showing that we also use it to remember, to reflect and organise our thoughts, to communicate, to make meaning and to understand our world. Teachers need to 'model the creative process for pupils with all the attendant risk taking this involves' (OfSTED, 2003: 8), since when our children see how we struggle, structure, think, re-read, revise and edit as we write, they are supported in their writing. Calkins asserts that 'our drafts are not the cutting edge – the growing edge – of writing, but the results of it', and suggests that the cutting edge of writing is the reflective interaction between the writer and the developing text (Calkins, 1986: 20).

Gradually, as their experience of writing at their own level and their assurance grew, the teachers began to reflect upon their ideas and demonstrated the important principle of writing to learn, which involves writing, rewriting and restructuring as meaning evolves and understanding develops. Writing is not a linear process, as the use of the word processor and whiteboard overtly indicate, for as we write we shift ideas around within our emerging text, juxtaposing parts and inserting new ideas to strengthen the organisation of the whole. In using writing to reflect upon our thinking, we become authors and increase our control and choice over our writing.

Re-reading during writing

The very act of writing enables us as writers to figure out what we know and demonstrates that the process of putting pen to paper involves considerable re-reading at the point of composition. Writers deserve to be introduced to this interactive process and to be taught to re-read and sub-vocalise as they compose, since such monitoring allows them to hear the tunes and rhythms of their work and increases their syntactic awareness. All writers need to become alert to their inner voice evoking their words, meanings and feelings. As one teacher observed, *I need to re-read as I write to feel where my voice is going* and another noted, *I find re-reading a vital strategy, not just for drafting, but in order to hear my own voice, and reinforce my angle.* This compelling dialogic process to which many of the teachers referred, is insightfully described by Murray.

> The self speaks, the other self listens and responds. The self proposes, the other self considers. The self makes, the other self evaluates. The two selves collaborate: a problem is spotted, discussed, defined; solutions are proposed, rejected, suggested, attempted, tested, discarded, accepted.
>
> (Murray, 1982: 165)

The teachers in the project were aware that they did not profile this in class. As Kaufer *et al.* (1986) have shown, when writers are composing with pen and paper, they often review the first part of their sentence before composing the rest. The teachers' awareness of constantly reading back and forth through their own writing as they composed was perhaps heightened by writing more regularly and reflexively at their own level. They were sometimes aware of asking themselves questions as they wrote, and some began to share these questions with their classes.

- What am I trying to say?
- How does it sound?
- Why did I choose ...?
- What do I want say/do next?
- How might I convey that?
- How else could I do so?
- What will my reader be thinking or feeling as they read this?

Repeated re-reading as a piece of writing unfolds can help direct and redirect the author's focus, as well as underline the meanings they are trying to convey and it should, we believe, be recognised as a relevant and teachable skill. In this way, writers become readers and then writers again, as they move back and forth in the compositional process, editing and reshaping and reflecting upon the sounds, tunes and visuals their words convey. In many of the project focus classrooms, teachers challenged themselves to model this process authentically, shifting from one stance to another and more spontaneously voicing out loud the plethora of options available to them. They declared their doubts and demonstrated to the children the complex dialogic nature of writing. In the process, they were explicitly showing the children that re-reading one's writing and listening to one's voice has a significant role to play in shaping writing. They were also helping the young authors develop a shared understanding of the craft of writing.

> When closely observed, students appear to write by shuttling back and forth from their sense of what they wanted to say to the words on the page, and back to address what is available within them.
> (Perl and Egendorf, 1979: 124 quoted in Britton, 1982)

This shuttling is a critical and ongoing skill and not one to be left to the end of the compositional process. As the teachers found, in learning to listen to our voices emerging off the page we get a feel for the potency of our own particular message and develop a more critical and self-evaluative ear. As writers, re-reading our writing at the point of production can increase our conscious control over the process, enable us to hear the tunes and patterns of our text and help us avoid the writing spiralling out of control. It can also help us exercise our authorship more fully. In the classroom the teachers began to profile this practice, share their insights, and re-read their children's drafts back to them, since as Barrs and Cork (2001) have shown this can reveal the texture of the writing and heighten the learners' awareness of their voice in action. Through profiling the reflexive and emergent nature of writing and the need to re-read and reflect in order to hear one's authorial voice, these teachers moved forward themselves as writers and tried to help their young writers discover what they were trying to say, enabling them to focus on different ways of communicating their meaning.

Autonomy and involvement

In a third of the teachers' writing workshops, the content and the genre of the writing undertaken was imposed, whilst in the remaining sessions support was offered, but the teachers' exercised their own choices. Their commentaries, both on individual pieces of writing and on the process of writing, consistently raised the issue of choice. They clearly valued this autonomy, finding our 'imposition' both inhibiting and infuriating. At the onset of the research, as reported in Chapter 4, the children too had expressed strong views about autonomy in writing, particularly those aged 7–11 years (Grainger et al., 2002). Writing journals had subsequently been established for them and more choice was gradually offered in other writing

Figure 9.1 My Bob's a Heart-throb 1

contexts too, but it wasn't until their teachers were involved themselves as writers, some twelve months later, that this desire for agency and personal choice was experienced first hand. As one of them commented, *the supported choice – but freedom to do as I wanted was critical for me – even now I don't give enough choice.*

The teachers' personal involvement was evident in the many opportunities seized to reflect upon themselves, their families and friends, for example, after an animated sharing of the picture book *Clarice Bean that's Me* by Lauren Child, one teacher, Angela, decided to make a book about her husband, see Figures 9.1 and 9.2. *My Bob's a Heart-throb* was a labour of love, 16 pages long, full colour and in the magazine style of Clarice Bean, it was an opportunity to reflect upon their relationship and celebrate 36 years of marriage. *If you'd said we had to write one I wouldn't have wanted to,*

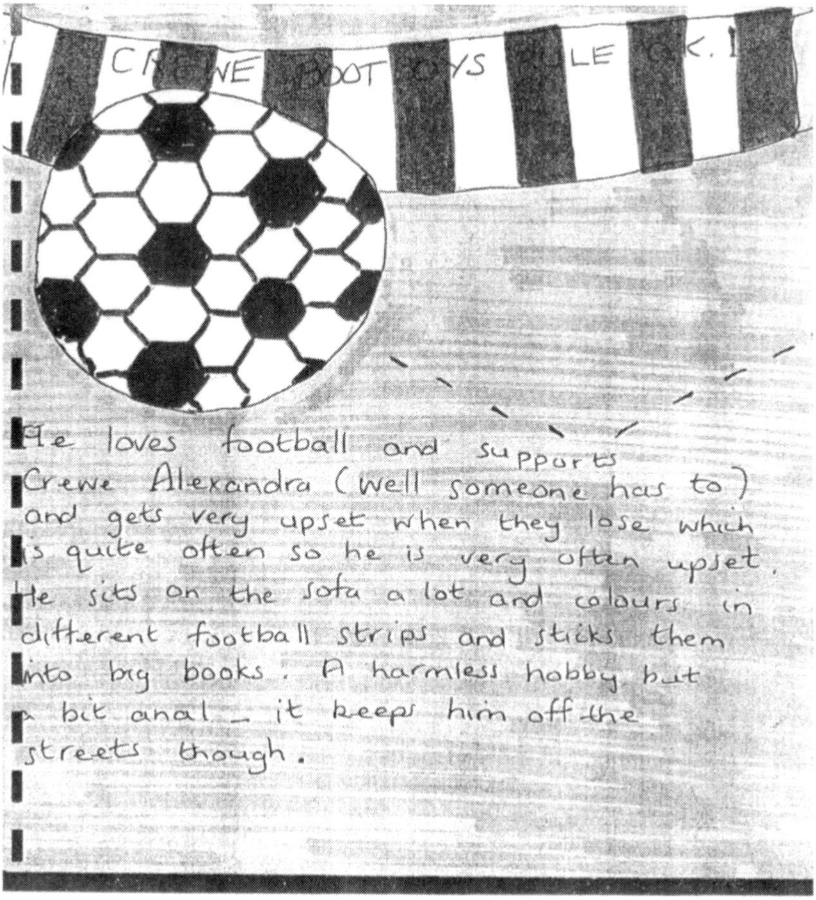

Figure 9.2 My Bob's a Heart-throb 2

but given the chance to do my own thing, I found I was free and somehow more determined, Angela commented. The space to shape her own writing made a marked impact on this professional, who invested considerable time and energy in producing this book which she shared with her class, some of whom in turn were inspired to create their own autobiographical/ biographical picture books. She wrote with voice and verve, energy and creativity, and created full colour illustrated double page spreads about Bob's favourite hobbies and habits, his dreams and desires and her love for him. Her voice is her own, ironic, engaged and humorous but is also influenced by the post-modern style of Lauren Child. She employs amusing asides, diagrams and visuals, satire, photo montage effects and a real sense of the zany.

Figure 9.3 'Did my Grandad go to war?' says Clarice Bean I

Understandably Angela's class were impressed and in Figures 9.3 and 9.4 extracts from Sarah's picture book are shown; this was entitled *Did my Grandad go to War? says Clarice Bean*. It effectively combines two of Lauren Child's key characters with young Sarah's own knowledge of her great-

Figure 9.4 'Did my Grandad go to war?' says Clarice Bean 2

grandfather's involvement in the war. This 9-year-old took great delight in sharing her work with her teacher and friends; she too has borrowed and inhabited Lauren Child's irrepressible voice, her modes and manners of telling, but Sarah has found her own voice too, with hilarious asides such as *Harry says his dad has declared a war over money* and *Miss Wilberton shaves her legs*. Her artistically involved teacher had modelled the production of such a text very fully and had undertaken half a term's work with the class on the work of this contemporary author, so Sarah was prompted to join her and create her own book deliciously linked to her own life and amusingly told in words and images.

In re-reading their writing and reflecting upon the writing workshops, many of the teachers observed that the writing prompts (which included for example, retold tales, object stories and old-fashioned sweets), and the discursive atmosphere and sense of collegiality in the sessions enabled them to make connections, revisit memories and reflect upon their lives. Several commented that they often chose first person writing as they found this easier and more satisfying. This work began to develop their awareness of the relationship between the writing and their sense of self and subjectivity.

> *I don't think much of what I wrote today, but that doesn't matter – what does is that it has reminded me of my dad – his love of walnut whips, [a fondant chocolate confection] and his love of me.*

> *I feel I've met myself again through these writing sessions, I hadn't realised writing was so much about oneself, even when I'm writing in role I can see myself, my life, my views in the writing.*

> *I wrote all these for myself really – that was my choice I guess, although an unconscious one. The best ones are when I was retelling my life experiences. I found them most satisfying – It's like re-reading my life. Thank you.*

It would seem that some of the teachers were finding their outer voices through choosing to converse with their inner voices, they were listening to themselves and beginning to hear what they had to say. The writing workshops became for some an opportunity for time out of the rush of the curriculum and of life, a personal space, in which they could pause, reflect, question, consider and connect. The heart of writing, Moffett (1968) claims, beats deep within the subjective inner life of the writer and in a manner similar to their children, some of the teachers felt they had achieved most in their writing when they were doing something for and of themselves, something which made dynamic sense of their own lives. As they did so, they began to experience the liberating power and pleasure in writing.

Writing in role

Many of the teachers noted that the drama sessions made a considerable contribution to the quality and fluency of their writing. When they were asked to identify which piece of their writing showed the most voice and verve, the majority selected an example from one of the group's drama sessions. Several described this writing as flowing onto the paper with ease and insight. They had become so involved in the drama that the activity became spontaneous, and when the transition to writing was made it was relatively effortless since many of their ideas had already been rehearsed and reflected upon. In hearing their own and others' voices in the drama and sensing the flow of ideas, their later writing had begun to take shape in both form and content. The drama also appeared to provide a period of active contemplation, incubation and percolation in which their feelings were to the fore. *When I was in character, it just flowed onto paper. I couldn't be wrong, it was what I felt, what I believed*, commented one colleague, whilst another observed, *Putting myself in someone else's shoes and experiencing her dilemma really helped me form what I wanted to say.* The drama time may have enabled the teachers to develop their ideas and begin to hold a perspective long enough to unlock its potential. Often the writing during drama was undertaken in complete silence and a marked stillness descended upon the group, perhaps because the intensity and engagement in the drama transferred into the writing time. This may also have allowed more focused mental engagement on the writing itself. The impact of this stillness, in contrast to the active physical involvement evident in drama, deserves investigation. Perhaps a flurry of interactive artistic activity, such as drama, needs peace and quiet to be committed to paper effectively, although in contrast, the teachers also observed that the relaxed, collegial and humorous nature of some of the workshops enabled some of them to find words in comfort and in conversation.

The shape of the teachers' in-role writing seemed to emerge partly from engagement with and reflection upon the issues, and involved the dual processes of identification and transformation. There are perhaps parallels here with the 'closeness and distance – the pushing forward and pulling back, creation and criticism' that writing involves (Calkins, 1991: 91) which also links to re-reading one's writing. In drama, the teachers were operating as artists, generating and considering ideas through participating in an imaginary world. The impact of this experience enabled their thoughts to flow freely and produced passion in their prose. As one teacher noted in her journal, *I felt like the old woman and needed to write it all down quickly before the feelings went away. As I wrote, her pain seemed to ebb away. I suppose I was sharing her loss and remembering mine.* The act of composition, like any imaginative and generative process involves preparedness to take risks and to order and shape one's thinking; drama provided opportunities for both. The consequences for the classroom were clear; the teachers provided more time for the children to draft their ideas in role, enabling them to inhabit the narrative and become the characters. It is evident such insider engagement can enrich writing for all learners and create a clearer sense of voice.

Conclusion

If teachers are committed to encouraging creativity in writing and honouring their own and the children's imaginative potential, then they must develop sufficient assurance to take risks in safe and supported contexts and operate as artists in the language classroom. Teachers need to extend their own experience of creative and artistic endeavours and be prepared to step inside such contexts as learners, demonstrating their own engagement in the process and their emerging perspective as developing writers. The arts thrive on risk; on sharing the uncertainty of exploration and the satisfaction of discovery. In this way it may be possible for teachers of writing to extend their creative confidence as language artists and in the process develop a sense of ease and flexibility with written language.

> The artist's interpretation of experience is concrete; sensuous, emotional and intellectual. Yet it is not mere re-enactment either – it is a work of the creative imagination.
>
> (Britton, 1982: 21)

In interpreting their own experience both in the classroom and in the project group, the teachers were imaginatively engaged in making connections, sharing insights and evaluating their learning. They began to select powerful texts and explored their own responses to them honestly, thoughtfully and emotively. Some became storytellers, able to release themselves from the print on the page, and others took part in poetry and drama investigations, working creatively alongside their learners. In such language arts encounters, their emotional involvement and artistic engagement was evident and this appeared to replenish their spirits and renew their passion for teaching literacy. These professionals, most of whom were not literacy consultants in their schools, were given the chance to consider the complex process of writing, to engage in a range of artistic practices and to write personally and expressively, at their own level in the company of others. This opportunity to take part in the extended process of composition and reflect upon and evaluate their writing had several consequences. Some began to write diaries or kept their own writing journals; most, according to their own self-evaluations, became more positive about their writing, and seized opportunities to write in school alongside their children in different contexts, seeking further insights and opening themselves to new learning. In the final questionnaire and through discussion, many indicated that they were more aware of the relationship between writing, reflection and identity and had begun to perceive writing as a means of conveying and constructing meaning both in their own lives and the lives of the children. Such opportunities need to be built into both initial teacher education and in-service, so teachers can learn more about themselves, about writing and about the art of teaching writing in communities of adult writers. One year after the We're Writers project, the focus group is still meeting regularly; the teachers wanted to explore creative practice in cross-curricular contexts and have published various accounts of their work in professional magazines (Lambith *et al.*, 2004; Coles *et al.*, 2004). We hope this is only the beginning and in our last chapter we explore the nature of these and other creative teachers of writing.

Chapter 10

Creative teachers of writing

Creativity in children's writing does not occur independently of the skills, talents, motivations, knowledge and understanding of teachers. In recent years, the imposition of a prescriptive curriculum and tightly defined assessment system has arguably challenged professional autonomy, questioned teacher competence and reduced creativity (Burgess *et al.*, 2002). Teachers have been prompted to request permission to use their professional expertise and to work outside the apparent scripts offered. They have not felt fully involved in shaping, controlling or managing the extensive overhaul of the literacy curriculum and as a consequence some have appeared insecure, tentative and even distanced from the enterprise of teaching writing. Others have expressed concern about the loss of spontaneity in their teaching and the lack of time for children to reflect on their reading or to write at length (Fisher, 2004). Primary professionals have found themselves facing the contradictory curricula pressures of building on children's experiences and interests and responding to the axe of accountability and imposed curricula. If teachers are to find ways forward that maintain their professional integrity, make use of their knowledge of child development and achieve high standards in writing, then the adoption of a more creative stance and the assertion of their own agency in the classroom is essential. However, as Joubert observes,

> Creative teaching is an art. One cannot teach teachers didactically how to be creative; there is no fail safe recipe or routines. Some strategies may help to promote creative thinking, but teachers need to develop a full repertoire of skills which they can adapt to different situations.
>
> (Joubert, 2001: 21)

The repertoire of creative teachers of writing is complex and develops through focused experience, engagement and reflection, as we have seen through the We're Writers research and development project. This final chapter seeks to reflect on some of the critical skills and competences demonstrated by such creative teachers of writing. These include: the development of teachers' own creativity and playfulness; the role of pleasure and passion; the power of intuition; the importance of being learner focused; the need to profile meaning and purpose in writing; the value of risk taking and the construction of creative spaces in which the imaginative potential, voice and verve of the child can be developed. We conclude by trying to summarise insights from the project and return again to the voices of the teachers as they reflect upon their personal and professional journeys. Our discussion begins, however, with a consideration of the contested autonomy of the profession and the challenge of making appropriate pedagogical choices.

Teacher autonomy

The project teachers found that if children are given choice they become more involved and open to learning about writing and, as in the Reggio model, the teachers begin to consciously work towards 'a vision of children who can think and act for themselves' (Moss, 2001: 136). Teachers too deserve to be involved, to be honoured with professional space in which they can develop their skills and expertise and in which they can become both more assured and more autonomous as professionals. Surely 'successful schools do better when the professional learning is self-guided, discretionary and intellectually challenging ...?' (Hargreaves and Goodson, 2003: x). Any curriculum that prompts its teachers to seek permission to work outside a given framework misses the opportunity for such assuredness to develop and may constrain the intuitive potential of the profession (Hanke, 2002). As one of the evaluation reports of the National Strategies in England comments, 'the most effective LEAs and schools develop the ability to stay in touch with core values and goals and to take charge of change, rather than being controlled by it' (Earl *et al.*, 2000: 86). The core values and goals of teachers and their institutions, impact on curriculum, pedagogy and practice.

> The work we do (whether as practitioners or parents or policy makers or researchers) always takes a particular perspective – and therefore choices – or judgments of value – are always being made from which flow enormous implications in terms of theory and practice.
>
> (Dahlburg *et al.*, 1999: 119)

Layers of narrative influence pedagogy, ranging from individual classroom narratives to institutional narratives and the narratives of policy and politics at both local and national levels. Understanding the discourse employed by successive governments and policy makers helps us perceive how the will of politicians has influenced the pedagogy in our schools (Nutbrown, 1998). Practitioners' lives are dominated by realms of policy initiatives that exhort them to raise standards, to meet targets, to ensure excellence and enjoyment, yet some policies may disadvantage individuals or groups of children, as in the introduction of province-wide testing where cultural bias was seen to create injustice (Campbell, 2003). The narrative layers may seem both controlling and unremitting, but creativity has the potential to put 'a stutter into powerful narratives' and offers alternative and engaging possibilities for educators and children alike (Moss and Petrie, 2002: 185). In relation to writing, the extensive use of the catch phrase 'changing practice changes minds', which was used in NLS conferences and training (e.g. Stannard, 1999) indicates the intention to create a common set of pedagogical practices, such as shared and guided reading/writing. But teachers need to understand, to engage and reflect for themselves, and 'need principles, rather than routines, in order to be (or to become) confident teachers of writing' (Bailey, 2002: 33–4). Some research has shown that teachers have felt obliged to short change their principles in their anxiety to implement the NLS and be accountable to parents (English *et al.*, 2002), and government-funded evaluations have pondered on the depth of the changes in teaching and highlighted the need to 'increase the number of teachers who are expert – teachers who are learning about learning' (Earl *et al.*, 2001). Space urgently needs to be made for professional development built around teachers' own concerns and needs and the creation of increased pedagogical flexibility.

The time to work with one another gave the teachers in the We're Writers project focus group a feeling of ownership over their own work, since this was a bottom up initiative, involving the teachers as action researchers in their own classrooms, in contrast to imposed initiatives. Whilst they were challenged by the goals they set themselves, support was available and through affective engagement, reflection, collaboration and feedback they remained motivated, interested and determined to succeed. As a means of supporting professional development, Rowan (1990) proposes a commitment strategy which seeks to develop 'innovative working arrangements that support teachers decision making and increases teachers' engagement in the tasks of teaching' (Rowan, 1990: 354, quoted in Leithwood *et al.*, 1999: 18). Through increased involvement and commitment, these practitioners began to mediate the recommendations of the NLS within the context of their own beliefs and values, which many transformed and developed over time. Some colleagues made small pedagogical changes, others re-examined the theories of learning which implicitly underpinned their practice, all were empowered to make pedagogical transitions and use the insights gained in their own classrooms to question, discuss and reframe their practice. The teachers capitalised on the opportunities which the project gave them to 'problematise their own thinking, try out new conceptual tools and change their pedagogical practice' as they learnt to 'walk on two legs' and exert power over their own practice (Dahlburg *et al.*, 1999: 139). If primary professionals are reflectively involved in analysing both their own teaching and the children's learning, they may find the courage to reconstruct the literacy curriculum in a more open and imaginative manner, and are more likely to exert their right to choose pedagogic practices which develop creativity, flexibility and autonomy. Such creative teachers, as we have tried to show, move well beyond the basic requirements of national policies and exhibit resilience in the face of adversity, as they make their own informed choices and employ their own creativity in the classroom context.

Developing our own creativity

The challenge of using one's own creativity and developing more creative practice is considerable, especially for newly trained teachers who may have experienced very varied and even narrow frames of practice. In the We're Writers work, the triangulation of committed teachers, high quality children's fiction and a range of creative opportunities combined to afford space for humour, playfulness and risk taking. Prompted by their involvement in literature, in drama and in storytelling workshops and through writing at their own level, the teachers began to care for their own creative capacity and, as the previous chapter demonstrated, they developed more flexible practice and engaged as language artists. It appears that creativity arises out of a state of friendship, for as these teachers shared their writing and learning journeys, they built closer relationships and began to take risks together. In order to promote and enrich the children's creativity in writing, they began to explore their own creative talents both in the context of teaching and outside it, and in the process many, although not all, expressed considerable pleasure and intense satisfaction as they adopted more open and innovative stances. It seemed that part of their pleasure was derived from the amplified autonomy they experienced, part from their own engagement in the creative process and part from the response of their young learners who became more actively and creatively involved as writers. The group found that through living inside texts they were energised and animated as professionals, in contrast to discussing texts from the outside or from a distance, which had tended to characterise their previous practice.

One aspect of their creative engagement was being able and willing to express themselves which involved taking risks and being observed in this process. As Wilson and Ball (1997) found, risk taking is a common characteristic of highly successful literacy teachers, not merely in relation to their artistic engagement, but also in their capacity to experiment and remain open to new ideas and strategies which may benefit the learner. The role of posing questions is also essential, although these will need to be genuinely open to possibility not merely rhetorical questions employed for the purpose of testing knowledge. Within the project focus group it appeared that the least playful teachers, as identified in action and through self-reflection, were somewhat risk adverse; they tended to perceive taking risks as abandoning standards. Others however, seized opportunities to be non-conformist and independent and prompted their children to travel this road also. One teacher, working with 10–11-year-olds leant on William Carlos William's poem 'This is just to say ...' as a model for some work and asked the class to discuss possible risqué situations or actions in their families. These were later recorded as thoughts on post-it stickers. There were risks involved in inviting 11-year-olds to create such personal, anecdotal writing which pushed at the edges of what was seen to be tolerated in their homes and schools. However, they entered into the playful spirit of this imaginative act with delight and were highly motivated, asking for more time and opportunity to write in this somehow revealing and frequently amusing style (see Figure 10.1). Some also wrote post-it stickers for their teacher, which were teasing in tone, reflecting their close relationship and shared sense of humour.

This is just to say *I have taken the beautiful fountain pen* *from your desk* *which you were probably* *going to take hom e* *Forgive me* *but the nibs* *so smooth and* *the spelling so accurate.*	*This is just to say* *I have taken a tenner* *from your purse* *which you were probably* *going to spend on mum* *Forgive me* *the puppy* *won't be much trouble.*
This is just to say *I have taken the mark book* *from your table* *which you probably* *consider school property* *Forgive me* *but I have* *a right to know.*	*This is just to say* *That I have taken your car out* *for a drive* *and which* *you were probably* *going to show off* *in front of people at the disco* *Forgive me* *but it purrs like a* *jungle cat* *and the music's to die for.*

Figure 10.1 'This is just to say ...'

Demonstrating passion

We perceive that passion and affective engagement are both critical and underrated components of a creative teacher's repertoire. We have observed that teachers can be 'emotional, passionate beings who connect with their students and fill their work and their classes with pleasure, creativity, challenge and joy' (Hargreaves, 1998: 35) and we have seen the influence of this passion in the children's attitudes and their writing. The presence of passion has been documented as a critical component of learning groups, both in the classroom (Krechevsky and Stork, 2002) and in professionals' learning contexts (Woods, 1995). In successful schools too, teacher's obsessions and passions about literacy and literature are clearly valued and given space to develop (Frater, 2001). Such teachers realise that actively teaching for creativity is a complex, demanding job which is emotionally, physically and intellectually engaging, and they know that children too need to be motivated, affectively involved and inspired in order to wrestle with words and meanings and respond to the challenge of writing.

The modernist tendency to separate emotion and reason, in order to privilege the latter, needs to be challenged, and the emotional dimension of learning must, we believe, be recognised more fully. As Robinson claims, 'creativity depends on interactions between feeling and thinking and across different disciplinary boundaries and fields of ideas' (Robinson, 2001: 200). This opportunity for interaction across the curriculum, across texts and experiences has been emphatically supported recently (e.g. Bell, 2004), and our study shows that where teachers demonstrated creativity in teaching writing, this stance permeated other aspects of their classroom practice. The teachers began to forge productive curricular links and made many more connections as they adapted the organisation of the curriculum in order to facilitate learning, engagement and creativity. They drew extensively on their expanding knowledge of children's literature to enliven enquiries and to engage their learners in fictional contexts across the curriculum. In addition, their relationships with the children developed and a more affectively engaging classroom ethos was often observed. It would seem that teachers who are conscious of the potency and pleasure of their own energised participation often feel an accompanying responsibility to engage children with themes and possibilities in which they too can become thoroughly involved.

Being learner focused

Research in the field of creativity indicates that creative teachers adopt a learner-centred focus. This involves responding to children's feelings, engaging their interests, maintaining their identity and autonomy and encouraging their capacity to reflect critically by adapting to their performance (Jeffrey and Woods, 1997). Respect for each individual learner and their creativity is of primal importance, for those teachers with the strongest relationships celebrate diversity and are, we believe, oriented towards children, their personalities and individuality. Such teachers show ontological care for the learners, give time and space for the creative and authentic voice of the child to develop and notice what is imaginatively vital in children's language, knowledge and experience. These teachers are also able to reflect upon their own creative pathways and validate children's creativity in text construction, discussing and modelling creativity in writing, as well as providing feedback and celebrating alternative ideas and contributions. They see children as creative and critical thinkers, who deserve opportunities to enrich their potential. The strength of such confidently creative teachers allows them to support children in the transformation of ideas and texts, helping them to consider their chosen direction and adapt or modify texts, perhaps moving transductively between modes of expression. As OfSTED note, 'a willingness to observe, to listen and work closely with children, to help them develop their ideas in a purposeful way is not a radically new pedagogy, but is an essential part of creative practice' (OfSTED, 2003: 5). In order to nurture children's impulse for questioning and their mental play, teachers need to build upon the assurance and ability of the young and help them recognise their personal creative potential. They also need to build 'an appropriate attitude towards imaginative activity – a sense of the excitement, respect, hope and wonder at the potential for transformative power that is involved, accompanied by a sense of delayed scepticism and distance' (NACCCE, 1999: 91). Such attitudes cannot be fostered without a deep respect for each individual and a concern for the development of the whole child.

If teachers are objectives driven and concerned primarily with results, they may inadvertently straight-jacket creativity since summative assessment is likely to detract from creative teaching, whilst formative assessment can promote it (Joubert, 2001: 27). In a study of novice and expert teachers, one of the defining features that separated the two groups was their relative ability to adapt continuously to the children's performance. 'Going beyond the script' was part of the practice of the expert teachers, who were responsive to the learners' needs, although their teaching was still framed by their overall intentions (Tochon and Munby, 1993). Deep knowledge of children as emotional human beings, with particular personalities and interests, enables teachers to use their intuitive skills effectively and develop mutual respect, as together they value and evaluate their own and others' writing.

Using our intuition

Intuitive teaching is an informed and sophisticated practice, hard to define and often unconscious, although not invisible. Claxton, for example, refers to intuition as a 'family of ways of knowing' that includes:

the ability to function fluently and flexibly in complex domains without being able to describe or theorize one's expertise; to extract intricate patterns of information that are embedded in a range of seemingly disparate experiences; to make subtle and accurate judgments based on experience without accompanying justification; to detect and extract the significance of small, incidental details of a situation that others may overlook; to take time to mull over problems in order to arrive at more insightful or creative solutions; and to apply this perceptive, ruminative, inquisitive attitude to one's own perceptions and reactions – reflection.

(Claxton, 2000: 50)

As teachers we need to trust our instincts and listen to the tunes and rhythms of the classroom, responding to the children, and accepting that at times the creative buzz of fully engaged learners may create more movement and noise than usual. On other occasions, however, the serious play of creative endeavour may evoke a quiet intensity, a concentrated calm. In using our instincts, and years of experience, we must try to listen first and listen second and let the children initiate and propose alternatives more frequently, responding reciprocally and sensitively to their ideas and interests. In a craft such as writing, intuition is indispensable, since routines and techniques will often be transcended and transformed and interpretations have to be made (Laevers, 2000). As we teach, opportunities will arise to use our intuition and move away from the security of the known as we are diverted by a child's idea or an imaginary situation. Creative teachers of writing know that with our long-term intentions held firmly in mind, we can allow the children to take the initiative and lead, for there are many possible routes to the same goal. The teachers in the We're Writers project who began to show most agency as professionals, found themselves involved in problem solving and problem finding in the teaching of writing, and drew on intuitive and non-conscious as well as rational and/or conscious thoughts. This relates to Schon's (1983: 239) 'non-rational intuitive artistry', which he perceives as spontaneous intuitive performance, and is shaped and developed by reflective practice. As action researchers, these teachers realised that their understanding about creativity in writing was not fixed or static; it developed over time through a variety of meaningful classroom practices and through their own engagement as writers and reflective professionals.

Profiling meaning and purpose

Research into effective teachers of literacy suggests that such effective professionals are also creative; they perceive that the creation of meaning is fundamental, focus attention first on the content of texts and on composition, and actively help children seek to make connections between text, sentence and word levels (Medwell *et al.*, 1998; Frater, 2001). These teachers place considerable emphasis on children's awareness of the purposes and functions of reading and writing, and involve them in problem solving and thinking about language for themselves rather than being given facts to learn. Work in the United States has also confirmed that exemplary professionals highlight the meaningful components in any learning process and listen to their children (Block *et al.*, 2000). The teachers in the We're Writers project certainly heard the strident voices of their youngsters, sought to respond to their views and to create a more genuinely dialogic conversation about writing and learning. In examining the multilayered practices of those schools which bridge the gap between disadvantage and gender and raise standards in writing, Frater (2003) found that such schools are flexible, confident and autonomous, with teachers who make extensive use of quality children's literature, profile meaning and are able to graft new practices onto their own. The basics tenets underpinning the teaching of writing in such successful schools are worth examining. In these institutions it appears teachers know that pleasure and involvement precede full understanding and work creatively to balance the teaching of skills, knowledge and understanding, through integrating the language modes in order to develop the independence of their learners. Such effective professionals undertake this with energy (Faust and Kieffer, 1998) and teach with flexibility and understanding to meet children's needs (Ruddel, 1997). They perceive that literacy learning and, by implication, learning about writing needs to:

- build upon the social and cultural diversity and changing needs of the children;
- be a motivating and highly interactive experience for all involved;
- be purposeful, relevant and authentic, since language is most power-fully learnt in the context of purposeful use;
- centre around and encompass a wide range of significant emotive texts;
- acknowledge and demonstrate the integration of the language modes;
- promote engagement, reflection and critical evaluation;
- involve the creation of a community of learners/writers.

Working within the demands set by national agendas and the artificial nature of educational environments, teachers need to 'invest school writing with a relevance and purpose that learners can identify with, to invoke contexts that make sense to and engage pupils' (Frater, 2001: 52) and help them find their inner voices. The work of the teachers documented in this book indicates that both relevance and purpose in writing can be found in a variety of imaginative and playful open-ended creative contexts, as well as in personal writing journals. Diverse and meaningful writing outcomes in school contexts might also include the creation of emails between friends, school and class anthologies, play scripts which are read and performed, radio broadcasts, tapes of poetry, songs and rhymes, news sheets, parent information pamphlets, school brochures reflecting the children's views, comics, letters and writing for 'real' in the context of drama.

However, writing is more than a means of self-expression and a way to communicate with others, it helps us seek and build knowledge in literacy and in cross-curricular contexts and develop understanding about ourselves and the world in which we live. In life, what writing achieves or accomplishes is frequently far more important than the correct observance of its assigned conventions, although these do contribute to the communication. Their relative value needs to be recognised, for as Smith (1982) observed, the surface structure of language is its conventions and the deep structure of language is its meaning. Technical skills can and must be taught, for 'creativity and knowledge are two sides of the same psychological coin, not opposing forces' (Boden, 2001: 102), but such skills transfer more easily if they are embedded in a meaningful framework and are employed for real outcomes. Literacy is much more than the mastery of a particular set of predefined skills and learning about language needs to encompass a more artistic orientation than the somewhat mechanically oriented focus of recent years, in which developing linguistic knowledge has taken precedence and has been seen as 'the equivalent of getting under the bonnet of the vehicle of English, and looking at the engineering to understand better how it works' (DfES, 2000: 2). We do need to give children knowledge about genres of writing and set targets which relate to punctuation and spelling, for example, but in the context of treating children as authors, as communicators and as meaning makers. So the knowledge of creative teachers of writing needs to encompass considerable subject knowledge, as well as pedagogical knowledge and an awareness of the significance of creative contexts and purpose in teaching writing.

Developing creative contexts

Creativity can be engendered by environments of possibility, packed with ideas and experience, resources, choice and time for relaxation and rumination. As Greenfield (2002) has shown, the environment for learning is of considerable significance in brain development and there is evidence that the literacy environment, physical, social and emotional, plays an important part in learning (Hall, 1988; Fox, 1993; Wray et al., 2000). Teachers' attitudes are also very influential, their perceptions of what is important are reflected not only in the literal displays and imaginative contexts for writing, but in the climate and ethos that pervades the classroom. Increasing knowledge of the conditions required for their own creative development as writers, supports teachers in fostering equally satisfying conditions in which children's creativity may grow in the collaborative culture of a writing classroom. In such climates of anticipation and expectation, in which the intrinsic relationship between reading and writing is explored both implicitly and explicitly, children as well as teachers will seize opportunities to read aloud, discovering the music of literature and the flexibility and power of their own voices also.

Teachers of writing also need to ensure there is sufficient physical space for the children to converse, challenge and negotiate meanings and possibilities together, and interpretations and representations are feasible through material exploration, play, role play, performance poetry and storytelling. Resources of various kinds also need to be made available to children, including perhaps props for storying, gel pens, percussion instruments and drawing materials. The presence of a role play area, message board, home writing display, writing table, audio-cassette recorder, computer, and reading area, for example, can all influence opportunities. Providing for conceptual space is also necessary, so that children are able to explore ideas, to experiment and communicate in secure writing environments. Young people have an enormous capacity for pushing boundaries and taking risks, and nurturing this, while offering ample opportunities to disseminate their discoveries and negotiate new possibilities, is a key feature of creative teaching. In the early years, children often spontaneously make and shape stories, re-enacting their own lives or constructing fictional problems and possibilities. Simple spaces, such as boxes for example, have for generations become beds, cars, houses, hideaways and trains and continue to do so today. The art of 'becoming', in relation to resources or children's roles, is central to composition, to the creation of what is possible. So we need to develop an irrefutable respect for play contexts: play environments, play resources, play opportunities and play time. Such outer play encourages the inner play of the imagination and develops flexibility with language and ideas.

Giving choice

In environments of possibility, which recognise the social and intentional aspects of writing, choice is critical. It is a necessary part of the writing curriculum and opportunities must be provided for children to formulate questions about their own writing and seek solutions as they write and develop their voice and verve. If we encourage children and have faith in them, they will share much of their knowledge and experience of the world with us through writing. In a class of 6–7-year-olds in the project, a teacher who was undertaking a unit of work on instructional texts involved the children in a myriad of activities: reading, listening, talking, displaying, drawing, exploring, improvising, inhabiting and performing various texts on the journey towards constructing their own in written form. Wisely,

Figure 10.2 How to look after a budgie

she allowed the children to choose their subjects and as the examples in Figures 10.2 to 10.4 indicate, their individual voices, shaped by these experiences and their different interests and expertise, shine through.

As teachers we must listen carefully to the children's different voices, their tunes and concerns and hear what they have to say, ensuring they experience the functions and purposes of writing for themselves. 'Autonomous engaged writers' have power and control over their epistemic writing and can use 'writing as a tool for a reflective search for meaning – as a way of constructing knowledge through a variety of discourses and in a range of identities' (Packwood and Messenheimer, 2003: 149).Writing can motivate and entice, tease and engage, inspire and involve, but much of it must be writing that children do for themselves, at their own pace and writing that connects to their own interests, beliefs and values. Such writing reflects the ownership, relevance, control and innovation which we have explored in this book, and which can be garnered through imaginative engagement in a variety of ways. Writing that is imposed upon children in a mechanistic way and formally assessed may prompt the learners to 'play the game called writing' and write to please the teacher. Choice is also significant in the creation of policy, as Whitehead points out in strong terms:

> The choice is clearly between allowing children's playful explorations of literacy to enrich the curriculum and their lives or allowing the blight of meaningless tasks and bits of knowledge to trivialise the educational experience.
>
> (Whitehead, 1997: 178)

Whilst some may consider this a polarisation of perspectives, we perceive that we are fortunate to have such witnesses to policy and practice to stir our consciences and upbraid our policy masters. It is also fortunate that, in projects conducted both nationally and internationally, teachers too are being supported to make choices, to tap into cultural and personal values and to construct powerful imaginative spaces for children to creatively shape texts that map, reflect and influence their lives and educational experiences (e.g. Barrs and Cork, 2001; Graham 2003; Bearne *et al.*, 2004; Fang *et al.*, 2004). In the end the challenge remains with us as teachers, both individually and collectively, to research and reflect upon our experience, considering how we can make the most difference to young meaning makers, communicating in whatever mode they choose.

We're Writers: listening to others' voices

Creativity, Moss (2001) suggests, is fostered by a pedagogy of relationships which emerges in response to a pedagogy of listening to oneself and others.

How to ride a bke without stabilisers

what you need.
a helmit
and a bike
and a mummy

1. Get on the bike.

2. Get your mummy.

3. Get your mummy to hold to you.

4. Start to Pedal.

5. put your hands on the handbars.

Figure 10.3 How to ride without stabilisers

Figure 10.4 How to look after a baby

The We're Writers research and development project involved considerable talking and listening to teachers and children, and through it strong relationships were built which supported the gradual transformation of practice and led to new understanding. At the outset, the young people showed little voice and verve in their writing, had no choice over content or form, few chances to create social or personal references, and little opportunity to borrow from any but the approved voices of others. Their attitudes towards writing, whilst varied, were generally of concern, particularly those that expressed boredom, disinterest and disaffection. The voices of their teachers too were muted, and seemed to indicate that as professionals, they felt compromised, quietened, even cornered. At this time, the loudest noises came from the success criteria relating to the national assessment tests. However, when the children's surveys were analysed and their views about writing made known, the teachers stepped forward, tentatively acknowledged their concerns and worked tirelessly together to transform the status quo and find more creatively engaging ways of working that might change the children's attitudes, engage and motivate them and develop their voice and verve in writing.

Over the two years of the project, the teachers moved beyond imitation towards innovation and adopted more flexible and less restrictive practices; they took time to experiment, to talk, to learn and to reflect on their own development as creative professionals. The model of professional development adopted involved considerable collaboration, challenge and reflection, particularly for the project focus group members, but also for the schools who selected various areas of literacy to develop. For example, some explored the relationship between drama and writing, others set up story boxes and fiction based role play areas, still others provided support for story writing through extensive experience of storytelling and visiting artists also became involved. All the schools established writing journals in response to the children's request for increased autonomy and raised the profile of talk in their everyday practice. Many initially found the implicit pressure to produce constant written evidence of the children's learning constrained them, but as their assurance grew and their ability to tolerate the uncertainty of more playful practice developed, they relaxed and acknowledged the importance of long-term goals alongside shorter-term objectives. The teachers needed time for collaborative planning, for reflection upon practice, they learnt much from documenting their growing understanding of children's creative texts, for as the Stockholm Project demonstrated, 'documentation has the potential to reveal the embodied character of knowledge construction and as such functions as an emancipatory practice' (Dahlburg et al., 1999: 156). It was clear that through their own creative involvement and reflection and through the opportunities for dialogue, the teachers transformed their practice and re-examined their principles. The experiential and discursive opportunities in which they engaged, unleashed their energy, talent and creative capacity and in their view and ours they became more committed and more involved, personally and professionally in teaching writing.

The head teachers, who were involved at all stages, talked about the project as a 'watershed' in the development of their teachers and observed that a more questioning and critical stance had been adopted in classrooms and staff rooms. New documents delivered to the schools began to be questioned and problematised, local NLS consultants were challenged, new insights were defended, vigorous debates were held and some staff voices *'were heard for the first time in years'*. The teachers expectations of writing and literacy in general were raised and they not only expected more from the children, but also demanded more of themselves. In embracing the complexity of creativity and writing, these teachers were no longer prepared to accept others' perspectives and articulated their views with increased assurance. As professionals they began to voice their views in opposition to local discourses which they perceived limited the children's experiences and engagement and talked about trusting themselves more and planning creative spaces; one voiced the view that *unless you plan the opportunities they might not happen – you have to plan spaces for them.* The issue of trust was a common theme: *I've started to give more space to the children, I trust them now and go with the flow ... perhaps I trust myself more too* and *Before I did as I was told, now I feel I can trust myself more, I don't accept everything, I think about it and then decide, I have seen for myself how creative practice frees my children – they want to write – you can't stop them.*

Throughout the project, we prompted the teachers in the focus group to express themselves through their stories as a means of placing themselves and raising questions rather than answering them, reflecting openness not closure, and, as they reflected on the changing nature of the narratives of their own development, they began to critically evaluate the discourse around literacy and make more informed choices. We encouraged them to listen to their own voices and those of each other, to share their insights and the children's work. So used were they to listening to the voices of others: to politicians, advisers, inspectors and head teachers, that honouring their own perspectives took time to develop. The narratives and voices of these educators, as they engaged in dialogue with research and policy, with each other and with the children, revealed over time the adoption of more creative stances, for example, *I feel I have become more creative with ways to approach writing now and I see it differently, more holistically perhaps* and *I feel rejuvenated and inspired, the children have taught me so much, I've been astounded by their work, writing I would not have thought possible.* As their understanding about the creative potential for transformation and transduction in writing grew and their conception of composition expanded, they experienced a sense of liberation from perceived constraints and became distinctly more willing and able to value, promote and describe creativity in writing. *The children's enjoyment has fuelled my enthusiasm to take risks and try new things – I now encourage their originality and celebrate ideas in writing much more* and *I read what they've written first and then consider how they wrote it, that's a complete reversal for me* as well as *I feel I've learnt to play, to see things differently, to value difference.*

The bank of evidence we accumulated, indicated the growth of a group of enthusiastic and talented teachers and the development of more positively engaged young writers. The final sharing conference was led by these extended professionals who ran workshops for the consortia and shared their undoubted expertise and creative capacity. They appeared to have several attributes in common, which we tentatively share, acknowledging that the picture is a complex one and that each individual adopted a unique combination of these. However, on the basis of this work we believe creative teachers of writing are:

- learner focused and responsive to the children and their interests;
- artistically and playfully involved in the extended process of composition;
- able to develop creative contexts and affectively involving spaces for writing;
- open, flexible, passionate and intuitive;
- conscious risks takers;
- writers themselves;
- aware of the importance of meaning, purpose and agency in writing;
- knowledgeable, but with a questioning stance;
- independent individuals who demonstrate a degree of autonomy and value this in others.

Postscript
Engaging voices

The research and development project We're Writers documented and analysed in this book represented a fascinating journey of recognition and discovery. Through revisiting previously dormant knowledge and engaging reflectively with teachers we developed new insights about creativity and writing and found our understandings variously confirmed, challenged and transformed. In this postscript we share our evolving understanding and examine an emerging theory-in-practice, an exchange between theory and practice: 'praxis' (Freire, 1985) which may enable creativity and writing to be thoughtfully and theoretically connected in the classroom. Implicitly, elements of this theory underpinned the research from the outset, but as we took part and watched teachers grow as engaged and empowered professionals, our thinking has developed more fully through action, incubation and reflection. We have come to realise the significance of active, experiential learning, and children's affective and creative involvement in writing, and have in the process begun to explore the relationship between inner and outer activity, building upon Bruner's two landscapes: of action and consciousness (Bruner, 1986: 14). The two main strands of this theory focus on learning and pedagogy and both in different ways pivot around the complex concepts of playfulness and engagement. Children talk their way forwards in generative and playful contexts and find their voices through creative engagement and considered reflection. The concept of voice 'like a fingerprint, reveals identity' (Andrews, 1989: 21) and comes to represent the concept of individuality, the uniqueness of the individual writer, who draws upon their own experience, knowledge, attitudes and engagement. In the extended process of composition children can, if fully engaged, generate and share ideas, try out possibilities, reflect upon and refine their thinking and develop their creative potential as they make connections between different domains and between thought and language. This process of making connections is central to creative endeavour, as is a genuinely playful attitude, active involvement and autonomy. It is to these issues that we now turn.

Playfulness and engagement

Creativity in writing is, we perceive, characterised by a kind of passionate and playful intensity and full cognitive and affective involvement. Vygotsky (1978) refused to take the pleasure out of play and focused on the concept of playfulness acknowledging that whilst play offers freedom it is also rule-governed. The serious play of writing is also framed by rules or conventions, which are purposefully employed in the context of playful engagement. When children engage in deep play they conjure up possibilities, manipulate objects and talk, draw and create meaning, exploring both their inner and outer experience in the process. Playing with ideas in action, children also play with words and sounds and develop their creative capacity to experiment with language, interpretation and meaning. Their visual and bodily play and their playful exploration of multiple modes of communication enriches this capacity. Such playfulness enables learners to disrupt or question the status quo, improvise within it and develop a new consciousness of the creative journey in the process. Motivated by their own knowledge and interests, and supported by the space and scope offered for exploration, children often travel further in play and in such contexts are 'a head taller than themselves' (Vygotsky, 1978), since in playful situations they extend boundaries and step into uncharted waters with engagement, interest and motivation. Such creative play is paradoxically serious and arises out of interactions with others, with ideas and experience set within a generative, problem-solving and imaginatively involving context.

The teacher's initial invitation to engage, and the sensitive interventions, challenges and constraints created for the children to overcome, act as scaffolds for learning and create space in which they can grow as writers. Young people's involvement promotes the examination of issues from different angles, and encourages them to listen to alternative voices and express their own thoughts and feelings. Their affective engagement in this 'third area', as Winnicott (1974) calls the deep play of childhood, prompts an openness to learning upon which teachers need to capitalise. Through developing confidence and ease in playful and creative contexts, children learn to take risks with ideas, words and images, which supports their ideational fluency and enables them to make divergent connections and solve problems collaboratively. Playfulness has a particularly significant role in the compositional process. Perhaps this role has not been fully recognised or consciously developed in recent years, yet it is at the heart of developing creativity in the classroom. Returning to Gurevitch (2000), we perceive that the poetic seriousness of the child at play needs to be given space, time and support to develop in order to help children write with voice and verve.

Textual play

Creativity in writing cannot be demanded or required, but it can be nurtured by steeping children in powerful literature and other texts and developing creative and exploratory contexts in which ideas are represented in a variety of ways and writing is purposeful. In such contexts, the desire to mean, to make, to understand and to write is fostered. Well told stories in books, films, live performances or other forms, which are both evocative and emotionally engaging, can make a real contribution to children's involvement, to their response and to their writing. The young play with the possibilities of texts that they have met and when given the chance they make full use of the visual, oral, physical and written dimensions of such texts. Composing can begin in any mode of meaning making and the exploration too will often encompass a variety of modes, with the eventual poems, parodies or persuasive arguments being captured, enriched, preserved, and bottled towards the end of the writing process. This process is often physically active and may take the form of the manipulation of images, gestures, body postures and objects, as well as spoken and written words. As learners travel towards new meanings, they are likely to change courses, adapt to new ideas, build alternative imagined contexts and explore constraints and possibilities, perhaps committing extracts of their journey onto page or screen in the process. Through creating and crafting physically, visually and orally, children move through the extended process of textual composition multimodally, representing and communicating ideas in different modes and leaning on what they know. In supporting and developing children's playful tendencies, teachers need to encourage them to explore the potential of different modes of communication and draw on the modes that best suit their intentions. This enables them to connect their own 'school of knowing' with the 'school of expressing' (Malaguzzi, 1998). Children can and do integrate their knowledge of text construction and design with their knowledge and experience of integrated technologies and narrative, and playfully use words, images and their own bodies to help them think and write. In their poetic compositions for example, they may be involved in finding words to fit the rhythm and beat evident in their physical creations and may fine tune their meanings as their choral refrains repeat and echo. In moving, tapping, dancing or singing poetry into existence, children are actively involved in creating and crafting their verse which may be further reshaped through conversation and reflection. If their poem is also performed, children may select visuals to screen on the interactive whiteboard as a backdrop to their performance, thus making the text even more multimodal in texture.

Autonomy as writers and learners

As already noted, mosaics of activities play a role in the extended process of composition, and as children interact, negotiate and experiment with possibilities, they move forward in their understanding, increase their volition and involvement as writers and make more of their own decisions. This is the real world of writing – a world where writing is employed as a tool for thinking and learning and is seen as 'an instrument not so much for solving problems as finding them' (Bruner, 2002: 15). Through experiencing and experimenting with language in use, the deep roots of writing are nourished and real reasons to write surface and grow. When children experience the potential power of writing and fully engage with issues, both imagined and real, they invest more of themselves in the process and direct more of their own learning journeys. In open-ended contexts, control is likely to be devolved, at least in part, to children and they are more likely to adapt and extend activities in unexpected ways, adopt different perspectives and construct their own tasks. In this way innovation and creativity are facilitated. Self-directed learning and the agency of the individual must be consciously encouraged, reflected upon and celebrated in order to foster creativity in writing. In writing journals for example, children often choose to write about their own lives and interests, and choice needs to be woven into other activities as well. Through providing more freedom, and framing 'challenges where there is no clear cut solution and in which pupils can exert individual and group ownership' (OfSTED, 2003: 9), teachers encourage authorial involvement in writing. In sharing their chosen writing with one another, children reveal something of themselves as young people, with a growing sense of self and identity and particular passions and desires. They may choose to write from the heart, share personal perspectives and inner concerns or may reflect upon their outer passions or interests. Writing 'from the inside' out also encourages the development of critical insight and can increase children's understanding about the interpersonal and ideational functions of writing, as well as reflect their ownership and control.

Regular space to make choices in writing, whether these are content, form or audience led, enables children to write *for* themselves and *of* themselves and to make connections which can affirm their social and individual existences providing both purpose and direction. If writers are given a range of authorial choices and are led towards taking increased responsibility for their writing then, perceived as experts in some areas, they can develop their preferences and extend their independence. Real choice in writing enables children to exercise their volition and agency as authors and encourages the development of voice and verve. Instead of playing the adult 'game called writing', framed by tests and targets, children should be encouraged to voice their views and interests and negotiate a writing curriculum that has genuine relevance to them. Such a curriculum would responsibly introduce a variety of genres and considerable knowledge about language, but would also ensure that the growing independence, autonomy and uniqueness of young writers is respected and developed.

Talk and drama integrating inner and outer experience

Through the imaginative use of talk and by bringing texts to life in a variety of ways, children try out, absorb and transform others' voices and begin to trust and stretch their own, this fosters the creative and aesthetic voice of the child (Bakhtin, 1986). In the extended process of composition, children use sustained talk opportunities to voice their views, express their feelings and talk their way forward; they create and transform their experience through imaginative engagement. In such contexts, talk is used to reconstruct events and reflect upon experience, share ideas and generate new understandings. The complex transformative nature of literacy is evident in the context of storytelling for example, for children initially imitate and lean on known tales, and gradually over time move to innovate and invent their own. In doing so, they internalise the form and structure of these narratives. The fluency and ease which resonates through their written tales provides both pace and shape to their texts, and emerges from the lived experience of telling, responding to an audience and feeling the form and tenor of the texts. The outer play of such textual encounters encourages children to travel inwards and fosters the inner play of the imagination, developing their flexibility with language, ideas and images.

Enticing and inviting children into imaginary worlds and problem-oriented activities enables them to cultivate, generate and incubate ideas. Children need time to explore, inhabit and reflect in a genuinely open manner, to follow through a train of thought and pursue and extend their ideas as well as critique them. This enables them to capture, shape and consider what it is that they want to say. This process of developing ideas deserves further attention, since what children are given the opportunity to do, say, make, co-construct and retell provides the frame for the development of their written texts. Layers of talk manifest themselves in creative contexts, and as children's emotive engagement deepens through interaction and empathetic involvement, their imaginations reverberate. Ricoeur (1978) describes this as a radiating process, reanimating earlier experiences and awakening slumbering memories. In such 'transitional spaces' (Winnicot, 1974) children move between their own lives and those of others – between the inner and outer landscapes to which Bruner refers.

In the context of drama, as children oscillate between engagement and reflection, they create connections between their inner and outer experience and develop empathy, that relational consciousness which will support them as writers. The active nature of the fictional frame prompts them to search within themselves and make resonant and reciprocal links and insights in order to take themselves and the imaginary situation forwards. The complexity of real-time living is reflected in the imaginary world of drama, where children 'think within the dilemma instead of talking about the dilemma' (Heathcote, 1980). In writing in role and evoking a sense of a character's perspective, children find themselves taking actions and trying out alternative voices and stances. In both experiencing and narrating a fictional first-person perspective in drama, they temporarily inhabit the thought processes of others and may begin to see and feel the world differently. This enables them to adopt a writer's perspective, writing of 'themselves' yet in role as others. The interplay between children's actions and intentions, between the inner and outer experience of living is integrated through imaginative talk and drama which can both motivate and raise standards in writing.

Creative spaces inhabited by divergent voices

Environments of mutual respect and openness, built on the diverse interests, languages, cultures and individualities of the children play a potent role in developing creativity in writing. If teachers use their intuition, experience and imaginative capacity, they can forge creative spaces and interact with children in transformative and transductive practices in order to generate authentic writing opportunities. Creativity flourishes in open and purposeful environments in which both teachers and children share their passions and personalities and where high levels of respect and support are combined with high expectations. In such environments of possibility, space to make choices, to talk and listen, and space to imagine and play with ideas and materials is consciously created. In making meanings in these spaces, children use 'what is to hand' (Kress, 1997). Influenced by their interactions, experiences and the resources available, their representations will also be shaped by the approval and encouragement received. In such open environments it is possible for the learners to seize the initiative and find their own way forwards.

Children deserve to have their individuality and uniqueness fostered, and need space to be themselves in the classroom, as well as the conceptual space to think, talk, enact, improvise, move, feel, create, craft and forge their ideas in collaboration with one another. They also need to feel some degree of ownership of this learning space, both physical and intellectual, in order to be able to shape it for themselves and try out their voices in the speech and writing that forms part of it. In this landscape of possibilities, children should not feel confined, but supported in expressing themselves in a variety of ways, in developing alternative ideas and taking oppositional stances. Through inhabiting the space actively and creatively they can find their voices. Sometimes in such spaces, children will experience paradox, ambiguity and indeterminacy, but the boundaries of a secure writing environment will help to sustain them. In writing contexts in which the teacher invites the learners to journey towards writing, to engage, respond, imagine and investigate texts through a process of deep immersion, playful investigation and considered reflection, then the social and intellectual environment in the classroom justifies recognition as a kind of 'third teacher' (Edwards *et al.*, 1998) that also facilitates the development of creativity in writing.

The principle of catering for and celebrating diversity is a key element of creative practice in such environments, since through valuing creativity and openness, diversity and difference, teachers increase children's awareness of the conviction, individuality and authenticity which their voices reflect. The playful stance of the teachers is closely associated with a flexible and creative pedagogical style that is open to children's ideas and questions, comments and contributions and recognises the importance of diversity in all its forms. If creative behaviour is reinforced, and explicit praise alongside focused evaluative feedback is offered, then children can learn about creativity and develop their potential as creative learners. Knowledge about creativity is critical and a language to describe creative endeavour: the generation of ideas, the asking of questions, the making of connections and combinations needs to be developed. In celebrating the unexpected, the playful and persistent, and modelling the evaluation of ideas and actions, creative teachers of writing construct a positive disposition towards creativity in the young, and develop their capacity to think and learn for themselves. In recognising the diverse voices on which children draw and the literacy capital which they bring to school, teachers enable young writers to connect the literacies of home and school and make more use of their popular text experience and their inner affective existence. This increases the salience and relevance of writing and motivates their engagement in the process of composition.

The integration of teaching and learning

Since education requires full participation and involvement, enticing invitations to engage and reflect need to be offered to children, prompting active learning and enabling them to employ understanding from their lives, from texts and from inner and outer experiences of living. By taking a full part and dwelling in different worlds of possibility with the children, teachers can also nurture their own creative development and take risks as they too learn through exploring, engaging and reflecting upon ideas and issues. As learners in their classrooms, teachers open up their own potential and extend this through joint imaginative activity and interaction. In adopting more flexible and playful approaches, they are in a position to 'possibility think' (Craft, 2000) alongside children and model the generative and evaluative processes of creativity in writing from inside. Prentice describes such creative teachers who, he perceives, display cultural curiosity, he notes that they,

> continue to be self-motivated learners, who value the creative dimensions of their own lives and understand how creative connections can be made between their personal responses to experience and their teaching.

> (Prentice, 2000: 155)

Their creative orientation supports collaborative exploration in the classroom and enables them to show that they are learners, artists and writers, who are also trying to find the words or visuals to convey their message, thoughts and ideas. As both participants and spectators in the process of meaning construction (Harding, 1964), creative teachers genuinely and personally engage affectively, intellectually, aesthetically and ethically.

Together, teachers and children can find intriguing and profitable ways forward, as they experience the electricity of the unknown and learn to lean on themselves and on each other. Teaching and learning combine here as the teacher leads but encourages the children to take the initiative and direct more of the learning journey. Clear long-term aims will be known and consciously travelled towards, but these need not determine every step taken, for whilst a route map may be outlined, the route travelled will depend on the children's interests, desires and questions. So, clear about their destination, creative teachers will venture into unknown territory with children, listening to them, observing their interactions and offering options and challenges as they play their way forwards. Writing opportunities may be seized as they surface and imaginatively framed in support of a long-term goal. Sensitive interventions, challenges and constraints may be introduced to problematise the learning situation which will increase the children's sense of commitment and energise and invigorate their voices. The critical pedagogical principle of such creative contexts is that the teacher leads by following, creating flexible route maps with the class which foster autonomy, volition and innovation. This active learning journey will include periods of play, considerable engagement and reflection and time for focused writing. The reciprocity experienced through travelling together on such creative journeys offers satisfaction for both parties, building as it does on genuinely shared experience, trust and full affective involvement.

If teachers value their creative capacity as individuals and professionals and adopt a playful and informed mindset, they can learn to teach writing more creatively and support the development of voice and verve in the classroom. The generation of curiosity, interest, pleasure and excitement are significant features of a community of writers and a genuine desire to take part, to understand and to relate writing to life is important. To develop creativity in writing, children do need a rich diet of reading and reflection, but perhaps more importantly they need to be actively engaged in their own learning, taking a full part in open-ended and imaginative contexts in which they can make connections, enrich their knowledge about language and develop their autonomy and potential. Real time and space urgently needs to be afforded for such creative endeavour, for playfulness, for possibilisation, for conversation and for critical evaluation.

Bibliography

Abbot, J. (2001) 'Battery hens or free range chickens: what kind of education for what world?', Gray Mattern Memorial Address to the European Council of International Schools Annual Conference, 16 November 2001, The Hague. Available online at: www.21learn.org (accessed on 25.10.2002).

Alexander, R. (2000) *Culture and Pedagogy*, Oxford: Blackwells.

Almond, D. (2001) 'Writing for children', Lecture given at NLS 'Writing and Creativity' Conference, 4 June, London.

Alvermann, D., Moon, J.S. and Hagood, M.C. (1999) *Popular Culture in the Classroom: Teaching and Researching Critical Media Literacy*, Newark, DE: International Reading Association.

Anderson, H., Digings, M. and Urquhart, I. (2000) 'Hourwatch: monitoring the inception of the National Literacy Strategy', *Reading*, 34(3): 113–18.

Andrews, R. (1989) 'Beyond "voice" in poetry', *English in Education*, 23(3): 21–7.

Andrews, R. (1991) *The Problem with Poetry*, Milton Keynes: Open University Press.

Auden, W.H. and Garrett, J. (1935) *The Poet's Tongue*, London: Bell.

Bailey, M. (2002) 'What does research tell us about how we should be developing written composition', in R. Fisher, G. Brooks and M. Lewis (eds) *Raising Standards in Literacy*, London: RoutledgeFalmer.

Bakhtin, M. (1981) *The Dialogic Imagination* (trans. M. Holquist and C. Emerson, ed. M. Holquist), Austin, TX: University of Texas Press.

Bakhtin, M. (1986) *Speech Genres and Other Late Essays* (trans. V.W. McGee), Austin, TX: University of Texas Press.

Barnes, J. (2001) 'Creativity and composition', in C. Philpott and C. Plummeridge (eds) *Issues in Music Teaching*, London: Routledge.

Barnes, J. (2003) 'Teachers emotions, teachers' creativity', a discussion paper, *Improving Schools*, 6(1): 39–43.

Barrs, M. (1988) 'Maps of play in', in M. Meek and C. Mills (eds) *Language and Literacy in the Primary School*, London: Falmer Press.

Barrs, M. (2000) 'The reader in the writer', *Reading Literacy and Language*, 34(2): 54–60.

Barrs, M. and Cork, V. (2001) *The Reader in the Writer: The Influence of Literature upon Writing at KS2*, London: Centre for Literacy in Primary Education.

Barthes, R. (1967) *Elements of Semiology*, London: Cape.

Barton, D. and Hamilton, M. (1998) *Local Literacies: Reading and Writing in One Community*, London: Routledge.

Bearne, E. (2002) *Making Progress in Writing*, London: RoutledgeFalmer.

Bearne, E. (2003a) 'End piece: building a professional space', in L. Graham and A. Johnson (eds) *Children's Writing Journals*, Royston: United Kingdom Literacy Association.

Bearne, E. (2003b) 'Rethinking literacy: communication, representation and text', *Reading Literacy and Language*, 37(3): 98–103.

Bearne, E. (2003c) 'Playing with possibilities: children's multidimensional texts', in E. Bearne, H. Dambey and T. Grainger (eds) *Classroom Interactions in Literacy*, Maidenhead: Open University Press.

Bearne, E. (2004) 'The write thing to say', Keynote address presented at Write Voice Conference, Kent.

Bearne, E. and Kress, G. (2001) Editorial, *Reading Literacy and Language*, 35(3): 89–93.

Bearne, E., Grainger, T. and Wolstencroft, H. (2004) *Raising Boys' Achievements in Writing*, Joint Research Project United Kingdom Literacy Association and the Primary National Strategy, Baldock: United Kingdom Literacy Association.

Bell, D. (2004) 'Richness within reach in wonder years', *Times Educational Supplement*, 19 March.

Bell, G.H. (2001) 'The place of creativity in school curricula', in J. De Groof, C. De Smet and H. Penneman (eds) *Arts Meets Law in Education*, London: Kluwer Law International.

Benton, M. (1984) 'Teaching poetry: the rhetoric and the reality', *Oxford Review of Education*, 10(3): 319–28.

Benton, M. (2000) *Studies in the Spectator Role: Literature, Painting And Pedagogy*, London: RoutledgeFalmer.

Benton, M. and Fox, R. (1985) *Teaching Literature 9–14*, Oxford: Oxford University Press.

Bereiter, C. and Scardamalia, M. (1987) *The Psychology of Written Communication*, Hillsdale, NJ: Lawrence Erlbaum.

Bernstein, B. (1996) *Pedagogy, Symbolic Control and Identity: Theory, Research and Critique*, Lanham, MD: Rowan & Littlefield.

Black, P., Harrison, C., Lee, C., Marshall, B. and William, D. (2002) *Working Inside the Black Box: Assessment for Learning in the Classroom*, London: Department of Education and Professional Studies, King's College London.

Block, C., Oakar, M. and Hurt, N. (2002) 'The expertise of literacy teachers: a continuum from preschool to grade 5', *Reading Research Quarterly*, 37(2), 178–206.

Boden, M. (2001) 'Creativity and knowledge', in A. Craft, B. Seffrey and M. Liebling (eds) *Creativity in Education*, London: Continuum.

Bolton, G. (1984) *Drama as Education*, London: Longman.

Bolton, G. (1992) *New Perspectives on Classroom Drama*, London: Simon and Schuster.

Booth, D. (1996) *Story Drama: Reading, Writing and Role Playing across the Curriculum*, Markham: Pembroke Publishers.

Booth, D. and Neelands, J. (eds) (1998) *Writing in Role, Classroom Projects Connecting Writing and Drama*, Hamilton, Ontario: Caliburn Enterprises.

Bourdieu, P. (1977) *Outline of a Theory of Practice* (trans. R. Nice), Cambridge: Cambridge University Press.

Bourdieu, P. (1986) 'The forms of capital', in J. Richardson (ed.) *Handbook of Theory and Research for the Sociology of Education*, Westport, CT: Greenwood.

Brice Heath, S. (1983) *Ways with Words: Language, Life and Work in Communities and Classrooms*, Cambridge: Cambridge University Press.

Britton, J. (1970) *Language and Learning*. London: Penguin.

Britton, J. (1977) 'The third area where we are more ourselves: the role of fantasy and the nature of the reader's satisfaction, response to literature', in M. Meek, A. Warlow and G. Barton (eds) *The Cool Web*, London: Bodley Head.

Britton, J. (1982) *Prospect and Retrospect: Selected Essays of James Britton* (G. Pradl, ed.), London: Heinemann.

Britton, J. (1993) *Literature in its Place*, Portsmouth, NH: Boynton/Cook.

Britton, J., Burgess, A., Martin, N., Macleod, A. and Rosen, H. (1975) *The Development of Writing Abilities*, London: Macmillan.

Bromley, H. (2002) 'Meet the Simpsons', *The Primary English Magazine*, 7(4): 7–11.

Bronowski, J. (1978) *The Origins of Knowledge and Imagination*, New Haven, CT: Yale University Press.

Brownjohn, S. (1982) *What Rhymes with 'Secret'?* London: Hodder and Stoughton.

Brownjohn, S. (1994) *To Rhyme or Not to Rhyme?* London: Hodder and Stoughton.

Bruce, T. (1987) *Early Childhood Education*, Sevenoaks: Hodder and Stoughton.

Bruce, T. and Meggitt, C. (2002) *Child Care and Education*, 3rd edition, London: Hodder and Stoughton

Bruner, J. (1962) *On Knowing: Essays for the Left Hand*, Cambridge, MA: Harvard University Press.

Bruner, J. (1984) 'Language, mind and reading', in H. Goelman, A. Oberg and F. Smith (eds) *Awakening to Literacy*, London: Heinemann.

Bruner, J. (1986) *Actual Minds, Possible Worlds*, Cambridge, MA: Harvard University Press.

Bruner, J. (1999) 'Reading for possible worlds', paper presented at the annual meeting of the National Reading Conference, Orlando, Florida.

Bruner, J. (2002) *Making Stories, Law, Literature, Life*, Cambridge, MA: Harvard University Press.

Buckingham, D. and Scanlon, M. (2003) *Education, Entertainment and Learning in the Home*, Buckingham: Open University Press.

Burgess, T., Fox, C. and Goody, J. (2002) *When the Hurly Burly's Done: What's Worth Fighting for in English in Education*, Sheffield: National Association for the Teaching of English.

Burgess-Macey, C. (1999) 'Classroom literacies: young children's explorations in meaning making in the age of the literacy hour', *Reading*, 33(3): 120–5.

Calkins, L.M. (1983) *Lessons from a Child: On the Teaching and Learning of Writing*, Portsmouth, NH: Heinemann.

Calkins, L.M. (1986) *The Art of Teaching Writing*, Portsmouth, NH: Heinemann.

Calkins, L.M. (1991) *Living Between the Lines*, Portsmouth, NH: Heinemann.

Cambourne, B. (1995) 'Towards an educationally relevant theory of literacy learning: twenty years of inquiry', *The Reading Teacher*, 49(3): 182–90.

Campbell, E. (2003) *The Ethical Teacher*, Maidenhead: Open University Press.

Campbell, R. (1999) *Literacy from Home to School: Reading with Alice*, Stoke on Trent: Trentham.

Carter, R. (2004) *Language and Creativity: the Art of Common Talk*, London: Routledge.

Chambers, A. (1993) *Tell me, Children, Reading and Talk*, Stroud: Thimble Press.

Clandinin, D. and Connelly, F. (1990) 'Narrative, experience and the study of the curriculum', *Cambridge Journal of Education*, 20(3): 241–53.

Claxton, G. (1997) *Hare Brain, Tortoise Mind: Why Intelligence Increases when you Think Less*, London: Fourth Estate.

Claxton, G. (2000) 'The anatomy of intuition', in T. Atkinson and G. Claxton (eds) *The Intuitive Practitioner*, Buckingham: Open University Press.

Cliff Hodges, G. (2002) 'Learning through collaborative writing', *Reading, Literacy and Language*, 36(1): 4–10.

Cole, M., Hill, D. and Rikowski, G. (2001) *Red Chalk: On Schooling, Capitalism and Politics*, Brighton: Institute for Education Policy Studies.

Coles, J., Lambirth, A. and Smith, T. (2004) 'Low control learning', *The Primary English Magazine*, 10(2): 19–21.

Cook, M.A. (2000) 'Writing and role play: a case for inclusion', *Reading Literacy and Language*, 34(2): 74–8.

Cook, M.A. (2002) 'Bringing the outside in: using playful contexts to maximise young writers' capabilities', in S. Ellis and C. Mills (eds) *Connecting, Creating: New Ideas in Teaching Writing*, Royston: United Kingdom Literacy Association.

Corden, R. (2000) *Literacy and Learning through Talk Strategies for the Primary Classroom*, Birmingham: Open University Press.

Corden, R. (2001) 'Teaching reading–writing links (TRAWL)', *Project in Reading, Literacy and Language*, 35(1): 37–40.

Corden, R. (2003) 'Writing is more than "exciting": equipping primary children to become reflective writers', *Reading Literacy and Language*, 37(1): 18–26.

Craft, A. (1997) 'Identity and creativity: educating for post-modernism?', *Teacher Development: An International Journal of Teachers' Professional Development*, 1(1) 83–96.

Craft, A. (2000) *Creativity Across the Primary Curriculum: Framing and Developing Practice*, London: RoutledgeFalmer.

Craft, A.(2001) 'Little c: creativity in craft', in A. Craft, B. Jeffrey and M. Liebling (eds) *Creativity in Education*, London: Continuum.

Craft, A. and Jeffrey, B. (2003) 'Teaching creatively and teaching for creativity: distinctions and relationships', *Educational Studies*, 30(1): 77–87.

Cremin, M. (1998) 'Identifying some imaginative processes in the drama work of primary school children as they use three different kinds of drama structures for learning', *Research in Drama Education*, 3(2): 211–24.

Cremin, M. (2004) 'The role of the imagination in classroom drama', unpublished dissertation, Canterbury Christ Church University College, Canterbury.

Cremin, M. and Grainger, T. (2001) *Resourcing Classroom Drama 8–14*, Sheffield: National Association for the Teaching of English.

Cross, G. (1999) Gillian Cross, in J. Carter (ed.) *Talking Books: Children's Authors Talk about the Craft, Creativity and Process of Writing*, London: Routledge.

Crossley-Holland, K. (2000) 'Different – but oh how like!', in G. Cliff Hodges, M.J. Drummond and M. Styles (eds) *Tales, Tellers and Texts*, London: Cassell.

Crumpler, T. and Schneider, J. (2002) 'Writing with their whole being: a cross study analysis of children's writing from five classrooms using process drama', *Research in Drama Education*, 7(2): 61–79.

Cziksentmihalyi, M. (2002) *Flow: The Classic Work on How to Achieve Happiness*, London: Rider.

D'Arcy, P. (1999) *Two Contrasting Paradigms for the Teaching and Assessment of Writing*, Leicester: National Association for the Teaching of English.

Dadds, M. (1999) 'Teachers' values and the literacy hour', *Cambridge Journal of Education*, 1(29): 1.

Dahlburg, G., Moss, P. and Pence, A. (1999) *Beyond Quality in Early Childhood Education and Care*, London: RoutledgeFalmer.

Dann, R. (2001) *Assessment as Learning*, London: RoutledgeFalmer.

David, T., Raban, B., Ure, C., Goouch, K., Jago, M., Barriere, I. and Lambirth, A. (2000) *Making Sense of Early Literacy*, London: Fulton.

Derrida, J. (1991) 'Interview with François Ewald', *Le Magazine Litteraire*, 286: 29.

DES (1967) *Children and their Primary School*, Report of the Central Advisory Council for Education, London: DES.

DES (1989) *English for Ages 5 to 16: The National Curriculum*, London: Department of Education and Science and the Welsh Office.

Design Council (1999) quoted in NACCCE (ed.) *All our Futures: Creativity, Culture and Education*, London: DfEE.

DfEE (1998) *The National Literacy Strategy Framework for Teaching*, London: DfEE.

DfEE (1999) *All Our Futures: Creativity, Culture and Education*, London: DfEE.

DfES (2000) *The National Curriculum for England and Wales*, London: HMSO.

DfES (2001) 'The National Literacy Strategy', *Teaching Writing: Support Material for Text Level Objectives*, DfES 0531/2001, London: DfES.

DfES (2003) *Excellence and Enjoyment: A Strategy for Primary Schools*, Nottingham: DfES.

DfES/QCA (2003) *Speaking, Listening, Learning: Working with children in Key Stages 1 and 2*. London: DfES.

Dias, P. and Hayhoe, M. (1988) *Developing Response to Poetry*, Milton Keynes: Open University Press.

Dobie, T. and MacBeath, J. (1998) *Pupil Councils: A Case Study of Pupil Councils in Fife*, Glasgow: University of Strathclyde Quality in Education Centre/Fife Council.

Doherty, B. (2001) 'Recognising yourself in what you read', keynote speech at 'Just let me think: reflecting on literacy learning', United Kingdom Reading Association International Conference, 6–8 July, Canterbury.

Dombey, H. (1998) 'Changing literacy in the early years of school', in B. Cox (ed.) *Literacy is not Enough*, Manchester: Manchester University Press and Book Trust.

Duffield, J., Allen, J., Turner, E. and Morris, B. (2000) 'Pupils' voices on achievement: an alternative to the standards agenda', *Cambridge Journal of Education*, 30(2): 263–74.

Dyson, A.H. (1997) *Writing Superheroes: Contemporary Childhood, Popular Culture and Classroom Literacy*, Columbia: Teachers College Press.

Dyson, A.H. (2000) 'Writing and the sea of voices: oral language in, around and about writing', in R. Indrisano and J. Squire (eds) *Perspectives on Writing*, Newark, DE: International Reading Association.

Dyson, A.H. (2001) 'Where are the childhoods in childhood literacy? An exploration in outer (school) space', *Journal of Early Childhood Literacy*, 1(1): 9–38.

Earl, L., Fullan, M., Leithwood, K. and Watson, N. (2000) *Watching and Learning: OISE/UT Evaluation of the National Literacy and Numeracy Strategies*, London: DfEE.

Earl, L., Levin, B., Leithwood, K., Fullan, M. and Watson, N. (2001) *Watching and Learning 2*, London: DfES.

Earl, L., Watson, N., Levin, B., Leithwood, K., Fullan, M. and Torrance, N. (2003) *Watching and Learning 3: Final Report of the External Evaluation of England's National Literacy and Numeracy Strategies*, Toronto, Ontario: Ontario Institute for Studies in Education, University of Toronto.

Edwards, C., Gandini, L. and Forman, G. (eds) (1998) *The Hundred Languages of Children*, 2nd edition, Greenwich, CT: Ablex.

Egan, K. (2003) 'The cognitive tools of children's imagination', in B. Van Oers (ed.) *Narratives of Childhood*, Amsterdam: Vrije Universiteit Press.

English, E., Hargreaves, L. and Hislam, J. (2002) 'Pedagogical dilemmas in the National Literacy Strategy: primary teachers' perceptions, reflections and classroom behaviour', *Cambridge Journal of Education*, 32(1): 9–26.

Essex County Council (2003) *Visually Speaking Using Multimedia Texts to Improve Boys' Writing*, Chelmsford: The English team, Essex Advisory and Inspection Service.

Fairclough, N. (1989) *Language and Power*, Harlow: Pearson Education.

Fairclough, N. (1992) 'Language awareness: critical and non-critical approaches', in N. Fairclough (ed.) *Critical Language Awareness*, Harlow: Pearson Education.

Fang, Z., Fu, D. and Lamme, L.L. (2004) 'From scripted instruction to teacher empowerment: supporting literacy teachers to make pedagogical transitions', *Literacy*, 38(1): 58–64.

Faust, M.A. and Kieffer, R.D. (1998) 'Challenging expectations: why we ought to stand by the IRA/NCTE Standards for the English language arts', *Journal of Adolescent and Adult Literacy*, 41(2): 540–7.

Fisher, R. (2001) *Inside the Literacy Hour: Learning from Classroom Experience*, London: Routledge.

Fisher, R. (2004) 'Embedding the literacy strategy: snapshots of change', *Literacy*, 38(3): 134–40.

Fisher R. and Lewis, M. (1999) 'Anticipation or trepidation? Teacher's views on the literacy hour', *Reading, Literacy and Language*, 33(1).

Fleming, M. (1992) 'Pupils' perceptions of the nature of poetry', *Cambridge Journal of Education*, 22(1): 31–42.

Fox, C. (1988) 'Poppies will make them grant', in M. Meek and C. Mills (eds) *Language and Literacy in the Primary School*, Lewes: Falmer Press.

Fox, C. (1993) *At the Very Edge of the Forest: The Influence of Literature on Storytelling by Children*, London: Cassell.

Fox, G. and Merrick, B. (1987) 'Thirty-six things to do with a poem', *Children's Literature in Education*, 12(1): 23–9.

Frater, G. (2000) 'Observed in practice, English in the National Literacy Strategy: some reflections', *Reading*, 34(3), November: 107–12.

Frater, G. (2001) *Effective Practice in Writing at Key Stage 2: Essential Extras*, London: Basic Skills Agency.

Frater, G. (2003) *Securing Boys' Literacy: A Survey of Effective Practice in Primary Schools*, London: Basic Skills Agency.

Frater, G. (2004) 'Improving Dean's writing: what shall we tell the children', *Literacy*, 38: 2.

Freire, P. (1972) *Pedagogy of the Oppressed*, New York: Herder and Herder.

Freire, P. (1985) *The Politics of Education*, London: Macmillan.

Fryer, M. (1996) *Creative Teaching and Learning*, London: Paul Chapman.

Furniss, T. and Bath, M. (1996) *Reading Poetry: An Introduction*, Hemel Hempstead: Prentice Hall/Harvester.

Gardener, H. (1999) *Intelligence Reframed: Multiple Intelligences for the 21st Century*, New York: Basic Books.

Gardner, H. (1999) *The Disciplined Mind: Beyond Facts And Standardized Tests, The K-12 Education That Every Child Deserves*, New York: Simon and Schuster; New York: Penguin Putnam.

Garner, A. (1984) *Book of British Fairy Tales*, Suffolk: Collins.

Geekie, P. (2003) 'Social and cultural influences on literacy', in E. Bearne, H. Dombey and T. Grainger (eds) *Interactions in Language and Literacy in the Classroom*, Maidenhead: Open University Press.

Geekie, P., Cambourne, B. and Fitzsimmons, P. (1999) *Understanding Literacy Development*, Stoke on Trent: Trentham.

Giroux, H. (1983) 'Theories of reproduction and resistance in the new sociology of education: a critical analysis', *Harvard Educational Review*, 53(3): 257–93.

Glassie, H. (1986) *Irish Folk Tales*, Harmondsworth: Penguin.

Goodwin, P. and Routh, C. (2000) 'A brief history of timing: the impact of the National Literacy Strategy on the marketing and publishing of resources to support literacy teaching', *Reading*, 34(3): 119–23.

Gopnik, A. Meltzoff, A and Kuhl, P. (1999) *How Babies Think: The Science of Childhood*, London: Weidenfeld and Nicolson.

Graham, J. (2000) 'Creativity and picture books', *Reading*, 34(2): 61–7.

Graham, L. (1999) 'Changing practice through reflection: the KS2 Reading Project', *Reading*, 33(3): 106–13.

Graham, L. (2001) 'From *Tyrannosaurus rex* to Pokemon: autonomy in the teaching of writing', *Reading, Literacy and Language*, 35(1): 18–26.

Graham, L. (2003) 'Writing journals: an investigation', *Reading, Literacy and Language*, 37(1): 39–42.

Graham, L. (2004) 'Autonomy in writing', Lecture at United Kingdom Literacy Association Regional Conference on Writing and Creativity, 22 March, The Davidson Centre, Croydon.

Graham, L. and Johnson, A. (2003) *Children's Writing Journals*, Royston: United Kingdom Literacy Association.

Graham, L. and Johnson, A. (2003) *Writing Journals*, Cambridge: United Kingdom Reading Association.

Grainger, T. (1996) 'The rhythm of life is a powerful beat', *Language Matters: Language Arts*, 2 (July): 30–4, London: Centre for Literacy in Primary Education.

Grainger, T. (1997) 'Poetry from the nursery and the playground: making time for rhythms and rhymes', *Language and Learning*: 12–16.

Grainger, T. (1998) 'Drama and reading: illuminating their interaction', *English in Education*, 32(1): 29–36.

Grainger, T. (1999) 'Conversations in the classroom: poetic voices at play', *Language Arts*, 76(4): 292–7.

Grainger, T. (2000) 'The current status of oracy: a cause of (dis)satisfaction', in J. Davison and J. Moss (eds) *Issues in English Teaching*, London: Routledge.

Grainger, T. (2001a) 'Drama and writing: imagination on the page I', *The Primary English Magazine*, 6(4): 12–17.

Grainger, T. (2001b) 'Drama and writing: imagination on the page II', *The Primary English Magazine*, 6(5): 8–13.

Grainger, T. (2002) 'Storytelling: the missing link in story writing', in S. Ellis and C. Mills (eds) *Connecting, Creating: New Practices in the Teaching of Writing*, Leicester: United Kingdom Reading Association.

Grainger, T. (2003a) 'Let drama build bridges between the subjects', *The Primary English Magazine*, October: 8–12.

Grainger, T. (2003b) 'Let drama build bridges to non-fiction writing', *The Primary English Magazine*, December: 19–23.

Grainger, T. (2003c) 'Exploring the unknown: drama, ambiguity and meaning making', in E. Bearne, H. Dombey and T. Grainger (eds) *Classroom Interactions in Literacy*, Buckingham: Open University Press.

Grainger, T. (2004) 'Introduction: travelling across the terrain', in T. Grainger (ed.) *The Routledge Falmer Reader in Language and Literacy*, London: RoutledgeFalmer.

Grainger, T. and Cremin, M. (2001) *Resourcing Classroom Drama 5–8*, Sheffield: National Association for the Teaching of English.

Grainger, T. and Goouch, K. (1999) 'Young children and playful language', in T. David (ed.) *Teaching Young Children*, London: Paul Chapman.

Grainger, T., Goouch, K. and Lambirth, A. (2002) 'The voice of the writer', *Reading, Literacy and Language*, 36(3): 135–9.

Grainger, T., Goouch, K. and Lambirth, A. (2003) 'Playing the game called writing: children's voice and view', *English in Education*, 37(2): 4–15.

Grainger, T., Goouch, K. and Lambirth, A. (2004a) *Creative Activities for Plot, Character and Setting, 5–7*, Milton Keynes: Scholastic.

Grainger, T., Goouch, K. and Lambirth, A. (2004b) *Creative Activities for Plot, Character and Setting, 7–9*, Milton Keynes: Scholastic.

Grainger, T., Goouch, K. and Lambirth, A. (2004c) *Creative Activities for Plot, Character and Setting, 9–11*, Milton Keynes: Scholastic.

Graves, D. (1983) *Writing: Teachers and Children at Work*, Portsmouth, NH: Heinemann.

Greene, G. (1947) 'The lost childhood', in J. Gross (ed.) (1991) *The Oxford Book of Essays*, Oxford: Oxford University Press.

Greenfield, S. (2000) *The Private Life of the Brain*, London: Penguin.

Gregory, E. and Williams, A. (2000) *City Literacies*, London: RoutledgeFalmer.

Gross, J. (ed.) (1991) *The Oxford Book of Essays*, Oxford: Oxford University Press.

Grugeon, E. (1988) 'Children's oral culture: a transitional experience', in M. MacLure, T. Phillips and A. Wilkinson (eds) *Oracy Matters*, Milton Keynes: Open University Press.

Grugeon, E. (1998) 'The singing game: an untapped competence', in M. Meek and C. Mills (eds) *Language and Literacy in the Primary School*, London: Falmer Press.

Grugeon, E. (1999) 'The state of play: children's oral culture, literacy and learning', *Reading, Literacy and Language*, 33(1): 13–16.

Grugeon, E. and Gardner, P. (2000) *The Art of Storytelling for Teachers and Pupils*, London: David Fulton.

Grugeon, E. and Harding, L. (2004) 'Discovering creativity on the playground', in P. Goodwin (ed.) *Literacy through Creativity*, London: Taylor & Francis.

Gurevitch, Z. (2000) 'The serious play of writing', *Qualitative Inquiry*, 6(1): 3–8.

Hall, N. (1995) *Exploring Writing and Play in the Early Years*, London: David Fulton.

Hall, N. (ed.) (1998) *Writing with Reason: The Emergence of Authorship in Young Children*, London: Hodder and Stoughton.

Halliday, M. (1973) *Explorations in the Functions of Language*, London: Arnold.

Halliday, M. (1978) *Language as a Social Semiotic: The Social Interpretation of Language and Meaning*, London: Edward Arnold.

Hanke, V. (2002) 'Improvisations around the National Literacy Strategy', *Reading Literacy and Language*, 36(2): 80–7.

Hannon, P. (2000) *Reflecting on Literacy in Education*, London: RoutledgeFalmer.

Harding, D.W. (1964) *Experience into Words*, London: Chatto and Windus.

Hardman, F., Smith, F. and Wall, K. (2003) 'Interactive whole class teaching in the National Literacy Strategy', *Cambridge Journal of Education*, 33(2): 197–215.

Hardy, B. (1977) 'Towards a poetics of fiction: an approach through narrative', in M. Meek, A. Warlow and G. Barton (eds) *The Cool Web*, London: Bodley Head.

Hargreaves, A. (1998) 'The emotional practice of teaching', *Teaching and Teacher Education*, 14(9): 835–54.

Hargreaves, A. and Goodson, I. (2003) 'Foreword', in E. Campbell (ed.) *The Ethical Teacher*, Maidenhead: Open University Press.

Harwayne, S. (1992) *Lasting Impressions Weaving Literature into the Writing Workshop*, Portsmouth, NH : Heinemann.

Haworth, A. (2001) 'The re-positioning of oracy: a millennium project', *Cambridge Journal of Education*, 32(3): 4–46.

Hayes, S. and Craig, H. (1991) *This is the Bear and the Scary Night*, London: Walker.

Heaney, S. (1980) *Preoccupations*, London: Faber and Faber.

Heathcote, D. (1980) *Drama as Context*, Sheffield: National Association for the Teaching of English.

Heathcote, D. and Bolton, G. (1995) *Drama for Learning: Dorothy Heathcote's Mantle of the Expert Approach to Education*, Portsmouth, NH: Heinemann.

Henry, M. (2000) 'Drama's ways of learning', *Research in Drama Education*, 5(1): 45–62.

Hewitt, P. (2002) *Beyond Boundaries*, London: Arts Council England.

Hill, D. (2001) 'The National Curriculum: the hidden curriculum and equality', in D. Hill and M. Cole (eds) *Schooling and Equality: Fact, Concept and Policy*, London: Kogan Page.

Hillocks, G. Jnr (1995) *Teaching Writing as Reflective Practice*, New York: Teachers College Press.

Hilton, M. (1996) 'The children of this world', in M. Hilton (ed.) *Potent Fictions*, London: Routledge.

Hilton, M. (2001) 'Writing process and progress: where do we go from here?', *English in Education*, 35(1): 4–12.

HMI (1987) *Teaching Poetry in the Secondary School*, DES: HMSO.

Hogan, T. (1980) 'Students' interests in writing activities', *Research in the Teaching of English*, 14(2): 99–126.

Hollindale, P. (1997) *Signs of Childness in Children's Books*, Stroud: Thimble Press.

Hoyles A. and Hoyles, B. (2003) 'Black performance poetry', *English in Education*, 37(1): 27–38.

Hughes, T. (ed.) (1963) *Here Today*, London: Hutchinson.

Hughes, T. (1976) 'Myth and education', in G. Fox, G. Hammond, T. Jones, F. Smith and K. Sterck (eds) *Writers, Critics and Children*, London: Heinemann.

Iser, W. (1978) *The Act of Reading*, Baltimore, MD: Johns Hopkins University Press.

James, A. and Prout, A. (eds) (1997) *Constructing and Reconstructing Childhood: Contemporary Issues in the Sociological Study of Childhood*, 2nd edition, London: Falmer Press.

Jeffrey, B. and Woods, P. (1997) 'The relevance of creative teaching: pupils' views', in A. Pollard, D. Thiessen and A. Filer (eds) *Children and their Curriculum: The Perspectives of Primary and Elementary School Children*, London: Falmer Press.

Jeffrey, B. and Woods, P. (2003) *The Creative School: A Framework for Success, Quality and Effectiveness*, London: RoutledgeFalmer.

Johnson, A. (2003) 'What I found', in L. Graham and A. Johnson (eds) *Children's Writing Journals*, Royston: United Kingdom Literacy Association.

Joubert, M.M. (2001) 'The art of creative teaching: NACCCE and beyond', in A. Craft, B. Jeffrey and M. Liebling (eds) *Creativity in Education*, London: Continuum.

Karmiloff, K. and Karmiloff-Smith, A. (2001) *Pathways to Language: From Fetus to Adolescent*, Cambridge, MA: Harvard University Press.

Kaufer, D., Hayes, J.R. and Flower, L.S. (1986) 'Composing written sentences', *Research in the Teaching of English*, 20: 121–40.

Kearney, R. (1991) *Poetics of Imagining*, New York: HarperCollins.

Kearney, R. (1994) *The Poetics of Imagining*, New York: Harper Collins.

Kiefer, B. (1995) *The Potential of Picture Books: From Visual Literacy to Aesthetic Understanding*, Eaglewood Cliffs, NJ: Merrill.

King, C. (2001) '"I like group reading because we can share ideas" – the role of talk within the literature circle', *Reading, Literacy and Language*, 35(1): 32–6.

Krechevsky, M. and Stork J. (2000) 'Challenging educational assumptions from an Italian–American collaboration', *The Cambridge Journal of Education*, 30(1): 57–75.

Kress, G. (1995) *Writing the Future: English and the Making of a Culture of Innovation* Sheffield: National Association for the Teaching of English.

Kress, G. (1997) *Before Writing – Rethinking the Paths to Literacy*, London: Routledge.

Kress, G. (2000) *Early Spelling, Between Convention and Creativity*, London: Routledge.

Kress, G. (2003) *Literacy in the New Media Age*, London: Routledge.

Kress G. and Van Leeuwen T. (1997) *Reading Images: The Grammar of Visual Design*, London: Routledge.

Kurtz, J. (1995) *Almaz and the Lion*, London: Puffin.

Kwesi Johnson, L. (1975) Quoted by Andrew Salkey in the New Introduction to Linton Kwesi Johnson, *Dread Beat and Blood*, London: Bogle-L'Ouverture: 8.

Laevers, F. (2000) 'Forward to basics: deep-level learning and the experimental approach', *Early Years*, 20(2): 20–9.

Lambirth, A. (2003) '"They get enough of that at home": understanding aversion to popular culture in schools', *Reading, Literacy and Language*, 37(1) April: 9–13.

Lambirth, A., Darchez, L., Noakes, H. and Wood, C. (2004) 'Infant story writing', *The Primary English Magazine*, 9(5): 8–10.

Lankshear and Knobel (2003) *New Literacies: Changing Knowledge and Classroom Learning*, Buckingham: Open University Press.

Lee, N. (2001) *Childhood and Society: Growing up in the Age of Uncertainty*, Buckingham: Open University Press.

Leithwood, K., Jantzi, D. and Mascall, B. (1999) *Large Scale Reform: What Works*, Toronto, Ontario: Ontario Studies for Education, University of Ontario.

Lewis, M. (1999) 'Developing children's narrative writing using story structures', in P. Goodwin (ed.) *The Literate Classroom*, London: David Fulton.

Luce-Kapler, R., Chin, J., O'Donnell, E. and Stoch, S. (2001) 'The design of meaning: unfolding systems of writing', *Changing English*, 8(1): 43–52.

Luke, A. and Carrington, V. (2002) 'Globalisation, literacy, curriculum practice', in R. Fisher, G. Brooks and M. Lewis (eds) *Raising Standards in Literacy*, London: RoutledgeFalmer.

Lupton, H. (2001) 'Betsy Whyte and the dreaming', in G. Cliff Hodges, M.J. Drummond and M. Styles (eds) *Tales, Tellers and Texts*, London: Cassell.

Macdonald, A., Saunders, L., Ashby, P. and Kendall, L. (1999) *Boys' Attainment, Progress, Motivation and Participation: A Report for Islington Council Education Department*. Slough: National Foundation for Educational Research.

Madaus, G. (1994) 'Assessment', in C. Gipps (ed.) *Beyond Testing*, Lewes: Falmer Press.

Mahy, M. (1996) 'A dissolving ghost', in S. Egoff, G. Stubbs, R. Ashley and W. Shilton (eds) *Only Connect: Readings on Children's Literature* (3rd edn) Ontario: Oxford University Press.

Malaguzzi, L. (1998) 'History, ideas and basic philosophy: an interview with Lella Gandini', in C. Edwards, L. Gandini and G. Forman (eds) *The Hundred Languages of Children* (2nd edn), Greenwich, CT: Ablex.

Mallett, M. (1997) 'Developing learning: can you say a little more about that?', *Education*, 25: 1.

Marsh, J. (2003) 'Contemporary models of communicative practice: shaky foundations in the foundaytion stage?', *English in Education*, 1(37): 1.

Marsh, J. and Millard, E. (2000) *Literacy and Popular Culture*, London: Paul Chapman.

Marshall, B. (2001) 'Creating danger: the place of the arts in education policy', in A. Craft, B. Jeffrey and M. Liebling (eds) *Creativity in Education*, London: Continuum.

Marshall, S. (1963) *Creative Writing*, London: Macmillan.

Martin, T. (2003) 'Minimum and maximum entitlements: literature at Key Stage 2', *Reading, Literacy and Language*, 37(1): 14–18.

Martin, T. and Leather, B. (1994) *Readers and Texts in the Primary Years*, Buckingham: Open University Press.

Maybury, B. (1967) *Writers' Workshop*, London: Batsford.

McNaughton, M.J. (1997) 'Drama and children's writing: a study of the influence of drama on the imaginative writing of primary schoolchildren', *Research in Drama Education*, 2(1): 55–86.

Medwell, J., Wray, D., Poulson, L. and Fox, R. (1998) *Effective Teachers of Literacy: A Report of a Research Project Commissioned by the Teacher Training Agency*, Exeter: University of Exeter.

Meek, M. (1985) 'Play and paradoxes: some considerations of imagination and language', in G. Wells and J. Nicholls (eds) *Language and Learning: An International Perspective*, London: Falmer Press.

Meek, M. (1988) *How Texts Teach What Readers Learn*, Stroud: Thimble Press.

Meek, M. (1990) 'Why response?' in M. Hayhoe and S. Parker (eds) *Reading and Response*, Buckingham: Open University Press.

Meek, M. (1991) *On Being Literate*, London: Bodley Head.

Meek, M. (1998) 'Why response?', in M. Hayhoe and S. Parker (eds) *Reading and Response*, Buckingham: Open University Press.

Meek, M. (2001) Preface, in M. Barrs and V. Cork (eds) *The Reader in the Writer*, London: Centre for Literacy in Primary Education.

Mercer, N. (2000) *Words and Minds, How We Use Language to Think Together*, London: Routledge.

Mercer, N., Fernandez, M., Dawes, L., Wegerif, R. and Sams, C. (2003) 'Talk about texts at the computer: using ICT to develop children's oral and literate abilities', *Reading Literacy and Language*, 37(2): 81–9.

Messenheimer, T. and Packwood, J. (2002) 'Writing: the state of the state vs. the state of the art in English and American schools', *Reading, Literacy and Language*, 36(1): 11–16.

Millard, E. (2003) 'Towards a literacy of fusion: new times, new teaching and learning', *Reading Literacy and Language*, 37(2): 3–8.

Mitchell, A. (1999) *Dancing in the Street: A Poetry Party*, London: Orchard.

Moffett, J. (1968) *Teaching the Universe of Discourse*, Boston, MA: Houghton Mifflin.

Morpurgo, M. (1995) *Blodin the Beast*, London: Frances Lincoln.

Mortimore, P. (1999) *Understanding Pedagogy and its Impact on Learning*, London: Paul Chapman.

Moss, P. (1994) 'Validity and high stakes writing assessment: problems and possibilities', *Assessing Writing*, 1(1): 109–28.

Moss, P. (2001) 'The otherness of Reggio', in L. Abbott and C. Nutbrown (eds) *Experiencing Reggio Emilia, Implications for Pre-school Provision*, Buckingham: Open University Press.

Moss, P. and Petrie, P. (2002) *From Children's Services to Children's Spaces*, London: RoutledgeFalmer.

Mroz, M., Smith, F. and Hardman, F. (2000) 'The discourse of the literacy hour', *Cambridge Journal of Education*, 30(3): 380–9.

Mullis, I.V.S., Martin, M.O., Gonzalez, E.J. and Kennedy, A.M. (2003) *PIRLS 2001 International Report: IEA's Study of Reading Literacy Achievement in Primary Schools*, Chestnut Hill, MA: Boston College.

Murray, D.M. (1982) *Learning by Teaching: Selected Articles on Writing and Teaching*, Portsmouth, NH: Boynton/Cook.

Murray, L. and Trevarthen, C. (1985) 'Emotional regulation of interactions between two month olds and their mothers', in T.M. Field and N.A. Fox (eds) *Social Perception in Infants*, Norwood, NJ: Ablex.

Myhill, D. (2001) Crafting and creating, *English in Education*, 35(3): 13–20.

NACCCE (1999) *All our Futures: Creativity, Culture and Education*, Report of the National Advisory Committee on Creative and Cultural Education, Sudbury: DfEE.

Naidoo, B. (2003) 'Out of bounds', Keynote speech at United Kingdom Reading Association International Conference, 8–10 July, Cambridge.

Neelands, J., Booth, D. and Ziegler, S. (1993) *Writing in Imagined Contexts: Research into Drama Influenced Writing*, ERIC Document Reproduction Service No. ED 355 576, Toronto: Toronto University Press.

Neisser, U. (1967) *Cognitive Psychology*, New York: Appleton Century Crofts.

Nichersen, R.S. (1999) 'Enhancing creativity', in R. Sternberg (ed.) *Handbook of Creativity*, Cambridge: Sternberg.

Nicholson, H. (2000) 'Dramatic literacies and difference', in E. Bearne and V. Watson (eds) *Where Texts and Children Meet*, London: Routledge.

Nutbrown, C. (1998) *The Lore and Language of Early Education*, Sheffield: University of Sheffield, Division of Education.

O'Brian, V. (1985) *Teaching Poetry in the Secondary School*, London: Arnold.

O'Neill, C. (1995) *Drama Worlds: A Framework for Process Drama*, Portsmouth, NH: Heinemann.

Oakeshott, M. (1959) *The Voice of Poetry in the Conversation of Mankind*, London: Bones and Bones.

Office for Standards in Education (OfSTED) (1993) *Boys and English*, London: DES.

Office for Standards in Education (OfSTED) (2002) *The Curriculum in Successful Primary Schools*, HMI 553, October, London: OfSTED.

Office for Standards in Education (OfSTED) (2003) *Expecting the Unexpected: Developing Creativity in Primary and Secondary Schools*, HMI 1612. E-publication. Available online: www.ofsted.gov.uk.

Olson, D. (1980) 'On language and authority in textbooks', *Journal of Communication*, 30: 186–96.

Olson, D. (1996) *The World on Paper: The Conceptual and Cognitive Implications of Writing and Reading*, Cambridge: Cambridge University Press.

Olson, D. (1997) 'From utterance to text: the bias of language in speech and writing', *Harvard Educational Review*, 47(3): 257–81.

Ong, W.J. (1982) *Orality and Literacy: The Technologising of the Word*, London: Methuen.

Orwell, G. (1936: 1989) *Keep the Aspidistra Flying*, London: Penguin.

Owen, G. (1988) 'Gareth Owen: an autograph', *Books for Keeps*, 107: 17–19.

Packwood, A. and Messenheimer, T. (2003) 'Back to the future: developing children as writers', in E. Bearne, H. Dombey and T. Grainger (eds) *Classroom Interactions in Literacy*, Buckingham: Open University Press.

Pahl, K. (1999) *Transformations: Children's Meaning Making in a Nursery*, Stoke on Trent: Trentham.

Paley, V. (1980) *Wally's Stories*, Cambridge, MA: Harvard University Press.

Paton Walsh, J. (1996) 'An autograph', *Books for Keeps*, 128: 22–3.

Pelligrini, A.D. (1984) 'The effect of dramatic play on children's generation of cohesive text', *Discourse Processes*, 7: 57–67.

Perkins, D. (1998) 'Thinking things through', in T. Blythe (ed.) *The Teaching for Understanding Guide*, San Francisco: Jossey Bass.

Perl, S. and Egendorf, A. (1979) 'The process of creative discovery: theory, research and the implications for teaching', in D. McQuade (ed.) *The Territory of Language: Linguistics, Stylistics and the Teaching of Composition Studies*, Carbondale, IL: Southern Illinois University Press; quoted in J. Britton (1982) *Prospect and Retrospect: Selected Essays of James Britton*, Montclair: Boynton/Cook.

Pickard, A. (2004) 'Dance the words', *The Primary English Magazine*, 9(4): 9–13.

Pirrie, J. (1987) *On Common Ground: A Programme for Teaching Poetry*, Sevenoaks: Hodder & Stoughton Educational.

Powling, C. (2003) 'Introduction', in C. Powling, B. Ashley, P. Pullman, A. Fine and J. Gavin (eds) *Meetings with the Minister*, Reading: National Centre for Language and Literacy.

Prentice, R. (2000) 'Creativity: a reaffirmation of its place in early childhood education', *The Curriculum Journal*, 11(2): 145–58.

PriceWaterhouseCoopers (2001) *Teachers Workload Study*, London: DfEE.

Pullman, P. (2002) 'Yes, but …', Keynote lecture, United Kingdom Reading Association International Conference, Oxford.

Pullman, P. (2003) 'Teaching and testing', in C. Powling, B. Ashley, P. Pullman, A. Fine and J. Gavin (eds) *Meetings with the Minister*, Reading: National Centre for Language and Literacy.

Puttnam, D. (1998) 'Puttnam fears for arts', *Independent*, 10 April.

QCA (1998) *Can Do Better – Raising Boys' Achievement in English*, London: QCA.

Ricoeur, P. (1978) *The Role of Metaphor*, London: Routledge and Kegan Paul.

Robinson, K. (2001) *Out of Our Minds: Learning to be Creative*, Oxford: Capstone Publishing.

Robinson, M. and Ellis, V. (2000) 'Writing in English and responding to writing', in J. Sefton Green and R. Sinker (eds) *Evaluating Creativity: Making and Learning by Young People*, London: Routledge.

Rogoff (1990) *Apprenticeship in Thinking: Cognitive Development in Social Contexts*, New York: Oxford University Press.

Romaine, S. (1989) *Bilingualism*, Oxford: Basil Blackwell.

Rosen, B. (1991) *Shapers and Polishers: Teachers as Storytellers*, London: Mary Glasgow.

Rosen, H. (1984) *Stories and Meanings*, Sheffield: National Association for the Teaching of English.

Rosen, H. (1988a) 'Postscript', in B. Rosen (ed.) *And None of it was Nonsense*, London: Mary Glasgow.

Rosen, H. (1988b) 'Stories of stories', in N. Martin and G. Lightfoot (eds) *The Word for Teaching is Learning*, London: Heinemann.

Rosen, H. (1988c) 'The irrepressible genre', in M. Maclure, T. Phillips and A. Wilkinson (eds) *Oracy Matters*, Milton Keynes: Open University Press.

Rosen, H. (1998) *Speaking from Memory: The Study of Autobiographical Discourse*, Stoke on Trent: Trentham.

Rosen, M. (1989) *Did I hear you write?* London: André Deutsch.

Rosenblatt, L. (1978) *The Reader, the Text, the Poem: The Transactional Theory of Literary Work*, Carbondale, IL: South Illinois University Press.

Rosenblatt, L. (1995) *Literature as Exploration*, New York: Modern Languages Association of America.

Ruddel, R.B. (1997) 'Researching the influential literacy teacher: characteristics, beliefs, strategies and new research directions', in C.K. Kinzer, K.A. Hinchman and D.J. Lew (eds) *Inquiries into Literacy Theory and Practice 46th Year Book of the National Reading Conference*, Chicago, IL: National Reading Conference.

Sachar, L. (1998) *Holes*, London: Bloomsbury.Sachs, O. (1985) *The Man who Mistook his Wife for a Hat*, New York: Simon & Schuster.

Schon, D. (1983) *The Reflective Practitioner*, New York: Basic Books.

Sedgwick, F. (2001) *Teaching Literacy: A Creative Approach*, London: Continuum.

Sharples, M. (1999) *How We Write: Writing as Creative Design*, London: Routledge.

Skidmore, D., Perez-Parent, M. and Arnfield, S. (2003) 'Teacher–pupil dialogue in the guided reading session', *Reading, Literacy and Language*, 37(2): 47–53.

Smith, F. (1982) *Writing and the Writer*, London: Heinemann.

Snyder, I. (2003) 'Keywords: vocabulary of pedagogy and the new media', in E. Bearne, H. Dombey and T. Grainger (eds) *Classroom Interactions in Literacy*, Buckingham: Open University Press.

Stannard, J. (1999) 'The National Literacy Strategy', Keynote speech at United Kingdom Reading Association National Conference, 18 March, Cambridge.

Steele, S. (1999) 'First persons: writing and role at KS2', *Language Matters*, Spring 1999: 7–12, Centre for Language in Primary Education.

Sternberg, R. (1997) *Successful Intelligence*, New York: Plume.

Street, B. (1997) 'The implications of the "new literacy studies" for literacy education', *English in Education* 31(3): 26–39.

Styles, M (1992) 'Just a kind of music: children as poets' in M. Styles, B. Bearne and V. Watson (eds) *After Alice*, London: Cassell.

Styles, M. (1998) *From the Garden to the Street*, London: Cassell.

Sutton-Smith, B. (1997) *The Ambiguity of Play*, Cambridge, MA: Harvard University Press.

Talley, G. (2000) 'Write away', unpublished dissertation for the Diploma in Writing and Action Research Davidson Centre, Croydon.

Tannen, D. (1985) 'Relative focus on involvement in oral and written discourse', in D. Olson, N. Torrance and A. Hilderguard (eds) *Literacy, Learning and Language: The Nature and Consequence of Reading and Writing*, Cambridge: Cambridge University Press.

Taylor, P. (1995) *Pre-text and Storydrama: the Artistry of Cealy O'Neill and David Booth*, Sydney: National Association for Drama in Education.

Taylor, P. (2000) *The Drama Classroom*, London: RoutledgeFalmer.

Teacher Training Agency (TTA) (2003) *Qualifying to Teach: Professional Standards for Qualified Teacher Status and Requirements for Initial Teacher Training*, London: TTA.

Tochon, F. and Munby, H. (1993) 'Novice and expert teachers time epistemology : a wave function from didactics to pedagogy', *Teaching and Teacher Education*, 3: 205–18.

Trevarthen, C. and Aitken, K.J. (2001) 'Infant intersubjectivity: research, theory and clinical applications', *Journal of Child Psychology and Psychiatry and Allied Disciplines*, 42(1): 3–48.

Troman, G. and Woods, P. (1999) *Primary Teachers' Stress*, London: Routledge Falmer.

Tucker, J. and Sharratt, N. (1996) *Do Knights Take Naps?* London: Walker.

Umek, L.M. and Musek, P.L. (2001) 'Symbolic play: opportunities for cognitive and language development in pre-school settings', *Early Years*, 21(1): 55–64.

Van de Kopple, W.J. and Crismore, A. (1990) 'Readers' reactions to Hedges in a science textbook', *Linguistics and Education*, 2: 303–22.

van Hensbergen, G. (2001) *Gaudi: A Biography*, London: HarperCollins.

Van Oers, B. (2003) 'Multiple narratives of childhood: tools for the improvement of early childhood education', in B. Van Oers (ed.) *Narratives of Childhood: Theoretical and Practical Explorations for the Introduction of Early Childhood Education*, Amsterdam: Vrije Universiteit Press.

Vygotsky, L. (1978) *Mind in Society*, Harvard, MA: MIT Press.

Wagner, B.J. (1994) 'Drama and writing', in A. Purvis (ed.) *The Encyclopaedia of English Studies and Language Arts*, vol. 1, New York: National Council of Teachers.

Wagner, B.J. (1998) *Educational Drama and Language Arts: What Research Shows*, Portsmouth, NH: Heinemann.

Wells, G. (1986) *The Meaning Makers*, London: Hodder and Stoughton.

Wells, G. (2003) 'Action, talk and text: integrating literacy with other modes of making meaning', in E. Bearne, H. Dombey and T. Grainger (eds) *Interactions in Language and Literacy in the Classroom*, Maidenhead: Open University Press.

Wells, G., Chang, G. and Maher, A. (1990) *Creating Classroom Communities of Literature Thinkers, Cooperative Learning*, New York: Praeger.

Whitehead, M. (1997) *Language and Literacy in the Early Years*, 2nd edition, London: Paul Chapman Publishing.

Wiggins, G. (1993) 'Assessment: authenticity, context and validity', *Phi Delta Kappan*, 75(3): 200–14.

Wilson, S. and Ball, D.L. (1997) 'Helping teachers meet the standards: new challenges for teacher educators', *The Elementary School Journal*, 97(2): 121–38.

Winnicott, D. (1974) *Playing and Reality*, Harmondsworth: Penguin.

Wood, D. (1988) *How Children Think and Learn*, Oxford: Blackwell.

Woods, P. (1995) *Creative Teachers in the Primary Years*, Buckingham: Open University Press.

Woods, P. (2001) 'Creative literacy', in A. Craft, B. Jeffrey and M. Liebling (eds) *Creativity in Education*, London: Continuum.

Woods, P. and Jeffrey, B. (1996) *Teachable Moments: The Art of Creative Teaching in Primary Schools*, Buckingham: Open University Press.

Wray, D. (1993) 'What do children think about writing', *Educational Review*, 45: 1.

Wray, D. and Lewis, M. (1997) *Extending Literacy*, London: Routledge.

Wray, D., Medwell, J., Poulson, L. and Fox, R. (2002) *Teaching Literacy Effectively in the Primary School*, London: RoutledgeFalmer.

Wright, P. (1999) 'The thought of doing drama scares me to death', *Research in Drama Education*, 4(2): 227–37.

Zephaniah, B. (2001) 'Poetry', in J. Carter (ed.) *Creating Writers: A Creative Writing Manual for Schools*, London: Routledge.

Index

Abbot, J. 1
affective engagement 22, 27, 118, 196
agency 17, 39, 46, 62, 122, 199
Ahlberg, A. 25–6
Alcott, L.M. 86
Alexander, R. 52
Almond, D. 120
Alvermann, D. *et al.* 39
Anderson, H. *et al.* 4
Andrews, R. 149
Arts Council 159–60
assessment 65, 91; influence of 5–6; and
    mixed mode communication 35
Auden, W.H. and Garrett, J. 140
authenticity 28, 101, 152, 166–7
authorial space 12, 34, 37, 39, 42, 68,
    98, 167, 199
autonomy 27, 164, 196; author 68;
    children's 33, 49–50, 57, 61, 76, 81,
    179; and collaboration/interaction
    17; desire for 65; development of
    17–21, 62; evidence of 17–18; and
    freedom of opportunities 64–5; and
    journal writing 81; need for 9;
    poetic 152–4; and role play 18–19;
    and teacher intervention 19;
    teacher's 157, 169–74, 179–81; as
    writiers/learners 199–200

Bailey, M. 180
Bakhtin, M. 25, 30, 36, 38, 90, 146
Barnes, J. 21, 157
Barrs, M. 37, 49, 59, 90, 99; and Cork,
    V. 8, 37, 38, 58, 88, 93, 94, 103, 109,
    116, 117, 127, 129, 169, 190
Barthes, R. 31, 113
Barton, D. and Hamilton, M. 32
Bearne, E. 7, 31, 33, 35, 52, 55, 57, 79,
    103; *et al.* 190; and Kress, G. 32

Bell, D. 183
Bell, G.H. 12
Benton, M. 139, 159, 161; and Fox, R.
    90
Bereiter, C. and Scardamalia, M. 59,
    93, 167
Bernstein, B. 39
Black, P. *et al.* 17
Block, C. *et al.* 186
Blythe, G. 93
Blyton, E. 85–6
Boden, M. 11, 58, 88, 187
Bolton, G. 116, 163
Booth, D. 116; and Neelands, J. 102
Bourdieu, P. xi, 21, 63, 76, 78
Brice Heath, S. 60, 121
Britton, J. 16, 25, 37, 51, 83, 89, 103,
    122, 166, 169, 176; *et al.* 12
Bromley, H. 39
Bronowski, J. 13
Brownjohn, S. 143
Bruce, T. 50; and Meggitt, C. 50
Bruner, J. xi, 30, 34, 47, 50, 56, 99, 112,
    200
Buckingham, D. and Scanlon, M. 43
Burgess, T. *et al.* 178
Burgess-Macey, C. 121

Calkins, L.M. 17, 56, 103, 122, 167,
    175
Cambourne, B. 51
Campbell, E. 180
Campbell, R. 50
CANCODE Corpus 41
Carter, R. 41, 48, 146
Chambers, A. 84, 162
children, affective/creative
    involvement 196; age differences in
    attitudes to writing 63–4; attitudes

confidence of 4; and shifting of roles 71–2; as storytellers 160–2; support for 180; teaching to the test 4, 5, 6; and use of conscientisation model 73; using intuition 184–5; as writers 164–75

teaching 95; as art form 10; balance in 11–12; creative/contextualised 62; formulaic approach to 11–12; integration with learning 202–4; mutual vs individual accomplishment 52; and oral culture of classroom 46; and persistence 72; redressing imbalance in 11–12; transmissive practice 52; understanding as optional extra 51–2

Teaching Reading and Writing Links (TRAWL) project 93

tests 4, 5, 6

text/s 20; analysis of instructional purposes 90–2; coherence, shape, meaning 95; construction/crafting of 89; conversations/discussions on 92, 93–4; creation of 92; engagement with 30; form/feature vs meaning/message 5; imaginative use of 100; inner 31; inside/outside experience of 181; and intentionality 49–50; interaction with 49; interpretation/production of 21; meaning of 58, 88; multimedia/multimodal 20, 21, 31–2; playful engagement with 52; quality 85–90; rhythm/tune in 37; and textual play 198; transformation of 97–9; understanding through drama 109; unnofficial 33

time 23

time and space 62, 94, 204

Tochon, F. and Munby, H. 184

traditional tales, and act of retelling 128; and development of writing 127; musicality of 128; as oral rather than visual 127; reader involvement 130; retelling of 131; rhythm/language of 128–30, 131; robustness/quality of 127; shape/pattern of narrative 128; structure of 128, *see also* storytelling

Trevarthen, C. and Aitken, K.J. 47

Tucker, J. 98

Umek, L.M. and Musek, P.L. 111

Van de Kopple, W.J. and Crismore, A. 43

van Hensbergen, G. x

Van Oers, B. 82

verve 1, 8, 9, 25, 27–8, 46, 101, 144, 175, 192, 199

voice/s 1, 8–9, 27, 81, 101, 174, 199; acknowledging diverse 32–5; artistic *see* drama; literature; poetry; storytelling; authentic 152; authorial 34, 37, 39, 42; changing landscape of 30–2; concept of 37, 196; conviction of 22; creating our own 42–4; development of 13, 42–4, 62; divergent 201–2; echoing 24–8; emergence of 11; and expression of feelings/ideas 145; finding 11–12, 153; formula for 28; and free verse 144–5; 'Hairy Potty' example 33–5; and image 31; imagined/inhabited 41–2; inner/outer 9; literary/storytelling 38–9; loss of 144; making it heard 89–90; muted 192–3; narrative 38; and other people's speech 36–7; others 38; pedagogy of 82; poetic/musical 40–1; popular culture 39–40; sense of 19, 38; social 38; and sociocultural differences 36; stretching of 20; technological 30–1; and writer's inner speech 90; written/oral link 25, 37

Vygotsky, L.S. 20, 24, 46, 47, 48, 51, 62, 99, 197

Waddell, M. 95

Wagner, B.J. 102, 114

Walsh, J.P. 38

Wells, G. 94, 121; *et al.* 58

'We're Writers' project 2, 3–4, 5, 6, 9, 13, 22, 31, 33, 36, 186; audit 3; as bottom up initiative 180; and choice/autonomy 62, 63, 67, 68; and creative writing 177, 178; development phase 3; educational/political context 3; evaluation phase 3; and literature 90, 95, 100, 158–9; and poetry 141, 142, 148, 151; in practice 192–5; Project Focus Group (PFG) 3; talking/writing 51, 56, 58

BRUNEL UNIVERSITY LIBRARY

Bannerman Centre,
Uxbridge, Middlesex,
UB8 3PH

Renewals: www.brunel.ac.uk/renew
OR
01895 266141

1 WEEK LOAN

60 4150383 X

'80415 328852"